Softspace

Following pages: Melting ice
field in the Chukchi Sea,
northwest of Alaska, 2002.

Softspace

From a Representation of Form to a Simulation of Space

Routledge
Taylor & Francis Group

LONDON AND NEW YORK

Architecture at Rice

Edited by Sean Lally & Jessica Young

First published 2007
by Routledge
2 Park Square, Milton Park, Abingdon, Oxon, OX14 4RN

Simultaneously published in the USA and Canada
by Routledge
270 Madison Avenue, New York, NY 10016

Routledge is an imprint of the Taylor & Francis Group

Published in association with
Architecture at Rice, the publication series of
The Rice School of Architecture
6100 Main Street, Houston, Texas 77005, USA

© 2007 Architecture at Rice, selection and editorial material
© 2007 the contributors, individual chapters

Designed and typeset by Jessica Young with Sean Lally.
Typeset in Arnhem Fine and Trade Gothic.
Printed and bound in China by Everbest Printing Co Ltd.

British Library Cataloguing in Publication Data
A catalogue record for this book is available from the British Library.

Library of Congress Cataloguing in Publication Data

Softspace: from a representation of form to a simulation of space / [edited by] Sean Lally and Jessica Young.
      p. cm.
    ISBN 0-415-40201-8 (hardback : alk. paper) –... ISBN 0-415-40202-6 (pbk. : alk. paper) 1. Architectural design. 2. Architecture–Research. 3. Architecture and technology. I. Lally, Sean, 1974- II. Young, Jessica, 1975-
NA2750.S594 2006
729.0285–dc22

ACKNOWLEDGMENTS

The editors thank and acknowledge the contributors for their sustained efforts during the preparation of this publication. We also thank the Rice School of Architecture Dean Lars Lerup and Associate Dean John Casbarian for the many opportunities afforded to us, beginning with an exhibition at the School in the Spring of 2004 which was the origin of Softspace. We gratefully acknowledge the Graham Foundation for Advanced Studies in the Fine Arts for their generous support, which permitted these ideas to move forward graphically and visually in the publication as we originally intended. Thanks to Christopher Hight, the managing editor of Architecture at Rice, to Melanie Pratt for her help during the early stages of this research, to Florence Tang for her help during the final stages, and to Mildred Crocker for managing the details. We also thank our editors at Routledge, Caroline Mallinder and Katherine Morton, for working with us to make this project happen.

ISBN10 0-415-40201-8 (hbk)
ISBN10 0-415-40202-6 (pbk)
ISBN10 0-203-96713-5 (ebk)

ISBN13 978-0-415-40201-9 (hbk)
ISBN13 978-0-415-40202-6 (pbk)
ISBN13 978-0-203-96713-3 (ebk)

2006013554

Contents

The stuff between, in & around

Sean Lally and Jessica Young

That architecture has often traditionally been preoccupied with the 'hard' (structure, forces, geometries of form), letting the 'soft' (qualitative environments, mood, atmosphere) become secondary, or residual, is a fairly obvious fact. Looking back, we find endless variations on form defined through structure and envelopes, often ignoring what's in between these fixed elements. This is due in some part to techniques of representation, which have reinforced pervasive (and conventional) notions of both *how* to make architectural space and *what* constitutes architectural space. These surfaces and structures, envelopes and skins, were considered to be the *material* pieces of architecture (yet are no longer the only elements that are definable and measurable), allowing space to be the 'stuff' that's left over between them – or, more simply stated, space is whatever form is not. Further, the distinction between the two has evolved into another simple opposition: form occupies the material, while space occupies the immaterial realm of design. This space, however, has always been imbued with endless qualities, behaviors, and effects, whether intentional or not – air, gas, fire, sound, odors, magnetic forces, electricity and electronics to name a few – which are, within the realm of 'softspace', distinctly material in nature. At the end of the day, isn't space the 'stuff' that we're after, anyway?

Softspace takes stock of a moment in design and research occurring now, and draws upon historical and ideological trajectories of projects that have been occurring over the past fifty years, while also foregrounding current architectural projects and essays that point to where these opportunities may take us. The work begins to break down the preconceived opposition between space and form, initially through the use of new tools and technology previously not part of the architect's vocabulary, but then moves beyond a fascination with the technologies and towards an exploration of the implications for space and its organization. *Softspace* looks to how architects can explore the *materials* that exist between the envelopes of geometry and structure. What potential role does something as seemingly omnipresent, inert and dependent as air play in the formation of space? Can emotions, sensations, temperature, humidity and scent, for example, be quantified, simulated and deployed as definitively as structural forces and descriptive architectural geometries? If we can visualize, quantify and instrumentalize qualitative effects and conditions as design materials, what then are the opportunities in the ways we may define boundary and edge in the spaces we inhabit?

Softspace is projective in nature, rather than documentary, and looks to suggest many possible futures rather than define discrete outcomes. Given that, we've refrained from organizing the book into distinct chapters, trying instead to present the material in a more continuous, somewhat linear progression where each contribution builds upon the subject matter of the others. *Softspace* is a body of research that looks *between, in and around* the structures and envelopes that capture space, and seeks to acknowledge its lineage in the past, act on the opportunities that exist today, and project what is still to come.

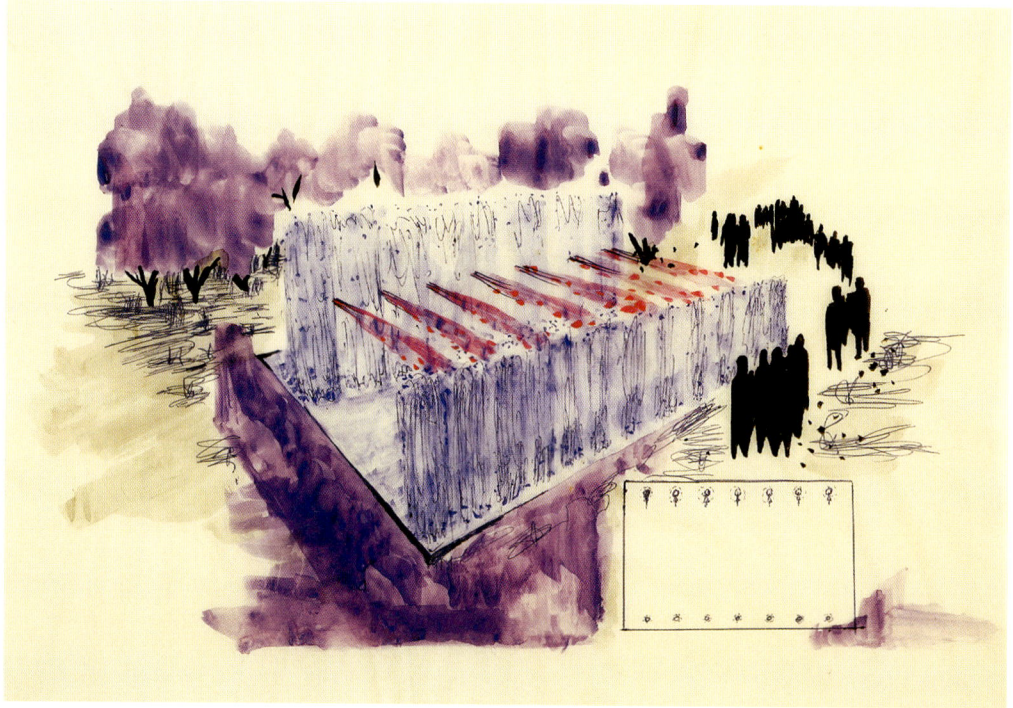

1.1: Yves Klein with architect
Claude Parent – *Fontaine de
Feu*, 1959.

INTRODUCTION

Energies, matter & the gradients of space
Sean Lally

Until now, the appropriation of digital tools to architectural design has been largely focused up-on innovating the generation of form. At the same time, advancements in the visualization and simulation of energies and material qualities have been relegated to design optimization, as a means to simply refine preconceived spatial and organizational conditions. Yet today, through these very technologies, energies and intensities such as air, gas, fire, sound, odors, magnetic forces, electricity and electronics have become architectural materials that can be visualized and operated upon as systematically and accurately as the forces that guide structure and geo-metry. *Softspace* examines the opportunities available today to employ such energy-matters as catalysts of innovation.

Caves to campfires

In *The Architecture of the Well-Tempered Environment*, Reyner Banham highlighted architects' continued fixation with defining a boundary or edge condition through formal strategies based on monumental skin and shell enclosures. In contrast to this cave mentality of capturing spatial organizations through form, Banham pointed to the campfire as a means for spatial organiza-tion. The campfire is both a source of energy and a territorial organizer, creating micro-climates of heat, light and darkness with the potential for variable conditioning. The radiating gradients of light and heat create a soft boundary that rises in intensity before slowly dying back only to

1.2: Robin Evans' *The Developed Surface*. Left: 'Section' of a stair hall by Thomas Lightoler, from *The Modern Builder's Assistant*, 1757. Right: The Etruscan Room, Osterley Park, with furniture as of 1782, Osterley Park by Robert Adams, 1775-9.

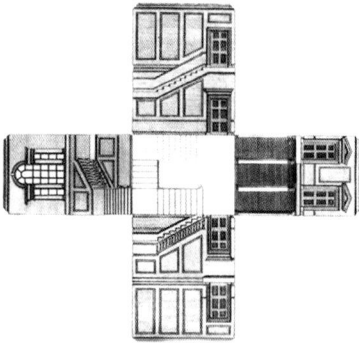

be activated once again later, all while organizing an individual's placement around a gradient and variable territorial boundary. It's these mechanical systems, responsible for making such spaces livable throughout the course of a year, that Banham sees as the facilitators of spatial configuration – not the skin or shell that constructs an envelope. Architects have continued to question and re-inform the role of architecture beyond the classical world view, often searching to represent the ever-evolving trends in our universal order or technological advancements to facilitate its realization. *Softspace* instead follows Banham's lead, searching not to question our world views or even the tools that order them, but rather the stuff they're made of – the energies and matter of space.[1]

Architects can look to the work of many artists (with the occasional architect in tow) to find a lineage of investigations that incorporate qualitative effects and energies as 'buildable' materials for design, including Hans Haacke's *Condensation Cube* of 1963, EAT's (Experiments in Art and Technology) *Pepsi-Cola Pavilion* at Expo '70 in Osaka, Olafur Eliasson's *Weather Project* in 2001 or Yves Klein with architect Claude Parent's

Fire Fountain of 1959. These examples, specifically the sketches and watercolors of Yves Klein, capture the imagination regarding how walls and roof exist not as inert massings, but as energies released through water and fire, simultaneously delineating boundaries and emitting qualities such as sound, light and heat. Found generally in the confines of gallery and spectator settings, these examples project the potentials of what has yet to fully infiltrate and interact with our daily activities. As Fredrick Kiesler's *Endless House* (1961) is to the formally smooth and spatially continuous that would influence architectural research born from the availability of a tool set in the early 1990s, so Klein and others can be seen as an impetus to research that has remained stunted in its pursuit of generating spatial and organizational implications within architecture.

These projects represent a field of research spanning the last half century, making it clear that the intentions raised within *Softspace* aren't novel. These are projects that question and stretch our imaginations as to how we engage another realm of materiality in the spaces we construct and occupy. As we question the materials we use to define and construct the territories we inhabit, we

1.3: The Optimization of Form
– Gehry Partners' Case Western
Reserve University building in
Cleveland, Ohio, 2002.

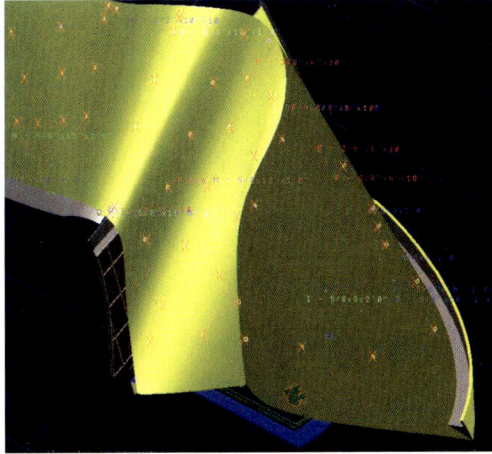

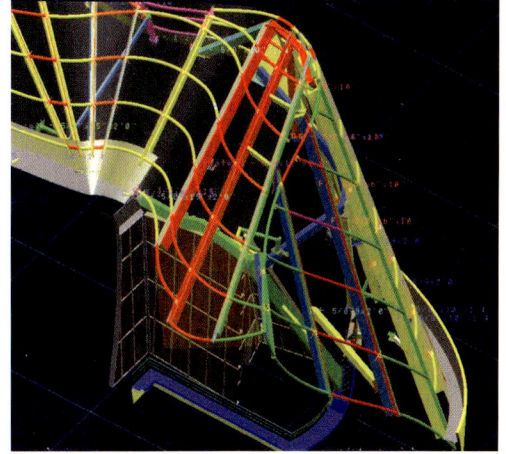

must also look to tools and technologies of today that permit us to visualize and operate upon them. Architects have yet to fully engage the opportunities available today or speculate upon the implications that such research will have on our spatial, formal and social constructs, let alone question how we live. With the imaginations of what could come, and the availability of tools and technologies that permit us to operate upon these 'materials', architects are now in a position to engage such opportunities with generative and projective research.

Technology transfer

One of the greatest strengths of the architectural discipline has been its ability to siphon the techniques and tools from adjacent and seemingly distant disciplines. One recent example of this appropriation has been the relationship between software and the ubiquitous availability and dissemination of CAD/CAM technologies that integrate techniques of visualization with tools for fabrication. This combination has opened doors for advancements within architecture; however, this collusion has also managed to fixate our explorations and subsequent discussions of spatial and organizational

investigations within an ingrained bandwidth of what constitutes boundary and edge. As Robin Evans points out, the techniques architects deploy are never 'neutral' in the information they convey. These techniques, whether hand sketches, orthographic projects (plans and sections), or 3-D modeling and animation, require the suppression of some kinds of information in order to highlight and communicate others. As we continue to use graphic techniques and tools focused on geometry and form as our primary means for delineating territories, architects have essentially suppressed spatial and material qualities as design strategies, reverting instead to tools and graphic representations that calibrate spatial organization as a capturing of space through form.

In *The Developed Surface*, Robin Evans brings to our attention the extent to which architectural techniques can have repercussions not only on formal but on spatial and organizational constructs, through an eighteenth-century graphic technique originally intended for the purpose of depicting exterior elevations of streets and town squares. The technique splayed the elevations flat as a means of depicting façade adjacencies along the street or square. However, as the technique's use shifted from

1.4: The Generative Form
– Greg Lynn Form's Port
Authority of New York and New
Jersey, 1995.

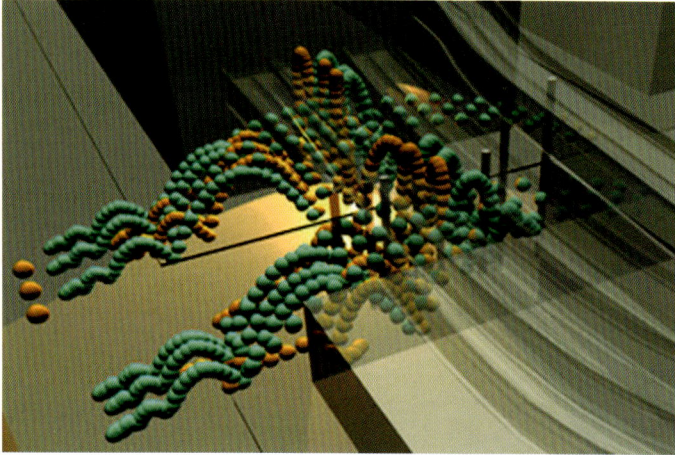

depiction of external elevations to showing the building's interior spaces, the subject matter of the drawings became the four walls of the individual room unfolded into discrete surfaces on a single plane. The technique of unfolding the room planes not only suppressed wall thickness and structure, producing a fixation on surface treatments that flattened materiality against these wall planes, but had larger ramifications in terms of how the rooms could be occupied and organized within the building, as the drawings appeared to create a 'hermetic' condition by suppressing connectivity of adjoining rooms.[2] Given this, the question we must ask today is this: With the advancements in technologies for how we visualize and operate upon information, what are we choosing to highlight and what have we managed to suppress?

Optimization vs the generative

The last ten to fifteen years have been crucial in terms of the techniques and operations architects have harnessed from other fields in the pursuit of design intentions. During this time there has been no shortage of writings documenting such technology transfers, including the integration of software packages from the automotive, aeronautical and naval industries and the animation studios of Hollywood, and the more recent use of scripting logics of computer science. However, it's worth reiterating an apparent schism that's developed within the architectural profession pertaining to how these tools are applied. There is one trajectory in which the harnessing of such tools is applied for the optimization and refinement of preconceived intentions and geometries, while another is concerned with tools for their generative strengths. The integration of these tools from the aeronautical and naval industries has made it feasible, both financially and logistically, to advance a trajectory that originated in hand sketches and physical models previously so geometrically complex as to leave one questioning their feasibility. These tools were engaged as a means to optimize what was essentially a predefined formal and organizational strategy, in which cues from adjacent disciplines were integrated to make preconceived visions viable and logistically efficient. This can be most clearly illustrated in the work of Gehry Partners. Originating as hand sketches and physical models, programs such as CATIA, which originated

1.5: Optimization of Energies
– Foster and Partners' City Hall
in London, 2003.

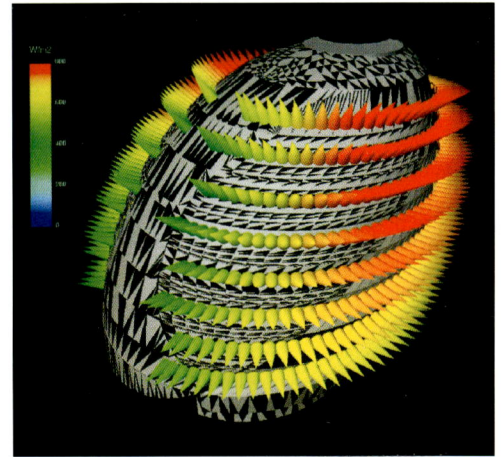

within the aeronautical industry, permit architects to visualize the geometries of the project for their structural analysis, cost feasibility and logistical organization during the construction process. The integration of the software at the terminus of the design phase limits the role of the tool to that of 'fine-tuning' preconceived geometries and formal strategies.

This differs rather significantly from the orchestration of animation software, scripted for generative potentials of design innovation. Here the inherent logics and proclivities of software packages and algorithmic operations are exploited in the pursuit of questioning organizational and aesthetic constructs through form. The integration of techniques originating in the animation industries furthered existing explorations in formal organizational logics in which the tools' 'Dynamic' and 'Animation' packages were exploited. Such an integration provided design tools for generating, questioning and informing a discussion of topology and form. While architects have advanced formal and geometric logics and organizations, similarly imaginative pursuits through qualitative and material energies have remained relegated mostly to optimizing certain preconceived spatial and

organizational conditions in search of the most efficient and optimal 72-degree interior temperature.

Larger architectural offices, including Foster and Partners and Grimshaw, incorporate specialist modeling groups that often partner engineers to document and analyze a project's energy performance. In the case of London's City Hall by Foster and Partners, the design was envisioned during the competition stage as a 'pebble' with a large lens overlooking the river. From its earliest stages the project was intended to be energy-efficient, and having won the competition Foster's Specialist Modelling Group, along with Arup's engineers, produced solar studies and analysis of the project's energy performance. With the ability to visualize the building's energy performance throughout the course of the year, they now had the responsibility of harnessing this information and making viable the original intentions of the project's formal scheme, while meeting the goals for energy efficiency.

The use of such tools within the architectural profession often occurs only later, during the project's development, as a means to optimize preconceived formal and organizational strategies while meeting the needs of

1.6: *Softspace* looks to practices using these material energies and generative techniques to explore spatial boundaries and the implications these approaches have on broader organizational and social constructs.

energy efficiency.[3] Under the slogan of 'sustainable design' and through various energy crises, architects and engineers have seen some of the greatest technological advancements in how we operate upon and make decisions related to environmental information that might otherwise have been dismissed. Yet the use of such information as a generative method and design tool has been largely overlooked in favor of its use as a tool for optimization. *Softspace* marks a shift from the use of digital tools to represent form to the simulation of spatial material behaviors.

The intention of the *Softspace* publication isn't to herald yet another 'new' within the architectural discipline, but instead to acknowledge and identify the 'now' that affords us opportunities to both operate upon and question the methods and criteria we use to define and explore the boundaries of our surroundings. The unique position that architects find themselves in today is not one lacking in precedents for the imagination, nor is it defined solely by the technological advancements of the past twenty-five years. Opportunities exist to visualize and operate upon information that questions what constitutes the material of architectural knowledge and its

operations in exploring and defining spatial, organizational and social occupancies. Techniques we deploy as architects are never neutral. Architects need to acknowledge that investigations that question something as rudimentary as what constitutes a boundary or edge condition on a local moment can have repercussions on much larger organizational and social behaviors. Therefore, architects interested in pursuing and advancing the profession cannot shy away from opportunities that give them the ability to visualize and operate upon a selection of information and criteria – air, gas, fire, sound, odors, magnetic forces, electricity and electronics – that were previously labeled as simply qualitative or ephemeral effects. Today, as architects continue to appropriate the tools of adjacent disciplines (from material engineers, software engineers and meteorologists), opportunities exist to quantify and manipulate such information through generative techniques, making it vital for projective research, practice and discourse.

GEOMETRIES & FORM

QUALITIES & SPACE

Kiesler's Endless House

Klein's Fire Fountain

OPTIMIZATION

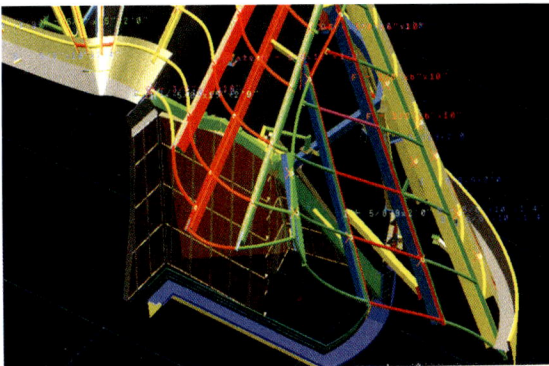

Gehry's Case Western Reserve Building

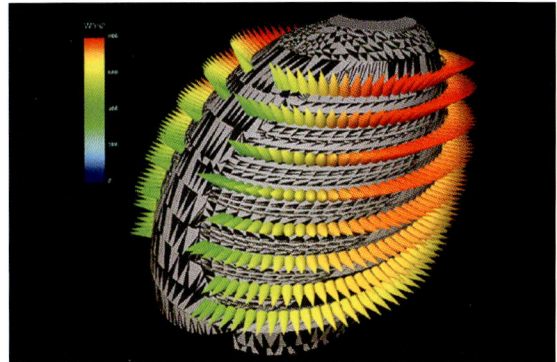

Foster's London City Hall

GENERATIVE

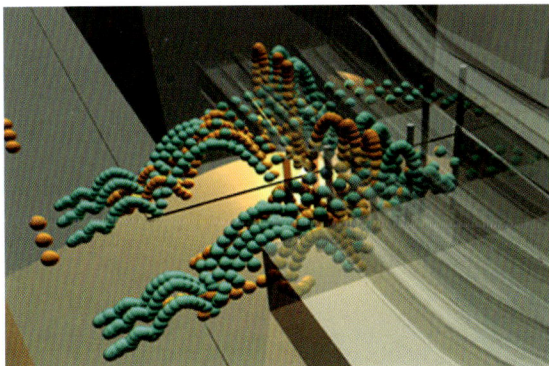

Lynn's Port Authority

SOFTSPACE

2.1: Brush fire, Northern Australia.

Putting out the fire with gasoline:

Parables of entropy and homeostasis from the second machine age to the information age

Christopher Hight

Reyner Banham's *The Architecture of the Well-Tempered Environment* is often understood as one of the inspirations for British High-Tech and certain aspects of 'green' architectural discourse, and is frequently referenced as historical material in technical courses on building systems.[1] It is far less frequently placed in relation to the genealogies of theories of material practices and responsive environments, which is where it belongs, for what is at stake in the book is not simply a supplementary history but a projective theory of architecture that treats its technical aspects not as supporting representations of abstract concepts (such as Giedion's space-time or Rowe's phenomenal transparency) but as the conceptual material itself.

Accompanying any proposition of new territories for practice are the potentials for re-territorializing the discipline's past. This is not because the present is some repetition of a given past or because the past can teach us something; rather, it is because these are virtual archaeologies of our present. Banham attempted to construct a history of modern architecture's relationship to the electro-mechanical systems that pervade the creation and existence of modern constructions but have been regularly ignored, or treated themselves as supplement to the crucial part of architecture: its form, its spaces and its ideologies. In that regard, the *Well Tempered Environment* remains an important precedent for all those interested in developing theories of architecture that derive from its material conditions and practices rather than from critical theoretical emphasis upon signification.

In many ways Banham's *The Architecture of the Well-Tempered Environment* was a response to the criticism he had laid at the feet of modern architecture and its historians in *Theory and Design in the First Machine Age*. In the latter's conclusion, he criticized architects for appropriating technology as representation rather than fully integrating technological processes into the practices of design and fabrication. The moderns had merely adapted classical representations of order with different referents.[2]

He more implicitly criticized those who had chronicled modern architecture as failing to recognize this and perpetuating the *aporia*. Siegfried Giedion comes under special scrutiny for *Mechanization Takes Command*. Banham mentions that many architects believed that after Giedion there was little to add to the history of technology and architecture, which he argues is itself symbolic of architects' naiveté. Giedion's text, while wide-ranging, almost entirely avoided discussing the architecture of the modern canon – one he of course had been crucial in determining. Instead, analyses are limited to industrial vernaculars and to a few second-rate propositions (which Giedion roundly dismisses). By presenting technology as having an anonymous history, and thus being at once autonomous and deterministic of human agency, modern architects were at least partially absolved of responsibility for what he saw as its dire effects, including –after the Holocaust and the atomic bomb – the imminent end of human history itself.

Indeed, Giedion sees the two as distinct and perhaps antagonistic fields, as his conclusion suggests in essentially arguing for aestheticizing technology through the imposition of design rules to align mechanization with human needs. This, he argues, would establish a new 'equipoise' between technology, nature and humanity, a term that combines the thermodynamic understanding of dynamic equilibrium with classical aesthetics of the human figure of proportional harmony and balance over the processes of technology, reversing the technological enframing of humanity so that it is machines that become framed, tamed, and domesticated to the needs of the human subject. Like Le Corbusier's Modulor, Giedion's concept sought to impose a transcendental humanist ordering upon technology, channeling the forces that seem to disrupt into supposedly timeless forms. Thus, Giedion's criticisms of technology are entirely comforting to architects' predilections and common sense rather than challenging, placing architecture once more as a potential savior.

The *Well-Tempered Environment* provided part of the history Banham argued had been entirely ignored, presenting a themed but roughly chronological analysis of projects in regard to the infrastructures of modern buildings – air conditioning and ventilation, plumbing, and so forth. For Banham, these were more than mere building services; they were motors to rethink practice, the architectural object and its subjects and social spaces. Indeed, he suggests that modern architecture is conditioned upon their possibility in every sense, from the most conceptual to the pragmatic. Extending these implications, he proposes, leads to a fundamental ques-

2.2: Two Diagrams of "primitive huts" from Reyner Banham's *The Architecture of the Well-Tempered Environment*. The top diagram depicts the nomad's campfire as the prototypical "power-based solution" to shelter, while the bottom schematic of a tent depicts what Banham argued remains the dominant "structure-based solution." Each, he argues, depends upon complex social and spatial organizations, which they in turn enforce as a feedback loop.

tioning of the privileging of form, circulation and discrete program in favor of the performative modulation of occupation. Banham's more optimistic assessment of technology and his skepticism of Giedion's Modernism (and that of Banham's former master, Pevsner) offers an inverted proposition: rather than domestic technology for the human figure, architects needed to develop an aesthetics of thermodynamic processes for a different sort of body, architectural or otherwise.[3]

Origin of the well-tempered environment

As with so many theories of architecture that are presented as a history of the discipline, Banham's opening pages offer a 'parable' of origin.[4] First he tells a story about the transformation of the human animal into a human subject:

> Mankind can exist, unassisted, on practically all those parts of the earth that are at present inhabited, except for the most arid and the most cold. The operative word is 'exist' … in order to flourish … mankind needs more ease and leisure … . A large part of that ease and leisure comes from the deployment of technical resources and social organizations, in order to control the immediate environment.[5]

Here is a familiar doubled origin: the conversion of the animal *Homo-sapiens* into a human subject through the invention of the means for doing so via prosthetic technologies that transform nature into a constructed environment. It is important that Banham withholds the terms of architecture or the city from this transformative moment. Unlike Aristotle's origin, which places

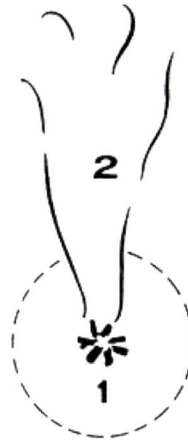

Environmental conditions around a campfire.
1. Zone of radiant heat and light.
2. Downwind trail of warmed air and smoke.

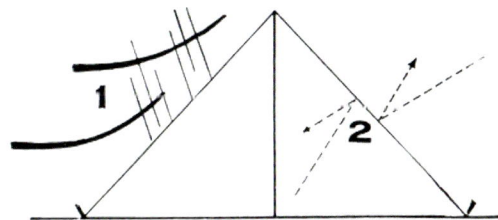

Environmental behaviour of a tent.
1. Tent membrane deflects wind and excludes rain.
2. Reflects most radiation, retaining internal heat, excluding solar heat, maintaining privacy.

the city as the necessary condition for 'culture' as such, or Heidegger's emphasis upon dwelling, Banham suggests architecture and cities as merely manifestations of more general social-technical infrastructures.

Banham then offers two different paradigms for the development of such technologies:

A savage tribe (of the sort that exists only in parables) arrives at the evening camp-site and finds it well supplied with fallen timber. Two basic methods of exploiting the environmental potential [energy] of the timber exist: either it may be used to construct a wind-break or rain-shed – the structural solution – or it may be used to build a fire – the power-operated solution.[6]

In his tale, humans use energy to maintain their biological equilibrium in the face of environmental change; they need, above all, to convert their labor into food to live. At the core, this means maintaining a regular body temperature even while the climate and other energy sources (i.e. food, temperature) fluctuate.[7] In the animal pre-history of humanity, humans are fully embedded within Nature, a part of its delicate processes, but unable to do more than maintain their bodily system within the larger ecologies of which they are a part because they expend all their energy just to maintain homeostasis. It is only by the creation of technologies that the potential energy of wood was released and instrumentalized to stabilize environmental conditions and allow humans to pursue non-subsistence activities. Banham returns to this theme at the end of the text, discussing how the body regulates its internal temperature and the cultural relativity of environmental comfort (citing all too fa-

miliar examples of cold being used as a tool of torture), replacing the image of the campfire and hut with that of 'space suits, with air-conditioners' that imply transcendence of the current human condition.[8] Dwelling in Nature is not only impossible; it is heat-death, maximum entropy.

Entropic horizons of humanity

This parable thus offers a thermodynamic explanation of life and the rise of civilization as the reverse of entropy. Entropy was figured by the second law of thermodynamics, derived from Carnot's studies of heat engines in the early nineteenth century. It states that in a closed system energy will flow (in the nineteenth-century understanding of heat as a type of fluid) from hot to colder regions. This differential is what allows engines (such as the steam engines of the Industrial Revolution) to produce work. Eventually equilibrium is reached; no more work can be extracted because heat is evenly distributed. This is the state of maximum entropy, a term invented in 1850 by Rudolf Clausius, who generalized it to any closed system. As physics shifted from a fluid model of heat to the statistical-energetic models of quantum mechanics and thermodynamics, maximum entropy came to be understood as that point at which highly energized and low-energy particles are evenly distributed. A popular analogy is the dispersion of an ink drop through a glass of water: at first there is clear water and the turbulent whirls of the ink, but given some time and without any movement of the water, the glass will become an even shade of grey because of the Brownian motion, or vibration, of the ink and water molecules.

Left on their own (i.e. without external energy), the ink and water will not separate because they have found their equilibrium, or average distribution throughout space. Rather than 'disorder', entropy is more correctly understood as the most probable state, or least organized condition. The second law states that because any closed system requires ever more energy to maintain its work or its organization, it will always tend towards this state.

Immediately, questions arose about phenomena that seem to stave off or even reverse entropy to produce greater order or organization. In 1867 James Maxwell constructed a thought experiment called Maxwell's Demon, in which an intelligent agent (the eponymous Demon) acts as a gatekeeper between two domains within a thermodynamic system; this Demon controls the flow between the two domains by sorting more energetic particles from lesser ones. In such a scenario, entropy could be arrested or even reversed (for example, by having two similar domains sorted into hot and cold regions). This presented a paradox: it seemed logically possible, but also to defy the second law. Like many paradoxes of science or mathematics, it was a motor of further research and has since been explained in various ways. For example, it was crucial in the transferal of entropy theory into cybernetic frameworks, which treated all these systems as information; Leo Slizard argued that the Demons required information about the particles they sorted, thus opening the system at some level. In this way, information became more important to physics and biological frameworks.

By the middle of the twentieth century, the problem of entropy and its apparent beguiling reversal was developed as a way to understand the creation of higher levels of order and complexity. For example, Schrödinger had argued in his popular book *What is Life?* that 'It is by avoiding the rapid decay into the inert state of "equilibrium" that an organism appears so enigmatic ... What an organism feeds upon is negative entropy.'[9] Negative entropy was understood as the free energy in the overall system of the organism and its environment. By the late twentieth century, Ilya Prigogine and Isabelle Stengers employed informational frameworks and Schrödinger's negentropy to suggest how in non-linear dissipative systems more complex ordering could arise from simpler conditions instead of their leading to less ordered states, as the second law of thermodynamics dictates for closed systems. An example of such negentropic informational processes includes life itself. In this work, energy that is stored within existing organizations can be released and used to create higher levels of organization and differentiation, such as that found in any organism or system. They defined this moment of the origin of order as follows:

> When the thermodynamic forces acting on a system become such that the linear region is exceeded ... [s]tability is no longer the consequence of the general laws of physics. We must examine the way a stationary state reacts to the different types of fluctuations produced by the system or its environment. In some cases, the analysis leads to the conclusion that a state is 'unstable' – in such a state, certain fluctuations, instead of regressing, may be amplified and invade the entire system, compelling

it to evolve toward a new regime that may be quali-tatively quite different from the stationary states corresponding to minimum entropy production.[10] This is the basis for theories of the 'thermodynamics of organized complexity' in which higher levels of organi-zation, for example forms of life or patterns of forma-tion, emerge.[11]

Banham's *Well-Tempered Environment* depends on these general principles of entropy and thermodynam-ics in two senses. First, of course, the technology for regulating the environment within buildings employs them as technical principles. Air conditioners and natu-ral ventilation systems work because of heat differential across spaces and surfaces. Second, and what I am con-cerned with here, is how these are used as existential explanations of human existence and, in turn, the social orders that such technologies of environmental modula-tion promote.

Moreover, as we have seen, in the opening passages of the book, society is presented as a vast heat engine. While prehistoric humans were in equilibrium with their environment, the creation of the higher-level or-ders of human subjectivity and culture come at the price of being in far-from-equilibrium with the environment. Transformation from animal existence to human society and subjectivity is enabled by the conversion of the po-tential energy within natural materials into technologies that serve as supplemental bodies. By regulating the environment into a more steady state (food is constant, cold kept outside), these prosthetic organs liberate ener-gy humans previously expended merely to maintain a sustenance level of existence.

In Banham's tale, as in a heat engine, the excess en-ergy released by the extension of the human body across its technologies neither disappears nor is lost; rather, it finds other outlets, for example what Banham calls 'leisure' – out of which higher cultural, social and politi-cal organizations emerge. These new social organs then act as capacitors to store more energy and thus allow ever-higher levels of human order to emerge in nested feedback loops. In short, human history is a thermo-dynamic process of neg-entropy as 'stored mobilizable energy in a space-time structured (organized) system'.[12] Banham's threshold between *Homo-sapiens* and human subjects is not singular but a thermodynamic process of becoming ever more human through the release of po-tential energy. The 'well-tempered environment' is not a well-designed architecture to ensure the comfort of its occupants so much as the existential infrastructure that allows the space of humanity to emerge from animal existence. Dwelling in Nature is not only impossible – it is the heat-death of Culture and the human subject.

The knowledge of power

Banham, as we have seen, offers two different paths for this evolution: 'the structural solution' and the 'power-operated solution'. These originate as different paths for the liberation of the energy stored as 'wood'. For Banham, the selection of either structural or power-based engines prescribes the sort of societies that emerge from the neg-entropic energy that the chosen technological solution liberates. Because any closed system will eventually 'run down' – that is, will lose capacity to perform work – and increase entropy, both choices require continual input of new energy through the expansion of their supplemental organs.

The structural solution requires a stable and massive orchestration and division of labor, producing a sedentary and striated social order of ever greater complexity. Also, once energy is stored into structures, they require ancillary organs for maintenance, lest they fall into entropically inevitable despair. This intensive amplification of available energy within the environment leads to increasing complexity of supplemental organs – from huts, to houses that are then assembled into neighborhoods, and these administrated by institutions and ordered into cities, and ultimately the nation-state.[13] Architecture's relation to social order as well as to the life of citizens was figured through this model as a sort of calcification of energy into monuments, fostering a discipline of architecture as the static containment of space, of subjects and of society: 'Cultures whose members organize their environment by means of massive structures tend to visualize space as they have lived in it, that is, bounded and contained, limited by walls, floors and ceilings.'[14] Design concerned the proper massing of these objects, their symmetries and balance as an image of equilibrium. This produces an ethical-aesthetic imperative of architectural permanence delineating bounded contours of political and social space, such as defined territories of the public and private.[15] As a result, Banham suggests, the structural solution has dominated European culture and architecture, whether Classical, Gothic or Modern (and here, we might want to add, Blobby).

The power-based solution, on the other hand, has produced no cultures that have 'shaped world architecture',[16] since they must always be in flight or they will deplete the energies of any one locale and die off.[17] This leads to the extensive vector of nomadic cultures. The lack of calcification also produces more supple social-spatial mapping, Banham tells us. The iconic campfire of the power-solution produces a heat and light gradient that interacts with the social order of the tribe (with the chief and elders at the center, and others arrayed according to rank).[18] Moreover, the heat gradient of the fire interacts with wind patterns to produce second-order effects. This leads to social ordering based on habit rather than territory, one that is performative and must be continually reinscribed through ritual, rites and ceremonies: in other words, institutionalized event structures.

The house of humanity or a house of cards?

We can now understand the broader implications of the *Well-Tempered Environment*. Banham proposes that this bifurcated path of human history reached a new state by the dawn of the second machine age. The structural solution no longer quite matched the technological conditions of modernity. Implicitly, the social and economic upheavals catalyzed by the technological revolutions of successive machine ages have effectively de-territorialized cultural, political and even epistemological boundaries. The structural solution no longer worked since the world had more to do with the temporary, ambient fields of the campfire. This was experienced as existential 'homelessness', or as solidity melting into the air. Implicitly, such expressions were only symptoms of being locked in the cave of the structural solution that could no longer effectively maintain homeostasis. Even as more and more energy was poured into maintaining ever more elaborate layers of the structural solution, the entire edifice began to teeter. The modern experiences of anomie and alienation are simply the subjective experience of the entropic mismatch of technological economies and social order.

Banham was writing as the 1960s were drawing to a close, just as the dream of an unending supply of cheap energy was beginning to be replaced by an economic scarcity that would reconfigure the social and political landscape of the 1970s and beyond. Thus, the 'power-operated solution' became paramount at the historical moment when the 'heat-death' of western civilization seemed at hand, both because the wealth of energy (as fossil fuels) available from the earth (the ultimate closed system) suddenly seemed finite and because the scope of human-made environmental disaster was beginning to be made apparent. As oil production in the United States was (correctly) predicted to peak by 1970, it seemed that human culture was reaching its homeostatic horizon.

Yet, the built environment and social order were both increasing determined by 'power-based' technologies rather than the structural solution. For Banham, one of the defining transformations from the first to second machine ages was the shift from large top-down industries of mass-production to consumer-based economies characterized by the proliferation of electric and electronic appliances that, he argued, were reshaping the social and cultural landscape.[19] At the end of the second edition of the book, Banham goes so far as to associate the development of automatically regulating architectural environments with feminist liberation movements.[20] In the first edition, he recounts the transformation of 'women-work' and the changing roles of the housewife in reference to Catherine Beecher's essays on domestic architecture and women. Banham was very critical of solar technology of the time that required frequent maintenance, warning that it would represent a step backwards for the bourgeois housewife because it would become a new kind of 'women's work'.[21] The incorporation of heating and washing apparatus into the household proper in the nineteenth century was, he emphasized, made possible largely though their miniaturization and safety regulation, but these also removed from architecture a great deal of the work it needed to perform in terms of environmental modulation and energy storage. This leads to a detachment of architectural design from its functioning as a calcification of thermodynamically produced social order.

> With little left to do, except to protect the tempered atmosphere within from blowing away, the outer shell of the American house, both in Catherine Beecher's early vision, and in later built fact from coast to coast, lost most of its detailed relationship to the internal economy and layout of the house and thus became susceptible to any stylistic diversification ... that came along.[22]

Architectural form, at least as understood under the 'structural solution', has lost its role within the thermodynamic expression of social and political order and has become a vestigial organ. Banham suggested abandoning the formal ethics of the structural solution in favor of the performative space of the fire.

Badly-tempered architecture

Banham was characteristically critical of modern architects' response to this condition. Air conditioning and lighting was reshaping architecture's relationship to the environment, and indeed was making entirely new sorts of space and occupation possible.[23] Most of these spaces were not the remit of 'high' architectural design, and the text is poised upon the tension between the development of low-brow environments that seem to exploit the energy-solution to maximum effect – for example, Las Vegas's light shows and speculative office building's generic open plans play a key role in the text. These structures depend on 'power-operated' solutions and downplay structural specificity. Indeed, the open office is presented as the modern equivalent of the campfire, constructed around a gradient of vertical circulation access at the core, natural light at the perimeter and even temperatures throughout. These fields, of course, configure office rank, the organization of furniture as a map of corporate organization and even economic regimes.[24] All this led to the a de-emphasis of structural solutions, for example with the development of curtain wall systems, and suggested a more flexible ordering of interior space and thus a less specific plan organization of architectural form.

This led to strange contortions of architectural expression. For example, Banham critiques the fire-prevention upstands and spandrel glass in SOM's Lever House and Harrison's curtain walls at the United Nations tower.

While Bunshaft's solution of hanging masonry at Lever House is, as he notes, more elegant, both are used, along with suspended ceilings, to conceal the vast mechanical systems that make these architectures possible, in favor of representational effects: 'the aim was to present a smooth rectangular envelope, mechanistic in its stylistic pretensions, but not mechanical in its expressed content'.[25] Like Beecher's American House, the envelope of the building only needed to contain the 'well-tempered environment within', like a soap bubble, and was detached from the technical-social ordering that it housed. Thus, from his point of view, the corporate architects of the second machine age were repeating with mechanical systems the mistakes many pre-war architectural heroes made in the first by representing technology rather than incorporating it.[26] The curtain wall becomes a stylistic fancy, not a real basis for an ordered architecture. According to the thermodynamics paradigm of the text, architects attempted to conserve architecture against entropic dissolution, rather than pursue its implications in earnest.

Banham also disagreed with Louis Kahn's dissimulations of service, which he quoted:

> I do not like ducts, I do not like pipes. I hate them really thoroughly, but because I hate them so thoroughly I feel that they have to be given their place. If I just hated them and took no care, I think that they would invade the building and complexly destroy it.[27]

Besides sounding like a page from Dr Seuss, the force of revulsion here is quite palpable. The 'power solution' is an anathema to Architecture. One must, Kahn declares, domesticate the fire, by containing it in its proper place as service. Otherwise, it would, as a representation of the energy solution, consume not just a discrete building, but the entire edifice of architectural discipline as the incarnation of the structural solution. In turn, it threatens the end of the human subject and social order as figured by the structural solution. Entropy was to be resisted by constructing ever stronger bulkheads, repetition of bounded spaces, and rigid geometries.[28]

The architectures of soft space

Finally, I want to explore the implications for architecture of the power-operated solution Banham proffered for our nomadic modernity. Within the text, Banham suggests a revised relationship between humans and their environment: indeed, that the choice lies between entropic decay of our structural-solutions culture, or the embrace of a 'power-based' solution to refashion our world. We are no longer bending olive branches upon some European peninsula to make an edifice, but gathering sticks upon a futuristic African or Mesopotamian expanse, or perhaps across the gridded expanse of a Superstudio photo collage.

To this end, Banham advocated a different relationship between aesthetic organization and technological function mediated through the corporeal perception. Elsewhere, he had argued that the *biological function* of architecture was to create a world of forms that synchronize the human experience with the technological environment in which this subject continually transforms.[29] This informational homeostasis is coupled to the thermodynamic ontology of the *Well-Tempered Environment* to suggest a revised notion of architecture and its relationship to social ordering. Charted through the case studies Banham provided, there are three implicit trajectories for the development of electronic and mechanical systems as a figure of a new social order.

The first implication was the sort of architecture manifested in Rogers and Piano's Pompidou Centre (itself an adaptation of Cedric Price's unbuilt Fun-Palace). Banham celebrated both in the second edition of the book as more sanguine responses than either Kahn's or SOM's structures. He argued that Rogers and Piano did not sublimate the energy systems into an image of structure but instead re-cast the structure as delivery system of services, operated by its users to produce fleeting social organizations and spatial conditions (the Fun-Palace and the Pompidou were supposed to have mobile partitions and floors).[30] It is largely because of this that Banham's text is seen as the foundation of the British High-Tech movement.

However, one can also extend it to Constant's use of similar architectural languages of scaffolds, space-frames and mobile platforms for his Situationist New Babylon projects, which were, after all, urban constructs and artificial and responsive environments for a post-revolutionary society, freed from the social ordering of bourgeois society and labor. Here Banham's thermodynamic parable about the elevation of humanity from an equilibrium state and the liberation of bodily heat as leisure is replayed and manifested as an architecture designed to induce purely ludic 'zones' of subjective intensity. The New Babylons were articulations of urbanism as fields of energy, not unlike the intensity of heat, smoke and wind in the original campfire, or for that matter the Paris of 'momentary intensity' mapped by Debord on his famous dérives. Within this energy field, unencumbered subjects would exists in an endlessly nomadic dérive made possible by the technological landscapes that stretch across national boundaries and environmental features. Higher orders would emerge from this negentropic liberation of energy from the calcified ruins of the structural solution. If the campfire mapped a stable social order for Banham's mythic nomads, in modernity the 'energy solution' seemed aligned with the de-territorializations of space, the de-stratification of social order. Inhabitable space frames are a cloud-like infrastructure for such gradient distributions of power.

A second path lay in the development of a surface architecture: a soft and responsive membrane of a technological organism. This option is less emphasized in the *Well-Tempered Environment*, perhaps because its moment seemingly had passed by the time of writing. Yet it is implicated in the privileged place at the end of the text given to the egg-shaped inflatable portable theater design by Victor Lundy and Walter Bird for the United States Energy Commission, as well as the second edition's large reproduction of Apollo-program spacesuits alongside orthographic drawings of an igloo. Under Banham's dichotomy of structure or energy solutions, the igloo is a hybrid, at once structural and dynamically responsive in terms of its modulation of light.

Hadas Steiner has described how the 1960s discourses on inflatable and mobile architectures offered soft structures as an antidote to architecture's hardware.

Architecture, it was argued, needed to acquire the fleeting existence of the soap bubble, and its sheen of scientific veracity. Steiner argues that architects rarely understood the distinction between programming and hardware, and thereby conflated the aesthetics of softness with transformability and feedback loops between users and their environment. She notes that Banham contrasted the inflatable environments of *Barbarella* with the computer-encrusted sets of *2001: A Space Odyssey*. He preferred, or as he put it, was 'turned onto', the former because it offered a 'responsive environment' that would adapt to its user's desires rather than serve the mad logic of HAL the computer.[31]

In the thermodynamic paradigm of the *Well-Tempered Environment*, the distinction between software and hardware becomes less important than architecture's role as a secondary osmotic membrane of information / energy, one that creates the opportunity for new spatial-social organizations.[32] Claude Shannon had by that time developed a cybernetic use of entropy, where the term was used to measure the amount of information in a system. In cybernetics, all organisms are simply systems interacting with other systems and sub-systems as homeostatic informational feedback loops that measure differentiation. Following Gregory Bateson's maxim 'information is the difference that makes a difference', the greater the degree of differentiation in a system – in other words its deviation from equilibrium – the more information the system contained.

Life itself had shifted from mechanistic and structural explanations to informatic processes.[33] And to close the loop from outer space to air-conditioned space, by Banham's time the ubiquitous air-conditioning thermostat was often used by cyberneticists to explain the concept of negative feedback and equilibrium to a general audience. The spacesuit, for which the term cyborg was invented, was nothing other than a externalization and amplification of the body's regulation of temperature and other critical parameters through complex feedback systems design to 'maintain the human user's homeostasis under extreme environmental conditions'. This homeostatic second skin is a model for the new sort of responsive information architecture that could catalyze new and higher forms of social organization and subjectivities.

Thus, the detached skin that Banham located in Beecher's American House or in the corporate office curtain wall is converted, in the inflatable, responsive and bubble architecture, from a vestigial organ of the structural solution into an osmotic cybernetic membrane for the power-based solution. This was most fully visualized in Webb's Archigram project, the Suitaloon, a hybrid of spacesuit and bubble-tent. The subject would operate his architecture, expanding or contracting its envelope, and even zipping into that of other users to produce temporary spatializations of social relations.[34] Often these pods and bubbles were rendered as giant organs. This was an image of a deterritorialized architecture, organs without the hierarchal body of structural-solution societies. Its territories were not defined by geometries of social and political boundaries but by mobile affiliations and networking of nodes. Moreover, like the scaffolds of the Fun-Palace, bubble architecture was in many ways an attempt to reconfigure architecture into a model of industrial design that promised ever greater leisure time, and thus the possibility of more energy spent on developing new social and cultural formations. Unlike those scaffolds, which always premised a social order, the bubble emphasized a hyper-individualism. For Banham, this provided for an implicitly molecular body-politic more suited to post-war societies' social transformations and 'liberated' practices of the self. Thus, the pneumatic bubble was not a primitive hut but an appliance for this new subject in a cybernetic garden of Eden – the anti-*oikos* for the anti-Oedipus.

The third and most implicit trajectory lay in further intensification of the membrane as a taut skin of information and media. This is represented in the text via the illuminated and animated landscapes of Las Vegas, in Banham's discourses of electric light, and in his references to Sheerbart's celebrated paeans to colored glass atmospheric architectures, and to media theater productions in the early Bauhaus. Its trajectory comes to rest on an unlikely project, Philip Johnson's Glass House in New Canaan, Connecticut, a house that dispenses with complex expression of mechanical systems and instead depends upon the shading of the trees and the topography of the site to provide a normalized climate. At night, Banham notes, the trees are illuminated, further blurring any distinction between architecture and environment. The architecture in effect is a hybrid between a scaffold, a pod and an illuminated screen.

2.3: The igloo, at once structural and dynamically responsive in terms of its modulation
of light.

Conclusion: history and theory of the well-tempered environment

That Reyner Banham's *The Architecture of the Well-Tempered Environment* remains a relatively overlooked text within the histories of modern architecture and its discourses may prove that Banham's central criticism of modern architecture is correct, at least in relation to the socio-technical orderings of modern culture: that is to say, contemporary architecture and its histories continue to neglect exactly the same dimensions and realities of our subject of study that Banham argued the so-called Modernists repressed within their work.[35] In our accounts of the built environment, historical and projective alike, architecture continues to favor the static and the enclosed spaces of representation over the performative fields and their infrastructures. Just think of how circulation, flow and program continue to dominate the production of form. This is true even with the advent of 'digitally based design' in the 1990s and concepts of space such as animation and field-spaces, for what has been at stake in these discourses remains a conversation about the representation of these forces as a way to generate architectural form. This is more than amusing, since contemporary criticism of architecture depends a great deal on the supposed sophistication of critical theory and histories over the Modernists' naiveté and technological romanticism.

Whether Banham was correct in the particulars of his argument therefore becomes less important than the certain repetition of erasure of an entire dimension of the modern built environment. His text becomes useful in attempting to determine the relationship of our present, and of the future suggested by the projects in this current volume, to the unfolding histories of the discipline's modernity. Moreover, it is interesting to note how each of the three implicit trajectories of the 'power-based solution' charted in his text are being explored within contemporary architecture, though many would send a shiver down Banham's humanist spine. Others seem to extend the fantasy of transcendental liberation.

Ultimately, however, the usefulness of the text may lie in its attempt to confound the banal divisions of architectural knowledge that are limiting the field. In spite of a plea at the end of the second edition, his text continues to be filed under the Library of Congress categorization with technical manuals. A search reveals its occasional place within technical course bibliographies, but scarcely any sustained analysis within the histories and theories of architecture. With his thermodynamic ontology, the text challenges, above all, the simple dichotomies of theory and technique, space and service, that still configure architectural knowledge. The proposition that technical opportunities and problems can be the theoretical basis of architecture remains important, and potentially more productive and challenging to our conventions than critical theoretical, phenomenological or deconstructionist-derived approaches of semiotics and representation that continue to dominate the discourse. This is all the more pressing today, when architects need to convert ecology and environmental issues from technical problems with engineering solutions into engines for innovating and opening the discipline.

3.1: Detail of "Amplification' Installation.

Potential energies
Sean Lally (Weathers)

In *Animate Form,* Greg Lynn looks to the 'performative envelope' as a means of engaging the environment through forces that architecture and its surface are situated within. As an example in which this is clearly expressed he points to the construction of the boat hull, which is based on an understanding of the external forces applied to the form as it moves through the water (flow, turbulence, viscosity and drag) and its necessity for accommodating multiple 'vectors of motion' simultaneously within its shape. The focus of the 'performative envelope' is its ability to hold within its shape multiple and latent responses to various external forces that have yet to be applied. Based on the knowledge of the forces that will exist within the waters, the hull of the boat is prepared to accommodate a range of external forces exerted upon it. However, a boat designed for the shallow waters of the Mediterranean would be ill-prepared for the open waters of the Atlantic, and neither of these boat hulls in dry dock would be anything more than a carcass. As Lynn states, 'form is therefore shaped by collaboration between the envelope and the active context in which it is situated' [1]

Today architects have the resources to operate and design not solely on the basis of the needs of form as they pertain to structure, force and envelope, but instead on the environmental criteria and conditions that facilitate organizations and actions within the places we inhabit. Investigations today are no longer representations of forces that inform geometry and envelope, but simulations of the broader ecosystems and interconnected variables that make up the 'active context'. The design process focuses not only on the instrumentality of 'envelopes' as they pertain to the boat hull and the forces they index but on the 'active context' itself that architecture finds itself situated within and around.

The SIM Residence. RIGHT,
3.2: Reflected ceiling plan.
BELOW, 3.3: Physical model.

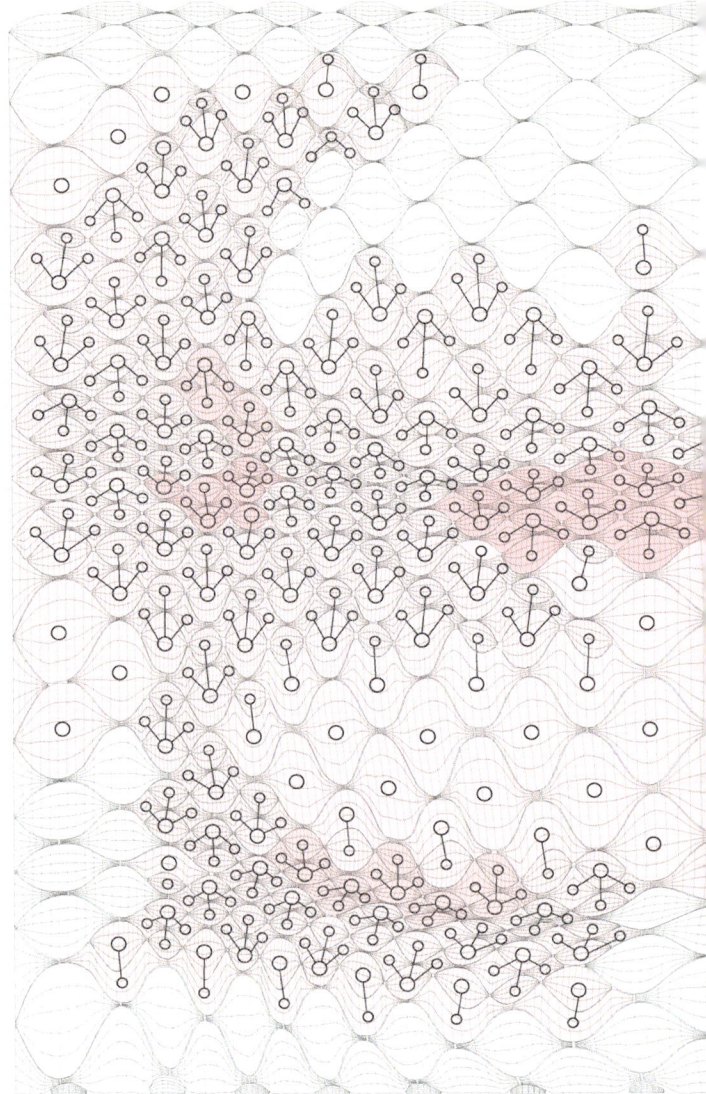

Variability: energies over form

There is a lineage within architecture committed to undermining an ingrained understanding of architecture as a discipline focused on the static. It's not necessary to look as far back as the Baroque, or to the Futurists' attempts to capture speed and movement, to recognize such attempts, as more recently architects have turned to techniques of 'the trace' or the 'self-similar multiple' as a means for indexing difference and variability. Extreme examples exist that employ the literal movement of form to accommodate and produce a multiplicity of conditions and responses, but it's precisely this type of approach to generating variability through form itself that's the 'red herring' in this discussion. As architects continue their long-standing history of borrowing and misappropriating the tools of parallel disciplines, including today's advancements in the visualization of atmospheric behaviors (developed by meteorologists and material engineers), there are more and more opportunities in how we visualize and operate upon our built environment that provide methods beyond the manipulation of geometries and formal logics for questioning and subverting architectural stasis. Previous attempts at achieving variability and adaptiveness have stemmed primarily from tools and techniques of representation focused on articulation and definition of envelopes and surfaces. Today's opportunities permit architects to engage a broader spectrum of environmental design, to engage a wider range of variables and to operate as designers on a thicker territorial context.

With the 'performative envelope' as the point of departure, this discussion will move from 'the kinetic'– relying on forces, vectors, and motion associated with form and geometry – and look towards 'the potential

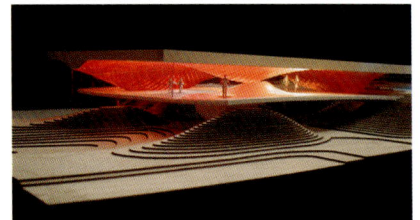

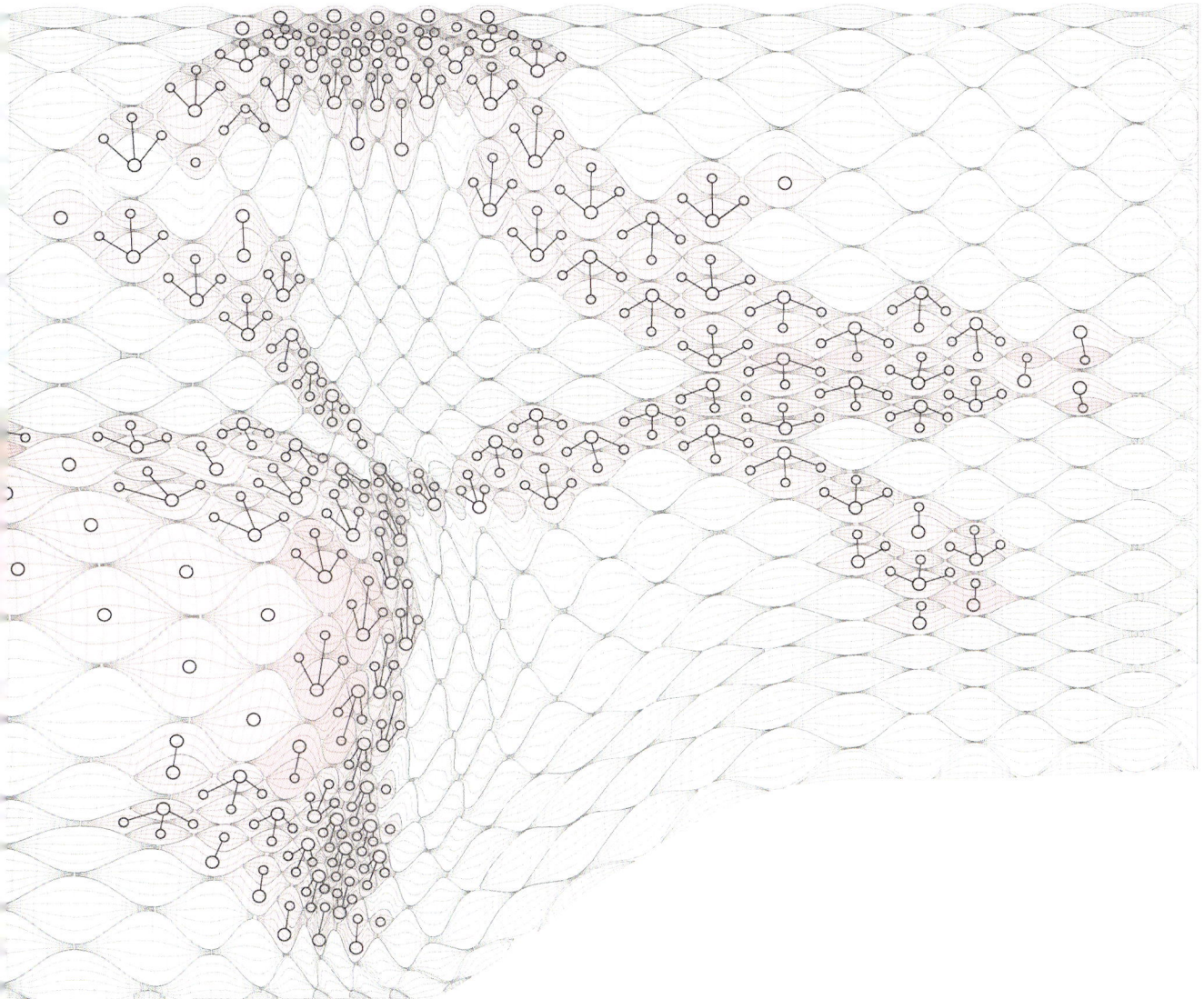

Project: THE SIM RESIDENCE

The SIM Residence Rigid in form, yet dynamic in its responsiveness to various scenarios of living, the SIM Residence displays a shift in energy from the kinetic to the potential. This is a shift in which form has the ability to become imbued with performative variation derived from multiple scenarios of configuration and position. These scenarios of living look to elastic and networked structures of organization (systems of display, illumination, and air flow and temperature) as a method to develop configurations that, while dormant, exist simultaneously within form until activated. In doing so, the SIM Residence develops a system of latent spatial conditions (scenarios) available to be called on for the varied needs of domestic living. The intent is to increase its capacity to support and diversity activities in time. These discrete systems and variations of display, illumination, and air temperature and movement network across local conditions to facilitate dynamic and responsive conditions, which define a house that is interested less in its form or massing within a site: the SIM Residence focuses on the internal conditions of living, the 'conditioned space' of the domestic.

energies of the latent, simultaneous and multiple that currently operate within our environment, yet remain under-utilized as generative spatial tools. Today's ubiquitous use of the term 'performativity' has been largely relegated to the surfaces of architecture, which act to mediate boundaries. A discussion of performance must therefore encompass a larger bandwidth of responsibility within approaches to environmental design. The intention is to shift the focus to the 'active context', and the variables of energies and material flows associated most

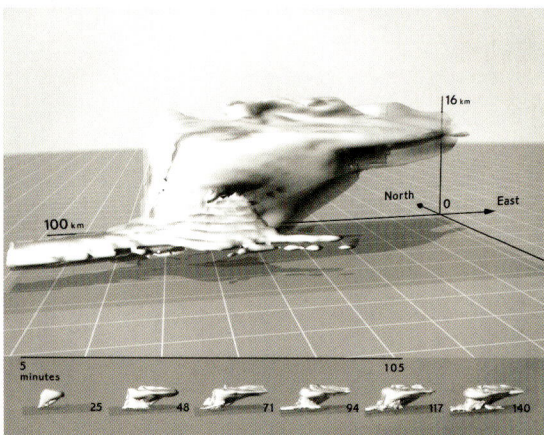

3.4: Initial investigations of Dr. Robert Wilhelmson focused on indexing forms and shapes of a tornado configuration that represented understood tornado behavior (funnels etc). With increased processor speed and data, the ability existed for the model to not simply index previously understood formal conditions that represented convection behavior but to simulate the tornado's behavior through an integration of independent variables, such as temperature, wind speed, pressure, etc.

commonly with spatial qualities (lighting, air flow, and moisture and heat transfer). Architects tend to assume that within buildings it's solely the solid surfaces that delineate and define boundaries.[2] However, advancements in the 1960s and 1970s that looked to building simulation as a means to operate upon a building's energy performance make it clear that we have developed other means for visualizing and defining such boundaries in architecture. Architecture and our inhabitable spaces are informed by more than envelopes and surfaces, and must begin to engage with ecosystems that incorporate a broader array of variables for the generation of our surroundings. These materials (energies and matter) are inherently not static but are instead variable, allowing us as designers to work within a broader bandwidth of spatial potentials.

Integrating variables and visualizing potentials

One of the most variable and least predictable common environmental behaviors belongs to the meteorologist to interpret and predict. In the late 1980s Dr. Robert Wilhelmson from the University of Illinois at Urbana-Champaign began to identify atmospheric conditions that resulted in the shift from common thunderstorms to tornados, using animation software. Though general organizational patterns of meteorology permit us a window into potential climatic conditions days in advance, scientists know less about the predictability of and relationships between severe weather systems and the conditions that permit their formations. The impetus for the research was the meteorologist's uncertainty as to why some storms produce tornados while others do not.

The SIM Residence. BELOW,
3.5: Soft-living scenarios. BOT-
TOM, 3.6: Physical model.

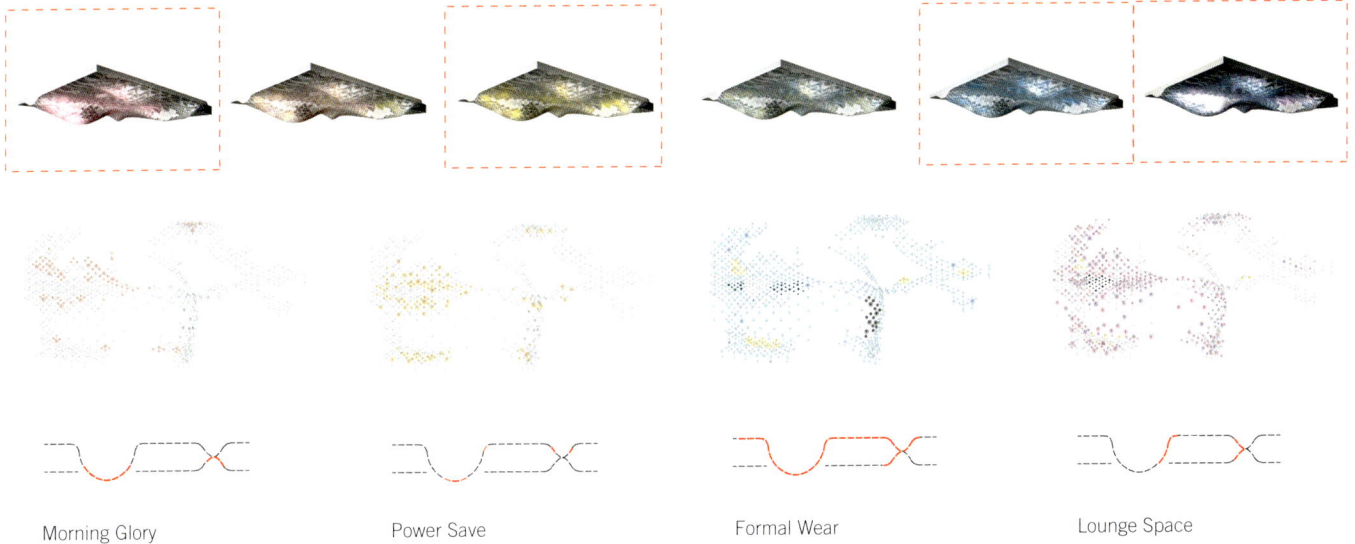

Morning Glory   Power Save   Formal Wear   Lounge Space

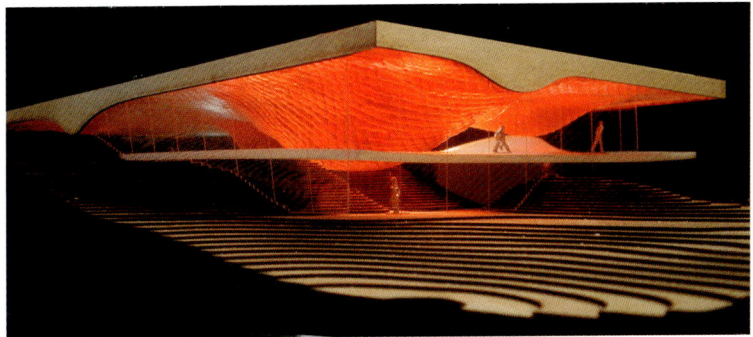

Territorializing space through light The SIM Residence looks specifically to qualities of light and air temperature as a point of departure to illustrate an ability to territorially define space through what might otherwise be dismissed simply as a quality. The dominant formal strategy is a reflected ceiling plan that consists of a network of nearly 300 interconnected points, which are a combination of lighting devices and air handlers. Lighting is used as a design strategy and material, incorporating a half-dozen scenarios for domestic living. These are configured to accommodate varied and multiple needs during the course of a day through light intensity, color and location. These configurations are not required to stay pure in their organization but can be tweened or blurred to meet the specific needs of an individual or activity within the residence.

The SIM Residence. RIGHT, 3.7: Simulations conducted in software packages that can visualize fluid dynamics, including temperature and air movement, help to broaden the bandwidth of what constitutes a material for defining boundaries and edges in architecture.

Vertices

1, 2, 3, 4, 5, 6, 7, 8, 9, 10, 11, 12, 13, 14, 15, 16, 17, 18, 19, 20, 21, 22, 23, 24, 25, 26, 27, 28, 29, 30, 31, 32, 33, 34, 35, 36, 37, 38, 39, 40, 41, 42, 43, 44, 45, 46, 47, 48, 48, 49, 50, 51, 52, 53, 54, 55, 56, 57, 58, 59, 60, 61, 62, 63, 64, 65, 66, 67, 68, 69, 70, 71, 72, 73, 74, 75, 76, 77, 78, 79, 80, 81, 82, 83, 84, 85, 86, 87, 88, 89, 90, 91, 92, 93, 94, 95, 96, 97, 98, 99, 100, 101, 102, 103, 104, 105, 106, 107, 108, 109, 110, 111, 112, 113, 114, 115, 116, 117, 118, 119, 120, 121, 122, 123, 124, 125, 126, 127, 128, 129, 130, 131, 132, 133, 134, 135, 136, 137, 138, 139, 140, 141, 142, 143, 144, 145, 146, 147, 148, 149, 150, 151, 152, 153, 154, 155, 156, 157, 158, 159, 160, 161, 162, 163, 164, 165, 166, 167, 168, 169, 170

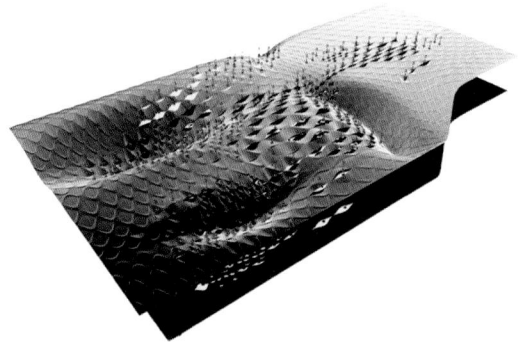

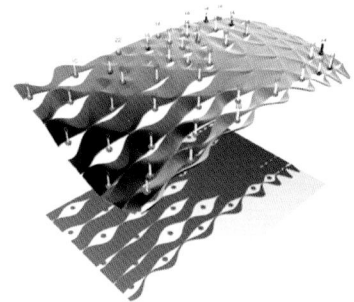

Wilhelmson wanted to investigate atmospheric conditions to understand what triggered such formations and behaviors and whether it would be possible to predict their formation through advancements in simulation software.[3]

The initial approaches focused on the animation of the storm's general structure and resultant formal conditions using available software. Much of this was based on the limited information available as attempts focused on the formal indexing of perceived behaviors, notating, for example, the resultant geometries and shapes of a storm as they pertained to understood behaviors indicative of a tornado. As the investigations and research continued for an additional ten years that included the availability of more processor speed (provided by the NCSA – National Center for Supercomputer Applications), scientists gained the ability to develop models that didn't simply index formal conditions, but attempted to simulate the tornado's behavior. This process sought to move beyond a formal representation of an understood condition within the storm, and instead build a database of variables (atmospheric temperatures, wind speeds, atmospheric pressure, humidity, etc.) as a means for interpreting the potential conditions and organizations that could arise. The geometry and external form of both the earlier and most recent approaches remain similar, but it was this shift from using graphic notations to represent formal logics to simulating environmental behaviors as a means for understanding the resultant formal configurations that was crucial.

The investigations of Dr Wilhelmson and the NCSA demonstrate an approach to articulating form based on

Potential energies > 4^{170} These then are potential energies: an exponential number of possible spatial and territorial constructs based on a network of information vertices and the static form that negotiates these relationships to the territories beyond. They are defined and refined through simulations and scenarios of desired needs for living. The examples included are intended to illustrate the availability of difference and the sheer magnitude of potentials that exist within a system of limited variables. The gradient colors above don't represent formal configurations, but instead spatial organizations and gradients suitable and malleable for varied activities and actions of individuals.

4^{170} Permutations
> 170 Vertices
> 4 conditions

4^{33} Permutations
> 33 Vertices
> 4 conditions

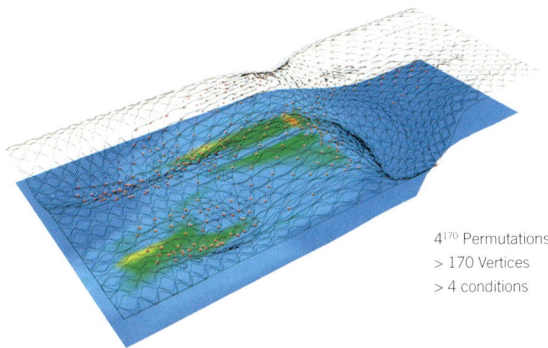

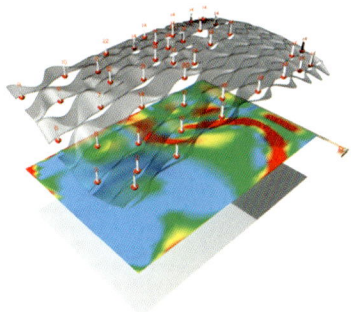

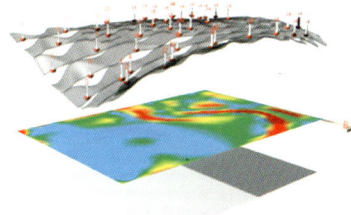

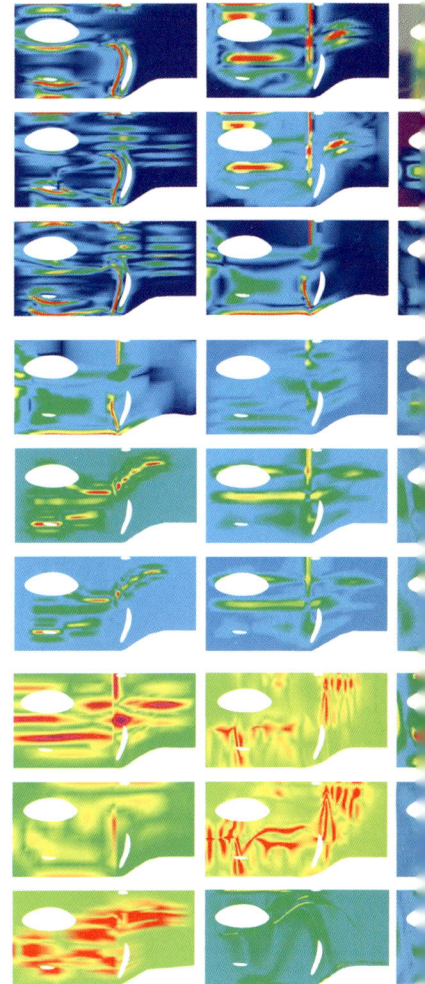

Territorializing space through air quality and temperature Even though form isn't the impetus for design decisions, it's never understood to be neutral in terms of its performance within space. The network of 300 interconnected points, which include air handlers, requires airflow and its gradient temperature to pass from the handler, through varied formal configurations and into the space beyond. Criteria for material and formal configuration is provided through simulations that provide feedback as to how that air moves and behaves with various possible formal configurations and spatial dimensions. The formal configurations are therefore a negotiation between the vertices or points that emit the air and light and the territories beyond. It is a collaboration between its formal configuration and the desired spatial qualities and conditions it mediates between.

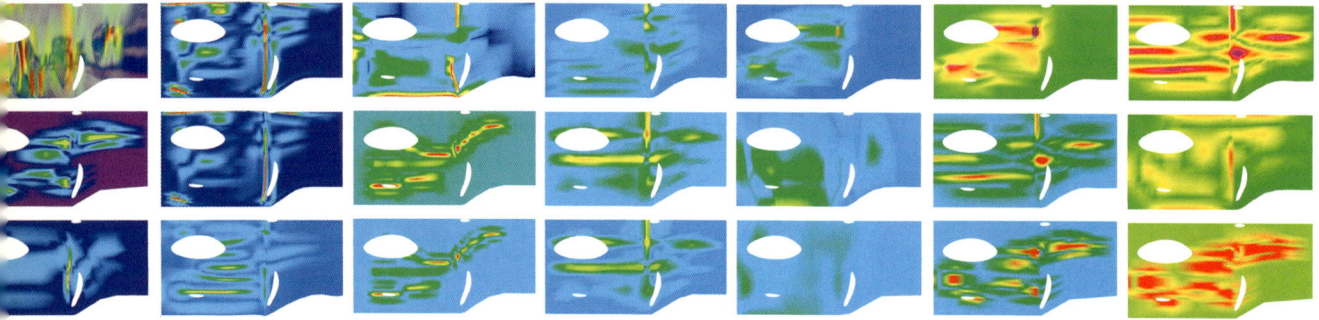

what many architects would quickly jump to dismiss as unusable, qualitative environmental conditions. Such investigations highlight the instrumentality of spatial qualities and effects as a means for articulating and constructing space and territory. These are implications that therefore have the potential to extend beyond the environmental needs associated with the conditioning of an interior space and into investigations focused on the understanding and instrumentality of the 'active context'. Dr. Wilhelmson's earlier visualizations and research relied on a geometric definition to represent an environmental condition – the use of form as a crutch to represent what was essentially definable not by borders and edges, geometries and solids, but by gradients and magnitudes, energies and variables. The simulations that permitted a diagnosis of the tornado's organizational system point towards an approach that provides architects with decision-making tools, enabling intensities, gradients and magnitudes of qualities to begin to play a role in the organization of resultant spaces and territories.

The research of Dr. Wilhelmson and the NCSA also highlights the potential design tools and methodologies available to architects for design exploration. Such investigations require the architect to have a means for choreographing relationships and interactions that might otherwise be understood as simply discrete qualitative effects. As a generative tool for questioning and researching the potentials of what constitutes spatial boundaries and organizations, the architect must be able to operate upon and visualize such information, and not simply represent a desired singular stasis but

simulate the behavior and interaction of these variables as latent and viable design scenarios. Unlike meteorologists, who have the unpredictability of climatic conditions to deal with, architects have the ability to control the stimulation of variables for spatial and design needs. If information including the behaviors of such energies can be quantified and visualized, then that information has the means for being made operative in the definition and qualification of the territories we construct and inhabit.

3.8: Enabling researchers to engage information in ways previously unavailable, the Cave provides an immersive virtual-reality room for visualizing and engaging spatial environments as they play out scenarios in front of you. See http://cave.ncsa.uiuc.edu

3.9: Site model, 'Amplification'
Installation, Schindler's Kings
Road House, East Courtyard.

Project· AMPLIFICATION INSTALLATION

'Amplification' Installation, Fall 2006, Schindler
House, Los Angeles Shifting from a focus on form-
finding and composition to an investigation of spatial
performance and behavior requires a progression in
how one defines desired and obtainable goals. Looking
to the courtyard and garden of the Schindler House,
the intention is to refrain from constructing or introducing a new system within the space but simply to
'amplify' and heighten existing domestic qualities of
living that characterize and define its locale. Vegetation offers a range of opportunities in its abilities
to introduce and provide spatial qualities, such as
variability in bloom, growth size, color, scent, and
filtration of light, as well as the micro-climates that

Vegetation   Facilitators   Climatic Zones   Space as Form

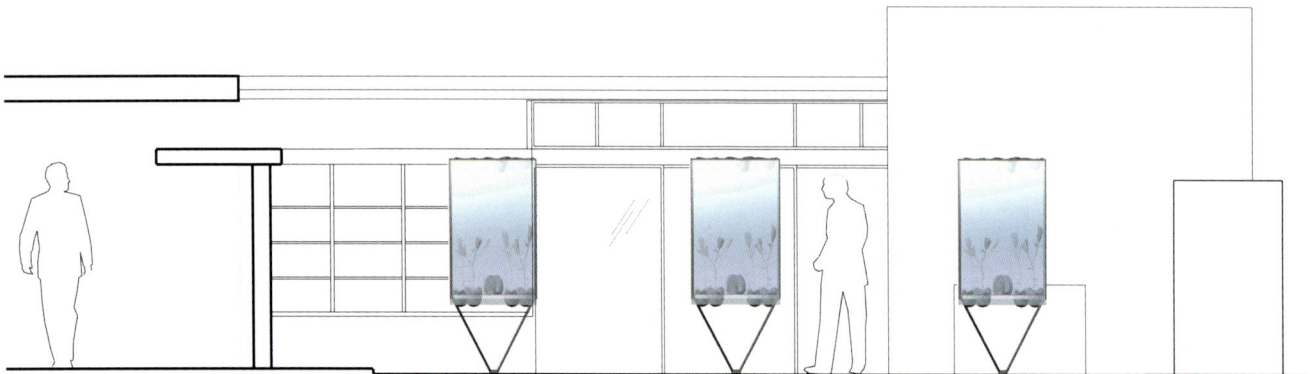

TOP, 3.10: Materials including
vegetation and the accompanying qualities of temperature,
light and scent are controlled
and amplified through facilitators such as heating devices,
fans and lighting which produce
resultant micro-climates of heat,
water vapor, condensation and
air particulates, creating spatial
boundaries and edges. ABOVE,
3.11: Section, 'Amplification'
Installation, Schindler's Kings
Road House, East Courtyard.

are required for varied plant types. The project is an
amplification device in which 'form' acts to mediate
between these quantified qualities and the spaces
they define and reside within. The project is an intervention that works to heighten and manipulate these
qualities and performances as a means to instrumentalize them. Qualitative aspects of the garden, including micro-climates of temperature, humidity, scent,
color and light, are identified through the physiology
of the plants and ecological systems responsible as a
means to amplify and operate upon these conditions.
The materials and operational strategies in this architecture and space are the physiology of the ecological
systems that encompass us.

3.12: Site model, 'Amplification'
Installation, Schindler's Kings
Road House, East Courtyard.

Vegetation, Climate and Facilitators Vegetation
is chosen from a range of climatic zones ranging
from humid, moist conditions to those of temperate,
shaded ones. These existing climatic conditions are
used as initial states from which they are 'amplified'
and 'altered' as design materials in the construction of new spatial territories and zones. Facilitators
– including heat sources in the water located below,
cooling agents in the top, air particulates introduced
between, lighting, and fans that control the velocity
of air movement – are quantifiable and controlled
to act upon the initial climatic conditions to create
varying and unique environments and internal spatial
boundaries. Each of these variables interacts and is
used to control and instrumentalize a range of criteria
generally dismissed as simply qualitative.

A   B   C   D

— A

— B

— C

— D

Temperature (°F)
Isosurface:
Pressure (lbf/in'2)

Fluid Temperature

Material Temperature

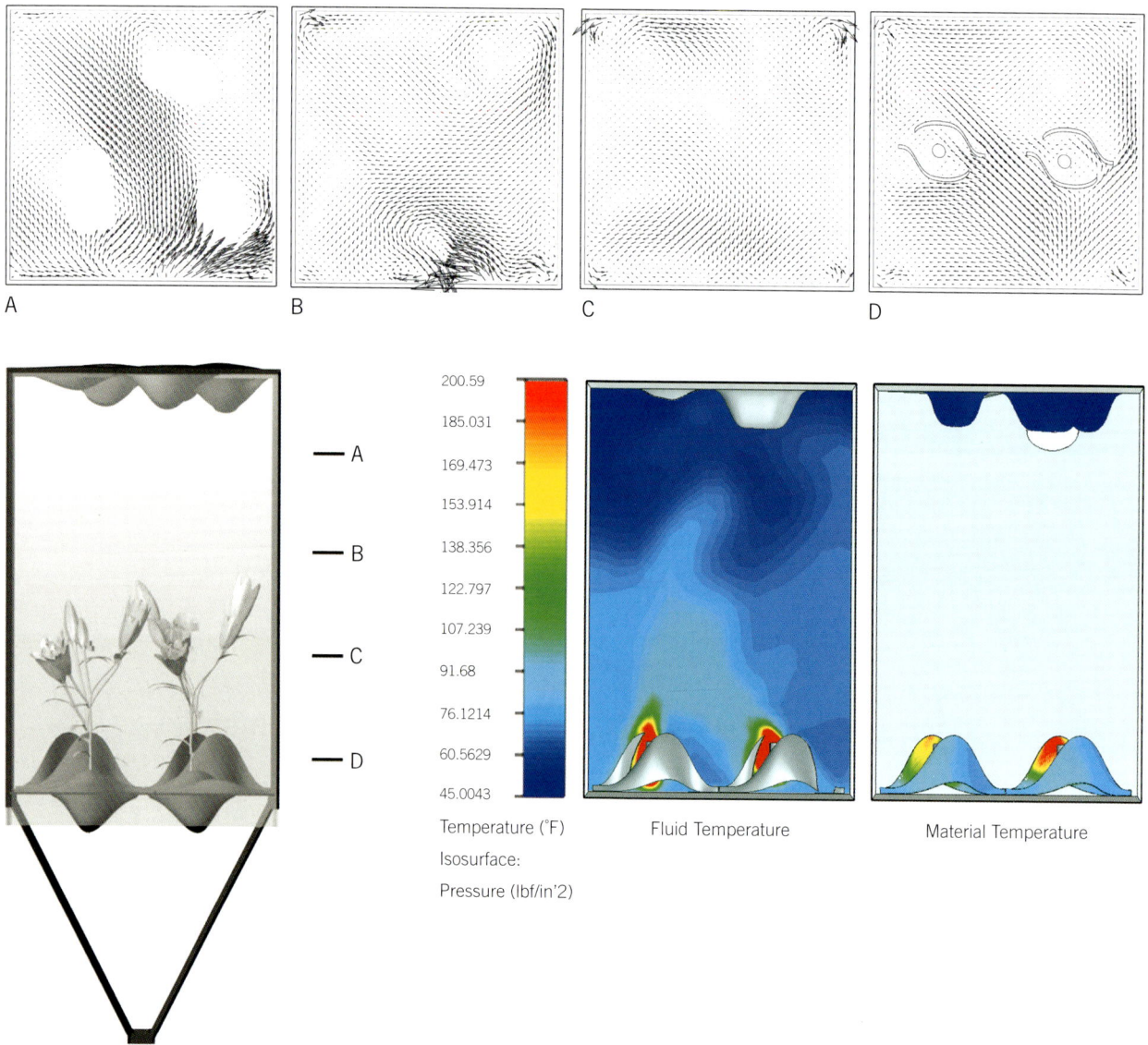

ABOVE, 3.13: Simulations in COSMOS permit each of the six "units" that make up the 'Amplification' Installation to appear identical in shape and form, yet unique and variable in terms of the interior spatial behaviors. This occurs through an understanding of material energies and fluid dynamics as design materials, rather than through the use solely of structure and geometry. OPPOSITE, 3.14: The elements of a typical "unit."

Tracer Humidity

Tracer colors are added to water and subsequent condensation, creating visual and spatial boundaries.

Fans

The fans control the movement and circulation of air for plant growth, including formations of micro-climates and air-flows visualized through colored dyes and humidity.

Acrylic Container

The container is engraved to trap water condensation on the interior in various sizes and patterns, trapping the water for recirculation.

Vegetation

Plant material grown in containers facilitates the varying climatic zones and systems.

Lighting

Fluorescent bulbs for plant growth, including the visualization and fluorescent dyes in vegetation and tracers in air and water.

Plant Containers

For the hydroponic growth of plant materials.

4.1: Photographed by a crew member on board the International Space Station, this image shows the limb of the Earth (at the bottom) transitioning into the orange-colored troposphere, the lowest and most dense portion of the Earth's atmosphere. The troposphere ends abruptly at the tropopause, which appears in the image as the sharp boundary between the orange- and blue-colored atmosphere.

The phenomena of the non-visual
Michelle Addington

Orthographic projection produces the objectified surface – fixed in Cartesian space and endlessly reproducible. What cannot be easily reproduced is the perception or experience of the environment that is always transient, always unique. Defining the surface does not define the environment. We traditionally design to create an image or sequence of images rather than a visual response; we design to replicate interior conditions rather than for a thermal experience. Perception becomes incidental, and yet we presume to design experience through the avatar of the surface. A discussion about light in an architectural work will focus on the materials and their placement. Any discussion about heat will revolve around the façade. When phenomena are foregrounded, they are described as the preternatural results of carefully designed architectural artifacts. Essentially, we have assigned environmental causality to an image on a picture plane.

This objectification of the surface as both the progenitor and the representative frame of environmental phenomena keeps us tautologically bound to a Renaissance definition of space even while our surface forms have become progressively articulated and non-orthogonal. Escaping this bind requires that we subordinate the hegemony of the picture plane representation, and begin to understand the surface as fluid and contingent rather than fixed and constituent. Only then can we begin to apply the unprecedented array of tools now available, which allows for the representation of phenomenological behavior.

Perceptual environments – those that determine what we feel, hear and see – are all thermodynamic in that they are fundamentally about the motion of energy. Furthermore, as energy is not visible, thermodynamic systems are not legible. As such, our normative mode of spatial representation has left us ill-equipped to design for perception. The tools do exist, the knowledge is available, but we must shift our contexts through which we define the body's environment in a building. The contexts in question are those that are premised on formal determinism. The concept of boundary, the use of scale, and the choice of the reference frame seem pro forma to us, but the presumption that the building, particularly its form, serves as the point of origin for defining these is antithetical to the description of energy systems. In these systems, boundaries are behaviors, not walls, and scale relates to the phenomenon and not to the size of the building. More difficult to untangle is the issue of the reference frame, being shifted from one in which the building is the objective determinant to one in which the subject operates as the center. The following essay steps away from our normative representation of the perceptual environment, and begins to ask how we might reconfigure these contexts in order to produce architecture as a construction of subjective effects rather than an assembly of objective artifacts.

Boundary as behavior

The term 'boundary' in architecture traditionally connotes limits – the boundary as a property line, as a building envelope, as the walls of a room. Its two-dimensional representation is a line that demarcates a discontinuity between adjacent entities. Inside and outside exist on opposite sides of the line in a plan, as do first floor and second floor in a section. Extruded, the line becomes our orthographic surface, and thus not only the limits of an environment but also its container. This boundary is static and defined, and its legibility for marking the limits is traditionally relegated to the visual artifact. In physics, however, the boundary is not a thing or a place, but an action that cannot be fixed or even designated in our conventional framing of space.

The boundary as action is the zone of thermodynamic energy exchange between two quiescent environments or energy fields. Collapsed into this zone of activity are a series of behaviors that serve as the means for transferring energy from one of these fields to another. We might be tempted to loosely describe it as a zone of transition or mediation, and thus presume that it can be equated to a threshold, perhaps as a region of ambiguity in which both fields co-exist, or even as a blurring where the edges may be indefinite. Transfer, however, is not the same as transition.

Our dependence on orthographic projection inherently privileges a spatial transition from one entity to another – regardless of whether that transition is scalar, linear or algebraic. A transition in direct sunlight can readily be plotted if the two-dimensional geometries are defined; a transition in the plane of view can similarly be constructed from perspectival projections. Notwithstanding the current preoccupation with descriptive geometry, in which extraordinarily complex geometric operations can negotiate between dissimilar and incongruous forms, the operations are still rooted in objective

4.2: Profiles of air temperature and velocity in two common types
of boundary layers:
(A) the boundary layer that develops between a heated surface
and cooler surroundings;
(B) the boundary layer that forms in open space above a heated
source (designated by the point).

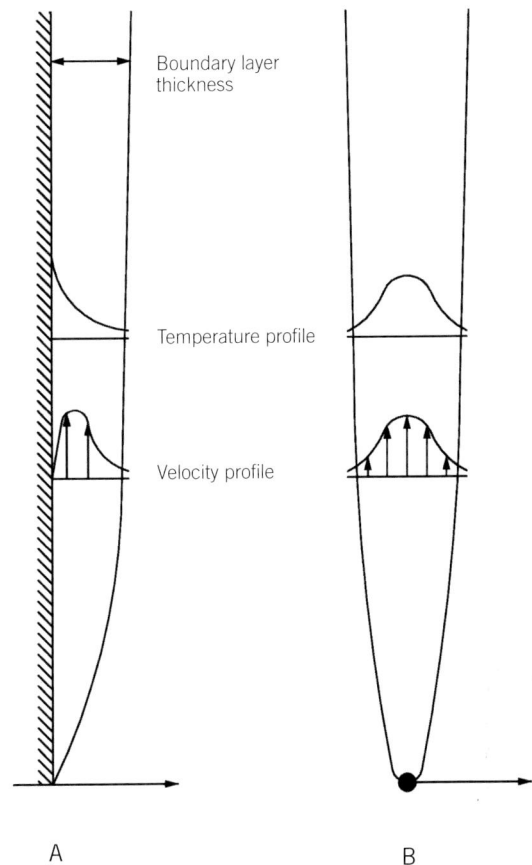

4.2: Profiles of air temperature and velocity in two common types of boundary layers:
(A) the boundary layer that develops between a heated surface and cooler surroundings;
(B) the boundary layer that forms in open space above a heated source (designated by the point).

Cartesian dimensions. Energy transfer, however, cannot be determined from geometries, and therefore we cannot neatly map these exchanges in relation to dimensioned entities. Heat, defined as the energy transferred as the result of a temperature difference, is transferred by motion, even though the temperature difference may be between two stationary entities. The boundary, then, is an active region of negotiation rather than a transitional space. As an illustration (see fig. 4.2), we can see that a velocity field will emerge and then disappear in the boundary between the static wall and adjacent, unmoving air. More importantly, the boundary of interest is not the wall as a discontinuity, but the moving layer that emerges between the wall and the adjacent environment.

The boundary layer comes into being only when there is an energy difference. This energy difference can be due to temperature, pressure, density, phase, height, momentum or concentration, and a unique boundary layer will appear for each difference and each magnitude of difference, and disappear when equilibrium is reached. Much more common than the boundary that appears next to a wall are those that develop in open space, known as free field boundaries. Among the most obvious of these are weather fronts, and we fully recognize that a cloud bank serves as the boundary layer in which two different-pressure air masses are negotiated. Not so easy for us to visualize are the free field boundaries that are continuously popping up and disappearing in our interior environments. All heat-producing entities – from computers, to lighting, to human bodies – produce a narrow boundary layer in which the energy is transferred

to the surroundings (fig. 4.2B). The pervasive image of environments as being relatively homogeneous belies not only the existence of these boundaries, but their importance in determining the body's perception of its surroundings. Essentially, the operative 'surfaces' in a building are these fleeting boundaries – not the fixed artifacts of walls, floors and ceilings. For the human body, then, the thermal environment is defined by the behavior of the boundary layer immediately adjacent to the body (see fig. 4.3). In spite of our incredibly bloated HVAC systems that condition huge volumes of air to maintain the building's environment at prescribed conditions, the effective surfaces of the body's thermal environment –that is, what the body 'reads' as its thermal environment – are all contained within the surrounding few centimeters of its boundary layer.

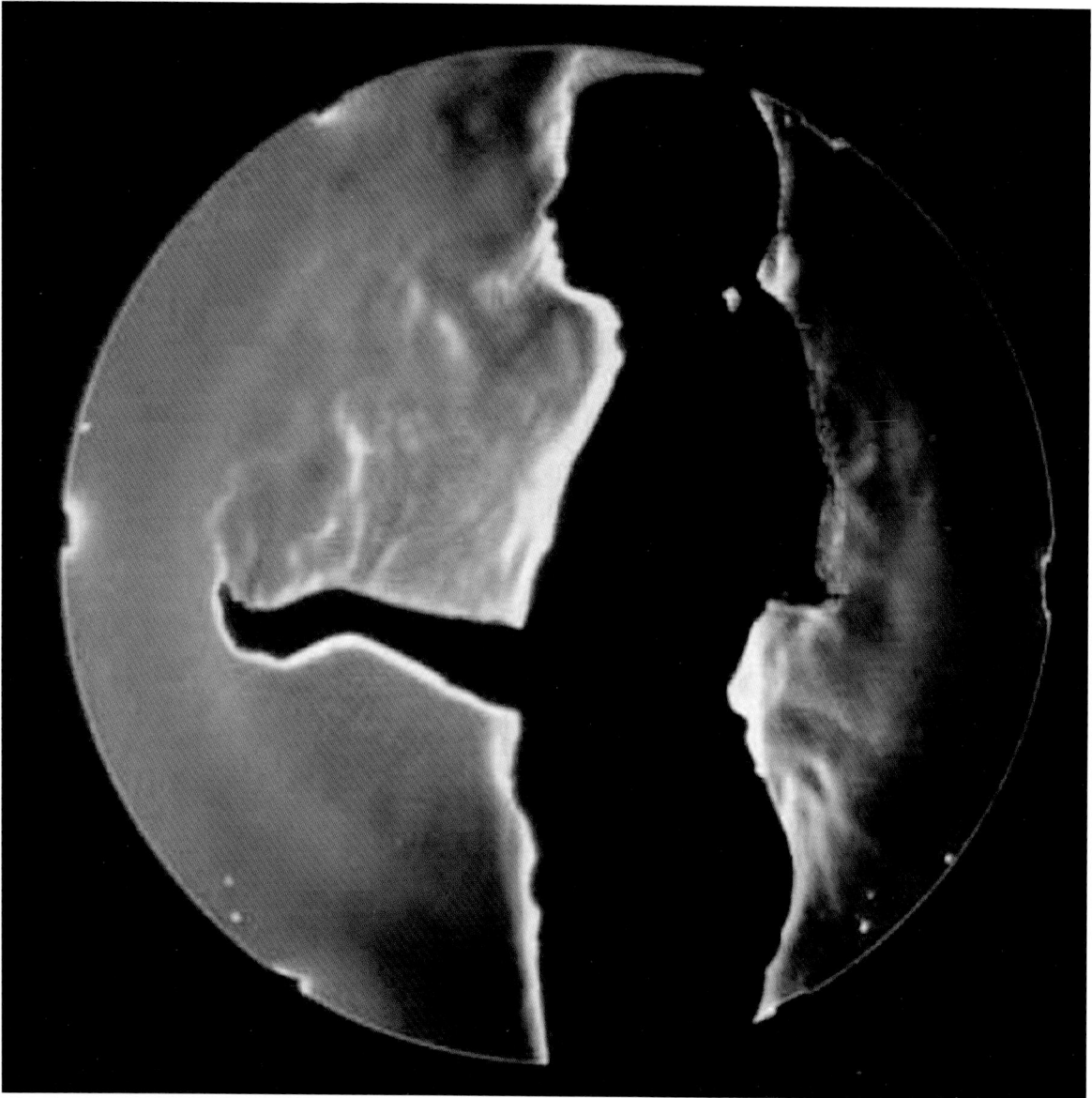

4.3: Schlieren image of the thermal boundary layer surrounding a girl.

Macro-scale ·········· Meter ··········
Meso-scale ·········· Centimeter ····
Micro-scale ·········· Micron ············
Nano-scale ············ Nanometer ·····
Pico-scale ············ Picometer ····

Convection (sound)

Radiation (light)

Conduction (diffusion-heat)

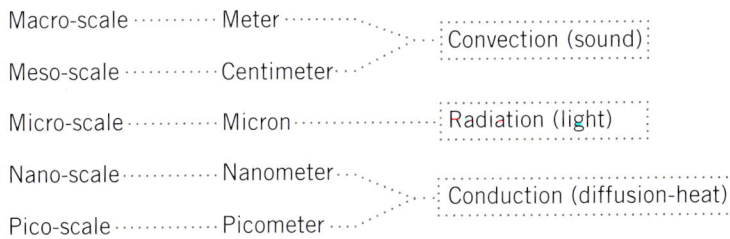

4.4: The scales at which thermodynamic phenomena are governed.

Scale

Perhaps even more difficult to conceptualize in regard to energy boundaries is just how little they have to do with the artifacts of design. Regardless of the complexity of a formal design, all the resulting artifacts can be described in geometric relationship to one another. As such, we can say that architectural form-making follows the rules of geometric similitude. Energy behaviors, and particularly thermodynamic behaviors, follow the rules of dynamic similitude. The magnitude of the forces determines how the relationship from one entity is negotiated. This is true even for boundary layers that are adjacent to a fixed wall – doubling the height of the wall will not affect the behavior of the layer, whereas a tiny change in temperature may instigate a radically different behavior.

Geometric dimensions are not inconsequential, but the dimensions of interest for energy boundaries are at scales that are several orders of magnitude smaller than those we associate with the built environment. In architecture, we use the terms micro- and macro scale analogously in relation to built objects – micro-scale might represent for us a room or a building, macro-scale might represent a site or an urban area. When we discuss the scale of energy behaviors, however, we use the dimensional scales quite literally – micro-scale describes those phenomena that are determined by micron-sized features. The behaviors that determine our perception of light, heat and sound are all produced by the basic mechanisms that drive heat transfer, and these mechanisms have a characteristic scale at which they are governed (see fig. 4.4).

Light, as a tiny subset of the electromagnetic spectrum, is wholly determined by features that are sized from 0.4 to 0.75 microns. When we design for light, we tend to design at the scale of a building – we think in terms of surfaces and their orientation. If south light is desired in a space, the building might be reoriented to face south, or an elaborate sunlight-directing system with roof-mounted heliostats might be used. But these strategies, even though typical, are exaggerated moves that indirectly produce the desired light conditions, and do so with substantial over-engineering. A thin film with a carefully designed 'texture' on any façade could easily deliver the desired light quality – an economy of scale matched to an economy of means. Herein lies one of the non-intuitive paradoxes of design: the artifacts that we see are not the determinants of their own visibility. Instead, what we recognize as a formal object, such as a wall, is tangible only coincidentally in that the surfaces of an object are generally the carriers of the micron-sized features. Indeed, when artists such as James Turrell operate intentionally at the level of light behavior to cause solid walls to seemingly disappear or make walls appear in thin air, we often describe the images as illusions or gestalt rather than as the fundamental manifestations of physics at its most basic level.

Among the energy behaviors of interest to the designer of human environments, only the convection of sound operates at dimensions similar to building scale. The wavelengths of audible sound vary from a centimeter to about 20 meters, and therefore the specific construction of wall sections and the volumetric positioning of surfaces become the primary determinants of sound

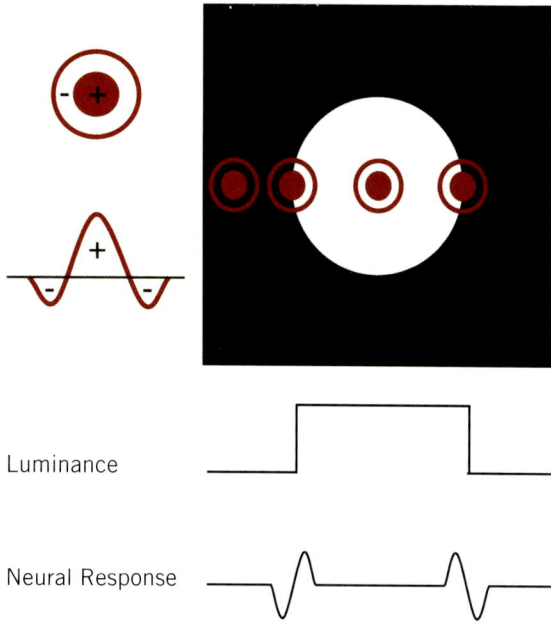

Luminance

Neural Response

4.5: Receptor field of the human eye. The receptor field 'zeros out' areas in which luminance levels do not change – the center of the field reads positive for photon interactions and the periphery reads negative for the same quantity of photon interactions. As long as levels are continuous, the neural response of the eye is unchanged, regardless of what the absolute luminous levels are. High luminance and low luminance produce identical neural responses. Only when difference is encountered 'within' the receptor field is there any change in response.

reception. Any wavelength of audible sound more than twice as large as the cross-sectional dimensions of the wall section will interact with the surfaces by rules of geometric optics. As such, this is the one exception in which the orthographic projection of picture planes can be translated directly into mapping the movement of sound in a space. Nevertheless, the orthographic projections of interest extend beyond simply the wall surfaces: about half of the audible range is small enough that the wall section dimensions will dominate. Rather than sound directly reflecting off the visible surface of a wall, different frequencies in the same bounce will 'see' different surfaces inside the wall, almost as if there were a simultaneity of many walls rather than only one.

The understanding of scale is important not only for the characterization of phenomena, but also for the determination of the appropriate means for manipulating those phenomena. The scales that govern the physical phenomena match directly with the scales of the human neurobiological system. Our perception of the visual domain is determined completely by a difference in photon activations in adjacent receptor cells. If there is no dif-

ference at this scale, or if the gradient of the difference is gradual, then the eye is incapable of distinguishing between black and white even insofar as there may be several orders of magnitude difference in the measured luminance levels at room scale (see fig. 4.5). Many aspects that we assign to a surface through its dimensions, such as position and distance, are 'read' wholly through microscopic rifts in luminance within the field of view. Just as light can best be controlled at the micron level, perception is also best activated at the micron level. One can design a room of surfaces at particular locations and orientations to indirectly create a desired visual reading of a space or one can take any arbitrary collection of surfaces and script tiny luminance shifts within the field of view to directly create the same effect.

Although less is known about the body's thermo-receptors (heat) and mechanoreceptors (sound), there does exist a similar specificity in these receptor fields at the scales of the relevant phenomena. Indeed, rather than immersing the body in a large surround of ambient air at a controlled temperature, one could selectively manage homeothermy (for example, using conductive

4.6: Frames of reference (t_0 is initial time, t_1 is some future time):
(A) Eulerian frame with objective coordinates for tracking motion;
(B) Lagrangian frame of reference – the present and future location can be one of many possibilities.

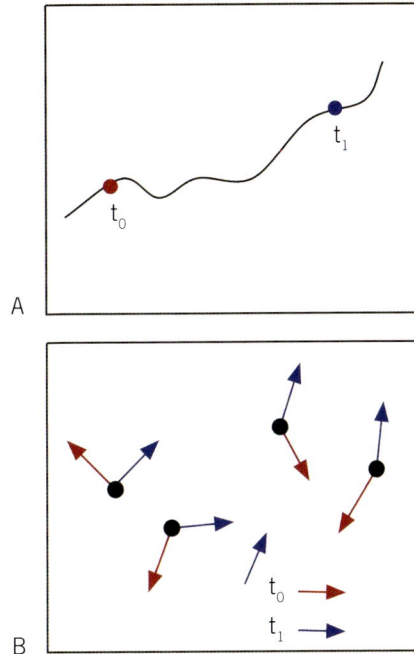

A

B

heat transfer near the carotid artery) while simultaneously articulating the perception of thermal events by selectively activating different receptor fields on different parts of the body. If we can operate directly at the scale of the phenomena to design receptor responses, then the surface, rather than being the primary determinant of its subjective reading, becomes almost incidental.

Lagrangian and Eulerian frames of reference

At the heart of subjectivity lies the concept of simultaneity. Although much of current architecture regards itself as posing conundrums, the objectification wrought by its translation into static forms, no matter how complex, privileges only the multiple, not the simultaneous. To be clear, simultaneity does not require movement of the forms – kinetic architecture is still represented by a sequence of multiples. It does require, however, a shift in the frame of reference.

In a Cartesian system, defining the coordinates of an object fixes the object in space, as defining the coordinates of a viewer fixes the viewer's place in the same space at any given time. When time is added as

a variable to a Cartesian system, the resulting frame of reference is said to be Eulerian. The spatial relationship between object and viewer may change, but for each moment of time there can only be one relationship. As a result, defining the location predetermines and thus fixes the 'view.'

Eulerian frames of reference are used extensively to objectify complex physical phenomena – by plucking out certain moments, one can develop a series of still 'pictures', and since every picture refers back to the same coordinate system, one can track a behavior (see fig. 4.6A). Tracking, however, is not substantively predictive, and more importantly, it is not explanatory. Furthermore, the fixity of the frame encourages the association of the artifact with the point of origin. As an example, a particular corner in a building will establish the locus for all other objects. The Eulerian frame is thus an idealized frame – pure geometries lead to closed mathematical relationships. As such, fields in which uncertainty plays a major role, particularly quantum mechanics and fluid dynamics, require an additional frame of reference that allows for the messiness of an intractable problem.

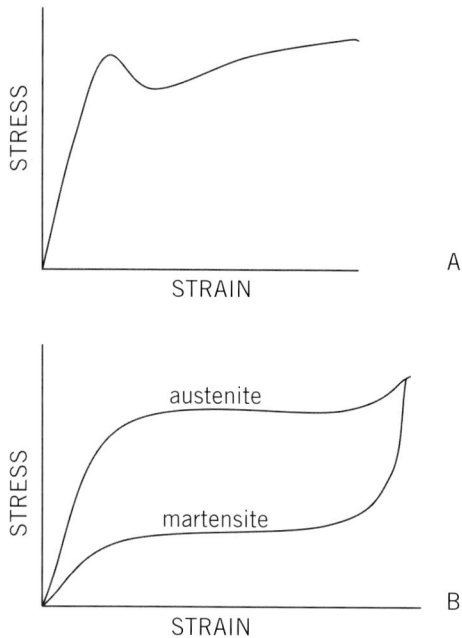

4.7: Comparison of stress–strain curves for conventional material (A), and for a shape memory alloy such as nitinol (B). Depending upon the starting temperature, the material will deform either in the martensite phase (low temperature) or the austenite phase (high temperature).

Lagrangian frames of reference, rather than being idealized, are premised on uncertainty and variability. The coordinate system has its origin not at a point fixed in space, but at the center of the subject (see fig. 4.6B). The frame is thus always subjective, and the artifactual objects are then viewed as fleeting entities of varying size and aspect, even insofar as they are invariant and stationary. Defining the positional coordinates no longer defines the artifact, and the subject must know where it has been, as well as where it is going, in order to know what it is seeing at any given moment. Lagrangian frames embed time as presenting simultaneous possibilities instead of as a linear march in which there can only be one position for each moment of time.

Perhaps the clearest example demonstrating the difference between a Lagrangian and a Eulerian frame involves stress-strain relationships in materials. Conventional materials fundamentally obey Hooke's law during elastic deformation. If the amount of stress on a material is known, then its position (as a result of deformation) is also known – there is only one possible path (see fig. 4.7A). In contrast, shape memory alloys such as

nitinol have two possible paths depending upon what stage of phase transformation the material is currently undergoing (see fig. 4.7B). Only by knowing where the material has been is it possible to know whether it is the martensitic path or the austenitic path.

Decoupling phenomena from form and foregrounding the subjective environment may yield unprecedented opportunities to design for perception. The understanding of human perception has typically been genericized in architecture, and described in relationship as qualities that belong to, and are therefore determined by, a building – the temperature of the ambient air, the footcandles on a surface. Perception, however, is active, and in Lagrangian terms wholly dependent upon the body's recent experiences – what one sees is determined not only by what is in the field of view at any one time but by what was in the field of view the moment before, as well as by which direction the eyes may be turning in: 'identical' images will be perceived differently if the eyes are moving from left to right rather than from right to left, and similarly so with up and down motions. Current research is demonstrating that even a tiny shift in the spectral distribution of light entering from the periphery of the eye rather than the center can completely reset the body's circadian rhythm. The thermal sensations of the body are due to changes in the rate of heat transfer on the surface of the skin and are perceivable only when the *rate of change* is changing from the moment before. The ambient temperature of the room is almost insignificant in determining sensation.

There has been an explosion in the amount of knowledge available regarding the functioning of the body in relation to its perceptual environments, and yet the architectural approach to perception remains wedded to assumption and anecdote. It is difficult for us to design what we can't see in order to determine what we do see, or to design for a tactility that is completely disconnected from an object. Regardless of how innovative our representational methods and building forms have become, we still address perception incidentally and statically. What would we make, as architects, if we could design for subjective experience?

Designing for perception

There is a wide array of computational tools that could allow us to make a small foray into this non-intuitive world. Computational fluid dynamics (CFD), originally developed in 1973 by NASA to replace wind-tunnel testing, has revolutionized many fields, from nuclear cooling to micro-electronics, because of its ability to characterize the transient behavior of air movement and heat transfer. Although its entry into the field of architecture didn't come until twenty years later, there already is a large body of experience with this tool, particularly in the major consulting firms. Indeed, very few large projects move forward without at least one CFD study that explores issues of wind or ventilation. Nevertheless, the application is heavily constrained by extant technologies – particularly HVAC systems – that produce stable, ambient conditions within the building volume. This assumption, that the thermal environment belongs to the building, prevents any substantive examination of individual behaviors, as the only boundaries in these models are the surfaces of the walls, not the numerous

layers against or around non-equilibrium conditions. Even the computational grids used for discretization are produced in the building's image as a container – boxes of conservative volumes that are several orders of magnitude larger than the phenomena supposedly being studied. In no other field that uses CFD would there be an *a priori* decision that the only energy boundaries of interest must belong to the largest solid surfaces.

Much of the difficulty we have in overcoming our innate prejudice that these tools should analyze building systems, and not thermal behavior, cycles back to issues of representation. In the other fields that use CFD, orthographic projection was never a common means of representation; indeed, most of these fields only use orthographic projection in association with the visualization of CFD data. As a result, there is no misunderstanding that the visualization is anything other than a means of simplifying the presentation of data. In the field of architecture, however, the automatic assignation of geometric form to an orthographic projection presumes that the representation and the object are one and the same. We are not able to extricate the visualization of an object from the visualization of behavior. The abstract representation of discretized data becomes instead a surrogate for our assumptions regarding the environment that surrounds us.

Our assumptions regarding the phenomena in our physical surroundings have been surprisingly resistant to reconfiguration, and this may well be due to the hegemony of the visual avatar. Phenomena, which are discrete and transient, are appropriated by the body's neurological system in an equally discrete and transient manner, such that all sensory experience is unique for each individual. There has been a long-standing effort to objectify sensory experience, particularly the thermal experience, and this is manifest through the various 'performance' measures that mandate the ideal interior conditions in a building. Indeed, much of today's current attention to the design of interior thermal environments refers to the PMV, or predicted mean vote, which attempts to quantity an ambient temperature that the majority of occupants will find neutral – that is, they will not *notice* their ambient surroundings. Sensation, however, does not provide a picture of the surrounding environment, nor does it necessarily serve as a means to communicate the construction of that environment. Our sensory systems activate only in the presence of change, and our cognitive awareness of heat, light or sound is not of the environment at all, but of the manner in which our own bodies are reacting to the environment. We directly sense ourselves, and only indirectly sense our environment.

The visual avatar becomes the language, and the only language, through which we can communicate that which is ostensibly private and personal. But we cannot draw what is perceptually present through the means of orthographic projection any more than we can draw what is physically present (with 'physical' referring to the phenomena and not to the artifact). As such, our representations of interior environments remain stunningly simplistic. As an example, the architecture field tends to 'validate' CFD simulations of room environments by comparing the results to reality, but this is a reality that has been determined by image, not physics. An image of

how air moves in a room that dates from 1844 (see fig. 4.8A), drawn long before the physics of air movement was fully understood, is little different from the visualization produced by a CFD package 150 years later (see fig. 4.8B), even though the CFD package represents the state-of-the-art understanding of heat transfer and fluid mechanics. In a similar vein, many of the tools that simulate light privilege photorealism – the image – over, ironically, vision. Photorealism is precisely what the term implies: the resulting image looks just like a photograph. We are fully aware that photographs represent what the camera sees, not what or how the eye sees, but we tend to abandon that distinction when we collapse photorealism into our orthographic projections. There has been some effort, however, directed toward using these tools to understand the construction of the visual field. The photorealistic images are still popular, but many architects are now investigating light via contour-level plotting, as it is the contours that determine what we see and not the surfaces (see fig. 4.9). Nevertheless, even these contours are generally plotted at building scale, and not at the scale of either light or vision.

The most advanced digital tools have been tautologically bound to reproduce that which we believe we know, rather than investigate that which we do not know. Escaping this constraint demands that we operate supra to the artifact rather than subordinate to it. Indeed, if we could use our digital tools to characterize physical behaviors, and not just to visualize them, the surface as both architecture and its representation might lose its hegemonic dominion. Instead of articulating the surfaces and filling the container with ambient (and

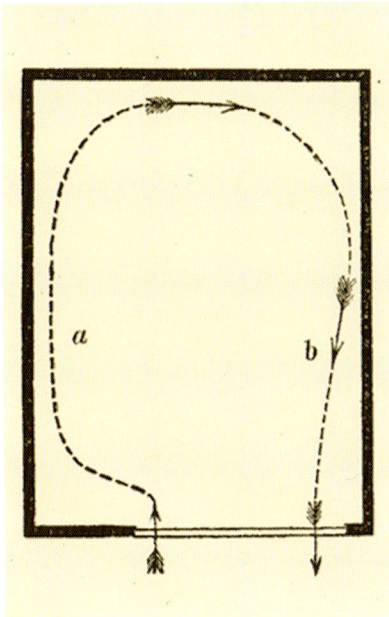

A

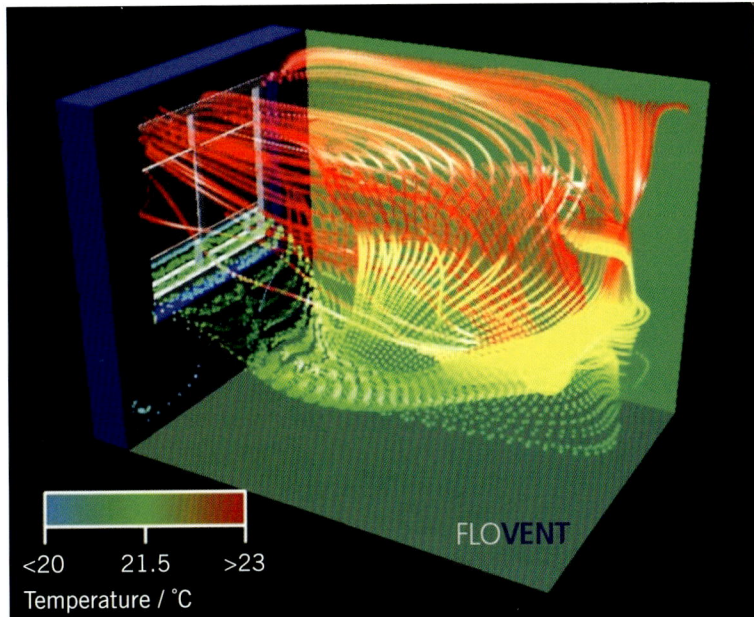

B

ABOVE, 4.8: Our image of how air moves is relatively unchanged over the last 160 years: (A) was produced by D.B. Reid in 1844 to illustrate how air circulates in a room with only one window; (B) is a sample image produced by Flomerics Corporation to illustrate their CFD package FLOWVENT™ and its simulation of air flow in a room with one window.

BELOW, 4.9: Nasser Albuhasan's and Joaquin Goicoechea's competition entry for the Tomihiro Museum used studies of light contours with the ray-tracing software Radiance to manipulate translucent surfaces within the field of view so that watercolor images would still be foregrounded.

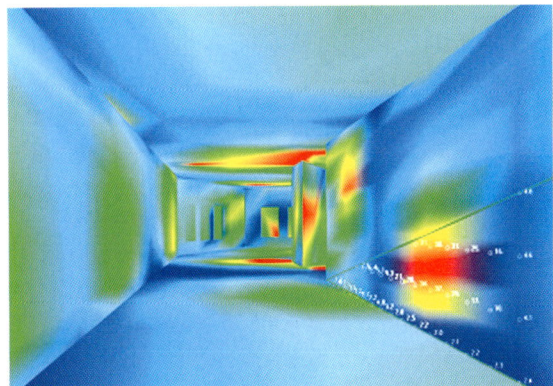

4.10: CFD 'experiments' in producing discrete thermal environments. The images on the left are sectional temperature profiles, demonstrating how the careful placement of a tiny heat source such as a halogen lamp (red dot in center of the left side) can produce distinct thermal zones within a larger space. The images on the opposite page are sectional velocity profiles, demonstrating how the use of multiple tiny heat sources (in centers of both sides) can cause the emergence of a highly active zone within a quiescent environment.

neutral) environments, the environments could become articulated and the surfaces would only be a neutral armature. A simple white cubic space could be read as an infinite number of spaces if we designed for perception by acting directly on the phenomena.

The actual sequence from objective phenomena to subjective perception can be understood as four distinct areas of knowledge, with two of these as operative:

1. Physical Phenomena – laws of heat transfer, mass transfer, electromagnetic radiation;
2. Inducement of Phenomenological Behaviors – selective technological or environmental manipulation;
3. Human Physiology – thermo-regulation, neurobiology;
4. Human Perception – receptor fields (zero-crossing), somatic sensations.

Figure 4.10 illustrates how one might begin to 'induce' phenomenological behaviors through very selective actions. The temperature profiles represented on the left part of the figure show how one might manipulate the surrounding environmental conditions to begin to differentiate thermal spaces within a larger space. The velocity profiles on the right part of the image demonstrate how tiny and discrete technologies can be manipulated to create different behaviors. These discrete zones and behaviors, and not the larger ambient environment, are what produce the conditions that determine the human response. The perceptions that ultimately emerge from the phenomena that surround us, then, are created through the design of an environment that bridges areas two and three, from phenomenological behaviors to human

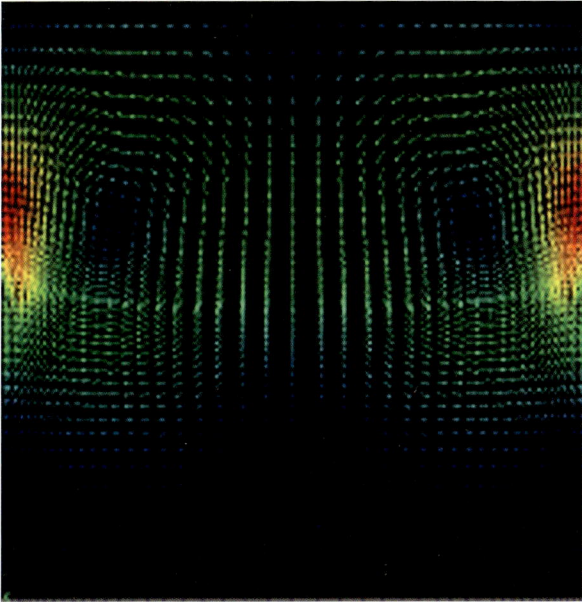

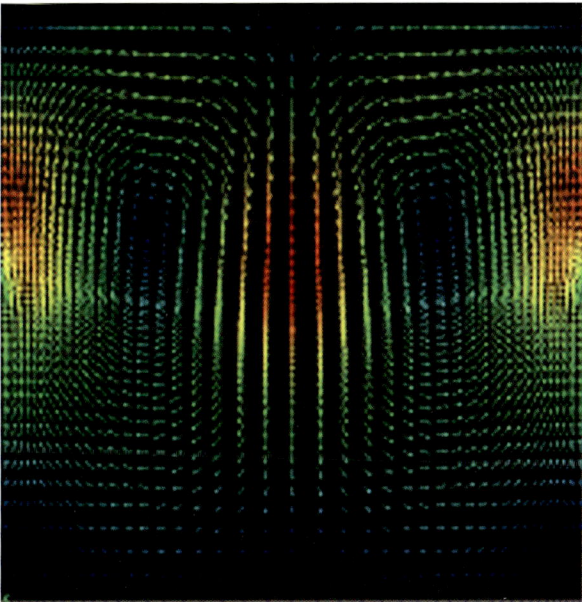

physiology. It is in this region that architecture, not as an artifact but as an action, resides.

The advent of the digital era promised a revolution in the production of architecture, and it delivered on that promise. The proliferation of highly articulated forms enabled by CAD/CAM are clear manifestations of the role that digital representation has played in the making of buildings. In regard to the experience of architecture, however, the switch from analog to digital representation is insignificant unless one can challenge the implicit privileging of surface that is embedded in orthographic projection. That challenge demands that we strip causality away from form. The boundary belongs to the phenomenon and not to the formal surface, and the phenomena that shape our perception of our surroundings operate by rules that have no grounding in our normative modes of spatial representation. The discrete phenomena of the physical environment are what directly determine the perceptual environment – as such, we would ideally design physical behaviors to create the perceptual response. The effect is decoupled from the surface; the surface becomes incidental. The building is no longer the incidental determinant of its environment, but the armature for its perception.

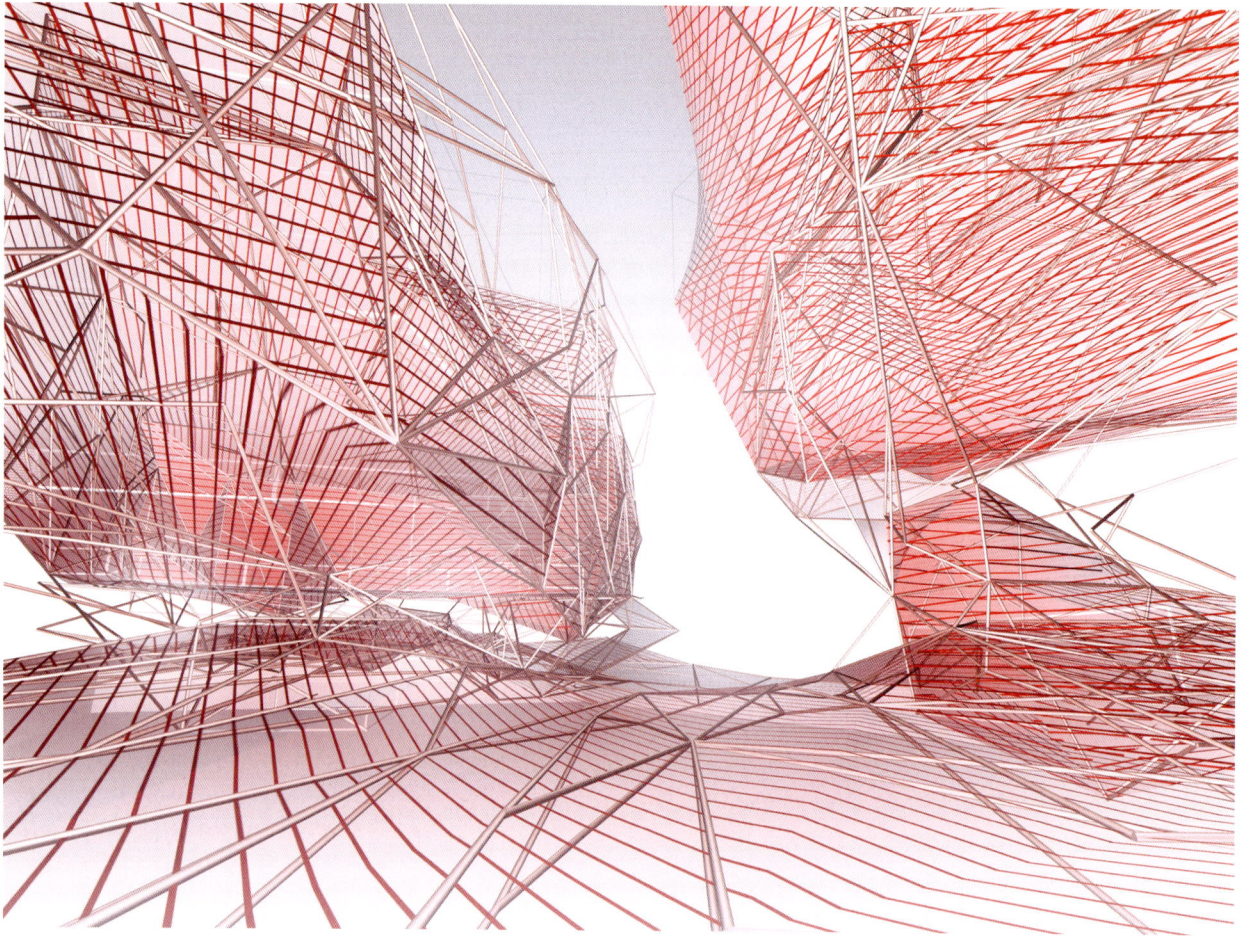

5.1: Jyväskylä Music and Art
Center concept rendering.

Nested capacities, gradient thresholds and modulated environments:

Towards differentiated and multi-performative architectures

Michael Hensel and Achim Menges
(OCEAN NORTH)

Contemporary architectural design characteristically deploys hard material thresholds to define spatial arrangements and areas for predetermined use of space. Within this context building performance is seen to relate to structural and environmental conditions, an area thought to be characteristic of engineering and thus largely seen and treated as some kind of post-design optimization. There is, however, an alternative approach to performance-driven architectural design based on a spatial paradigm that correlates material and gradient environmental thresholds and their capacity for mutual modulation. In this context notions of both 'structure' and 'environment' need to be understood in a wider sense, beyond the singular function of load-bearing and mechanical ventilation, air conditioning and heating. 'Structure' is here defined as the interrelation or arrangement of parts in a complex entity with particular spatial, formal and behavioral attributes and characteristics, the latter of which are indivisible from environmental performance. 'Environmental performance' is defined as the multitude of interactions between interrelated material and climatic constituents of the human habitat.

Based on this understanding, this article seeks to propose an architecture that actively differentiates environmental conditions by means of its morphological and material articulation. It does so by linking behavioral tendencies and performative capacities of material systems with environmental modulation and the resulting provisions and opportunities for inhabitation. In doing so, this approach engenders emergent and intensively choice-driven patterns of inhabitation and social formation, and approaches a new paradigm for social and environmental sustainability relative to the built environment. This is, however, a call not for kinetically enhanced architectures, but instead for an intelligent dynamic relation between a static yet highly differentiated morphology and a changing environment.

While contemporary architecture defines space through hard material thresholds, this has not always and everywhere been so. In his seminal work *The Architecture of the Well-Tempered Environment*,[1] Reyner Banham describes two traditions of architecture: one with substantial structures and one without. 'Societies who do not build substantial structures inhabit a space whose external boundaries are vague, adjustable and rarely regular,' wrote Banham, referring to the example of a campfire that provides a gradient of temperature and light that is at the same time dynamically affected by extrinsic influences, such as airflow and other environmental conditions. These dynamically differentiated spaces provide for individual preferences of inhabitants. Differentiation is thus expressed in gradient threshold conditions rather than a hard division between inside and outside, warm and cold, and so forth, which Ban-

ham posits 'might prove to be of fundamental relevance for power-operated environments' by suggesting a more sustainable approach to architecture. This article introduces a take on architectural design that incorporates Banham's varied and temporal spatiality into substantial yet equally varied structures, by shifting away from the homogeneous and largely mono-functional material systems that make up the built environment today towards heterogeneous and multi-performative systems. The aim is to show how these systems can modulate and, in turn, be modulated by environmental conditions and to suggest alternative spatial strategies based on gradient threshold conditions.

Modernist discourse postulated universal space as the key paradigm for democratic space. The open plan, ideally extended to an infinite homogeneous grid, for instance, was meant to deliver equal opportunity for inhabitation, while the ribbon window and glass curtain wall façade, were meant to replace privileged framed views. The preference for universal space brought with it the modularization of building elements and systems, as well as a homogenization of entire climates. In order to achieve universal space and intended uniformity, each building element or system was required to perform one principal function (primary structure, secondary structure, sun-shading, rain cover, climate envelope, to name a few) and was thus optimized towards that particular singular function.

This single-objective approach to optimization is based on an understanding of efficiency that entails the minimum use of material and energy to fulfill one single task. Single-objective optimization gave rise to

LEFT, 5.2 and BELOW, 5.3: View
of the 1/75 model showing the
primary, secondary and tertiary
lattice systems without the
building envelope. RIGHT, 5.4:
View of the 1/75 model with the
building envelope.

Project: JYVÄSKYLÄ MUSIC AND ART CENTER

Jyväskylä Music and Art Center by OCEAN NORTH The
Music and Arts Center proposed by OCEAN NORTH
aims for an extension of the Jyväskylä's landscaped
town square into a rich, acoustically animated and
climatically differentiated interior landscape that ca-
ters for formal symphonic and orchestral events and
art exhibitions, as well as for informal cultural events
and activities. The lattice structures, trellis-work and
surfaces articulating the interior space provide for ad
hoc stages and seating and exhibition areas, while
creating a dynamically articulated space of acoustic
and visual intensities, with the struts that make up
the lattices being locally sound-active. This extends
acoustic experience beyond the interior of the music

5.5: Diagrams showing the strategic constraints of the growth process, including the local search windows that determine the angles of each strut of the lattice in relation to the connection with the neighboring struts (this page), as well as the gradient maps that allocate search window constraints to regions within the building envelope (opposite page).

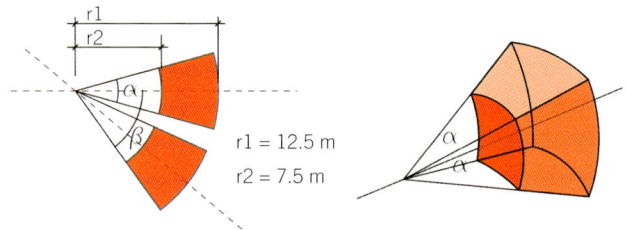

r1 = 12.5 m
r2 = 7.5 m

	α = 30	α = 40	α = 50	α = 60
β = 0				
β = 15				
β = 30				
β = 45				
β = 60				

the notion of lightweight structures with minimum use of material to achieve projected structural capacity and performance. With a desired decrease in the use of material, questions of liability appeared that led to an added percentage of performance capacity to guarantee functionality and safety. Redundancy thus was and still is largely understood as an unfortunate necessity. A critical view raises the question whether an alternative understanding of optimization, efficiency and redundancy in relation to multi-performative material systems can facilitate a very different take on spatial organization and environmental modulation.

Recent architectural discourse has largely moved away from universal space and declared a preference for heterogeneous architectures. This preference is evident in two distinct strategies The first strategy entails a two-step approach to varied space, commencing with generic shells that are subsequently tailor-fitted to the needs of their eventual inhabitants. The second strategy comprises the design of exotically shaped buildings that are right from the onset varied in expression and spatiality. The first strategy embraces modularized building systems, while the second operates from the differentiation of established building elements (individually articulated frame and tile elements, for instance). Both strategies concur, however, in embracing standardized requirements for interior environments, such as statistically determined homogeneous interior climates for public or office buildings, as well as a limited range of building systems. The latter is evident in recently developed parametric software that is bound to established engineering and manufacturing protocols relative to material

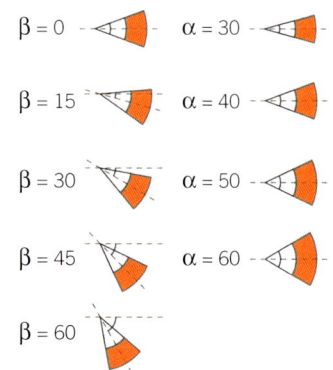

β = 0   α = 30
β = 15   α = 40
β = 30   α = 50
β = 45   α = 60
β = 60

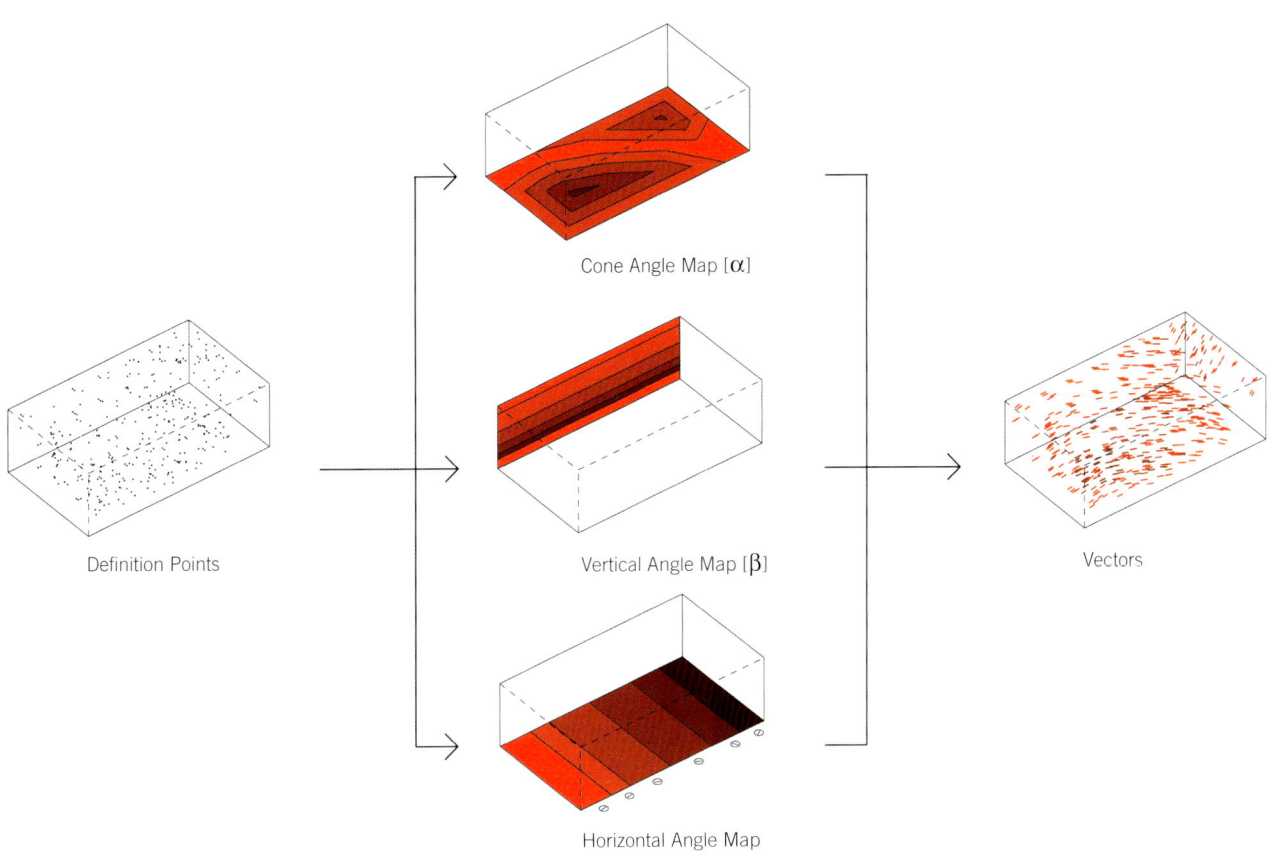

Cone Angle Map [α]

Vertical Angle Map [β]

Horizontal Angle Map

Definition Points

Vectors

hall and rehearsal rooms into the interior landscape of the building volume. The directionality, density and layering of the lattices, and the trellis surfaces and volumes that evolve from it, result in the perception of a locally differentiated yet vast space that is animated by gradient intensities of sonic experiences. The layered, transparent and reflective envelope continuously modulates gradients of reflection and transparency resulting from exterior and interior light conditions, which contribute to the perception of a boundless deep space.

In order to achieve such a high degree of morphological – and thus performative – differentiation, OCEAN NORTH deployed an iterative, digital growth process that articulates the lattices, informed by

rules pertaining to (1) the location, orientation and density of the struts that make up the lattice systems; (2) structural, sonic and luminous performance requirements; and (3) spatial design guidelines. The resulting lattice systems inform the geometries of the terrain, structure and envelopes of primary and secondary spaces and surface areas, the circulation pattern and the sound-active system. The deployed morphogenetic growth process commenced from the definition and distribution of virtual volumes informed by the programmatic requirements of the competition brief within the bounding box of the project site.

A series of gradient maps organised along the x, y and z planes, which delimit the growth area for the various lattice systems, informs the growth process

5.6: Chart outlining the rules
and spatial constraints resulting from the required volumes
and circulation that underlie
and inform the growth process
and the respective geometric articulation of the lattice
systems.

and machining technologies. Herein lies the problem.
While plan organization, the form of the envelope,
or the fittings and finishes might have become more
varied, material and building systems are not being
critically reviewed with respect to established types
and their mono-functionality, as well as building-type-
dependent interior climate requirements and uniform-
condition zoning.

The homogenization of interior environments had
its absolute peak with the advent of the office landscape
approach of the late 1950s through the work of the
Quickborner Team für Planung und Organisation, a
German management consulting group that proposed
vast open plan arrangements in which the anticipated
workflow is manifested in the furnishing of working
clusters arranged according to workflow.[2] Applying a
large number of rules to the furnished organization of
office space, circulation and workflow, it was argued
that a homogeneous interior environment would imply
the least visual, aural and tactile distraction that needed
to be removed. Subsequently this form of spatial-environmental homogenization migrated to other building
types, from public to private spaces. Ironically, it was
the deep open plan of the office landscape as the pre-
decessor of the 'scapes' of the 1990s, which operated
on a reduction of material threshold, that also sought
to fundamentally homogenize interior climates within
'sealed box' buildings. Space, according to this dogma,
becomes both deep and undefined, and environmen-
tally universal through its erasure of difference. The
ultra-modernist dream came to its climax and architecture became largely 'neufertised': appropriate values

with performative requirements according to the relation between and specific to the assigned zones.
These zones guide the morphogenetic development
by constraining the local search space for each strut
of the lattice system to be digitally grown in terms
of size and search angle, resulting in morphological regions with varying system capacities. For this
project the gradient maps are based on structural
performance, as well as the modulation of the luminous and sonic micro-environments of the interstitial
space between the outer envelope of the building and
the envelopes of the various interior volumes not to
be intersected by the lattice system. Once the overall
volume is established through different growth mi-
lieus, a first set of definition points and search rules

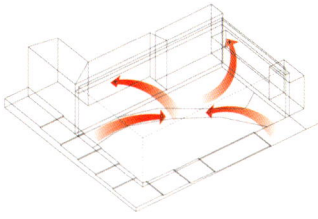

Circulation Concept

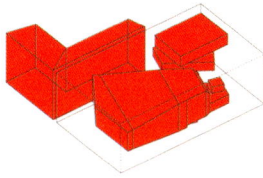

Program Volumes

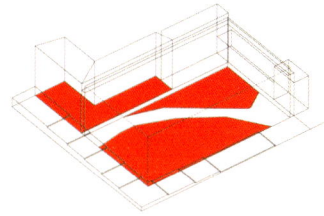

Site Concept

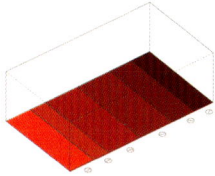

Horizontal Angle Map

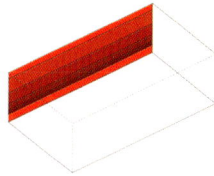

Vertical Angle Map

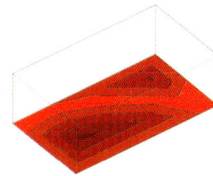

Cone Angle Map

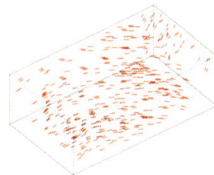

Vectors

Definition Points

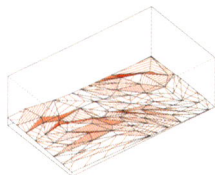

Tertiary Ground Lattic

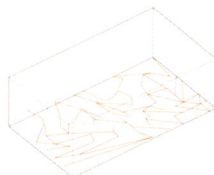

Secondary Ground Lattice

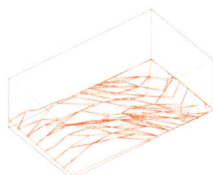

Primary Ground Lattice

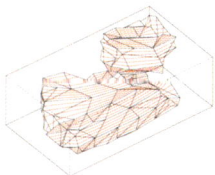

Tertiary Volume Lattice

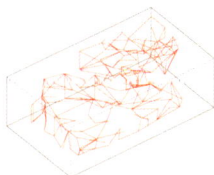

Secondary Volume Lattice

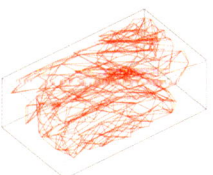

Primary Volume Lattice

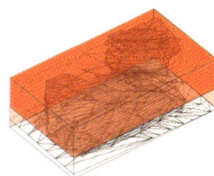

Composite

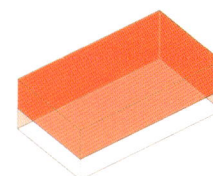

Exterior Surface

BELOW, 5.7: Three stages of
the iterative growth process
showing the distribution of
geometric definition points
and primary, secondary and
tertiary lattice (left to right),
which subsequently inform the
articulation of structure and
surfaces of the project.

OPPOSITE PAGE, 5.8:
Structural analysis of the digitally grown lattice showing displacement vectors (top) and
rotation vectors (bottom) for
the deformation resulting from
the self-weight of the structure,
mapped onto the un-deformed
geometry of the primary lattice
(red indicates highest deformation, blue indicates lowest
deformation).

for each purpose, program and type were once and for
all statistically established and listed in useful books.

However, the combination of optimized mono-functional elements or sub-systems together with homogenized comfort zones often requires an abundance of
heating, cooling, air conditioning, ventilation, lighting, and servicing equipment. While capital energy,
embodied in the materials and building processes, can
be kept relatively low, operational energy required for the
running of a building is extremely high, and is mainly
invested in the erasure of climatic differences to facilitate
a stable, 'ideal' interior environment. Environmental
design and engineering unfortunately remains a question of post-design optimization rather than informing
the design process from a very early stage as a strategic
and instrumental aspect that is central to the design approach. Moreover, a homogenized interior environment
can simply not satisfy the multiple and contrasting needs
of inhabitants.

An alternative understanding of architecture as ecology involves dynamic and varied relations and mutual
modulation between material systems, macro- and
micro-environmental conditions, and individual and
collective inhabitation. The proposed approach to
architectural design is based on the deliberate differentiation of material systems and assemblies beyond the
established catalogue of types, making them dissimilar
or distinct in degree and across ranges. Varied ranges of
material systems can provide for diverse spatial arrangements together with climatic intensities. This involves
the deployment of the inherent behavioral characteristics and modulation capacities of building elements

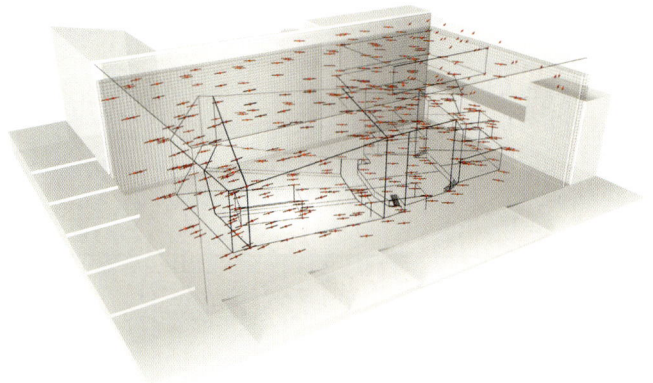

are defined that distribute and orientate the struts
that make up the primary lattice system in response.
From the primary system, a second set of virtual surfaces are derived on which a new set of definition
points are defined. In further digital growth iterations,
secondary and tertiary lattice systems are evolved that
define mesh-like enclosures for the required internal
volumes, circulation and sound-active systems.

While the iterative growth process is informed by
performance requirements, the synergetic impact of
the various systems working together needs nevertheless to be analyzed in stages. Digital structural,
luminous and sonic performance analysis was conducted repeatedly in order to evaluate the emerging

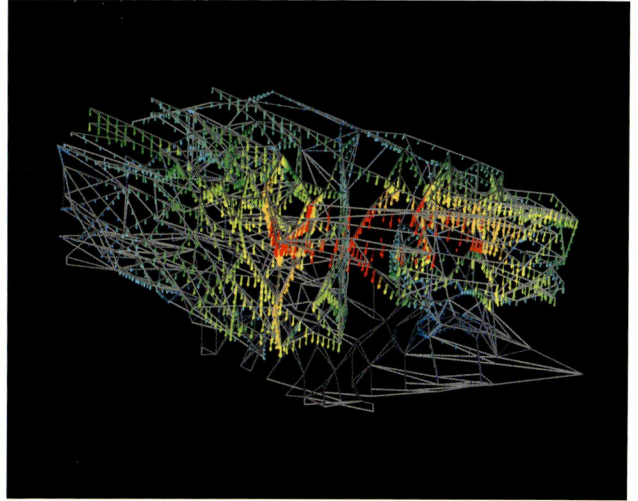

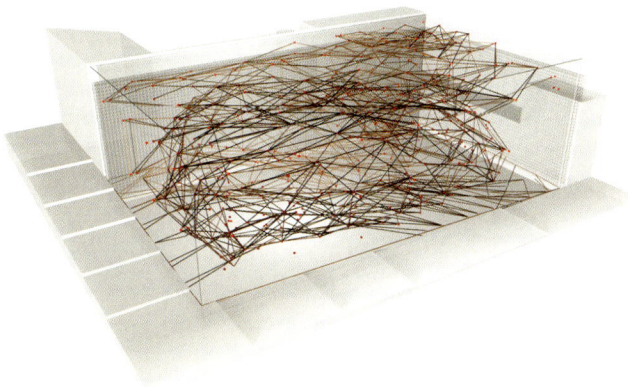

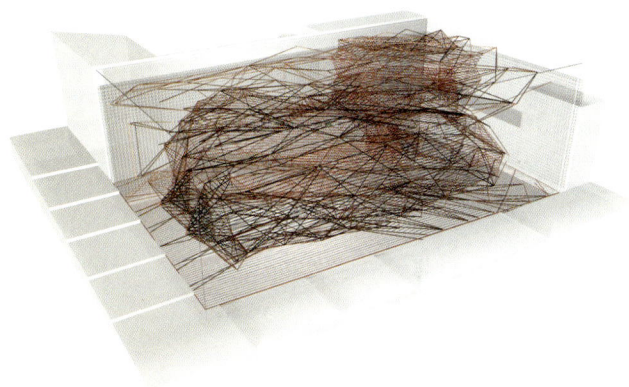

conditions and synergies between the various micro-
systems that make up the overall project. Through the
differential density, altering depth and angular variation of the lattice systems and the varied distribution
of sound-active elements, evolves a heterogeneous
space in which augmented spatial, ambient and climatic differentiation provide for choices between a
wide range of micro-environmental conditions that
can provide for time-specific, individual and collective needs and desires of the visitors, and an intense
cultural experience that conveys a contemporary and
synergetic spatial and musical sensuality and sensibility, and points towards the emergence of a new and
richly differentiated cultural institution.

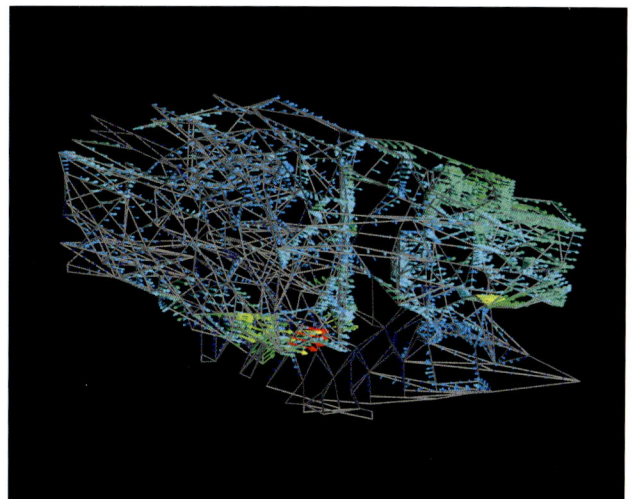

A

B

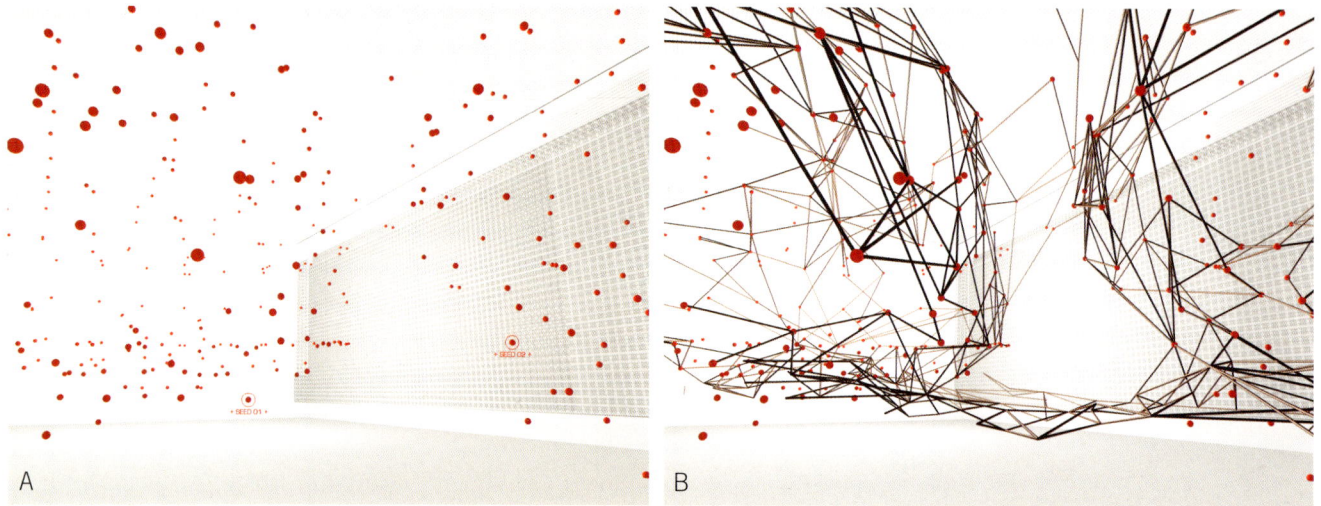

and systems, rather than a retrospective optimization process towards mono-functional efficiency. From this arises an understanding of efficiency as a dynamic characteristic of the effective, based on utilizing redundancy predominantly as latent capacity to perform a series of different tasks, rather than as a safety measure.

Instrumentalizing multiple-performance capacity requires an understanding of material elements and systems in a synergetic and integral manner. It considers these systems in terms of their behavioral characteristics and capacities with respect to the purpose they serve locally and within the behavioral economy of larger systems. Today's so-called sustainable design claims this understanding but operates on it mainly as a question of energy consumption, material life cycles and waste production. An instrumental approach to relational behavioral characteristics as a way of modulating spaces and environments, however, requires operative retooling for architects with respect to analytical and generative methods and techniques and their relation and phasing within the design process. Such an approach can learn from living nature, particularly the fact that most biological systems are articulated through higher-level multi-functional integration across at least eight scales of magnitude. This enables both scale-dependent and scale-interdependent hierarchical relations that result in higher-level functionality.

Take, for instance, the make-up of a tree: its hierarchical make-up from nano- to macro-structure ranges from glucose chains (in the angstrom range, 10^{-10} m),

to micro-fibrils (up to nanometer range, 10^{-9} m) and macro-fibrils (up to micrometer range, 10^{-6} m), to differentiated cells with equally differentiated cell walls (up to millimeter range), to the various features, such as leaves, roots, branches and the overall tree (in the meter range).[3] Whether the various regions of the timber of the branches perform better in tension (tension-wood) or in compression (compression-wood) depends mainly on an alteration of the cell wall, which serves to show an example of how differentiation on one scale will affect the performative capacity of the various larger scales of magnitude.

Performative capacities embedded within the material make-up and morphological articulation of the systems that comprise the built environment entail therefore the interrelation of performative constituents across a wide range of system scales. This realization suggests a radical shift from mono-functional modularized building elements, based on linear task-solution concepts, to integral systems with non-linear, complex behavior and properties.

In addition, architects can learn from connections and transitions between systems and sub-systems of biological entities. In the building sector connections between parts and elements are almost always discontinuous and articulated as dividing seams, instead of smoother transitions in materiality and thus functionality (such as is seen in the way tendon and bone connect, deploying the same fiber material yet across a transition of mineralization that affects the elasticity or rigidity of

ABOVE, 5.9: Morphogenetic growth process, left to right: (A) distribution of seed and definition points for the struts of the primary lattice system; (B) first growth step of the primary lattice system; (C) growth step defining the secondary lattice system in accordance with the primary system; (D) model view of the same location.

RIGHT, 5.10: Digital daylight analysis (red indicates highest intensity, blue indicates lowest intensity): top, midday 21 June; bottom, midday 21 December.

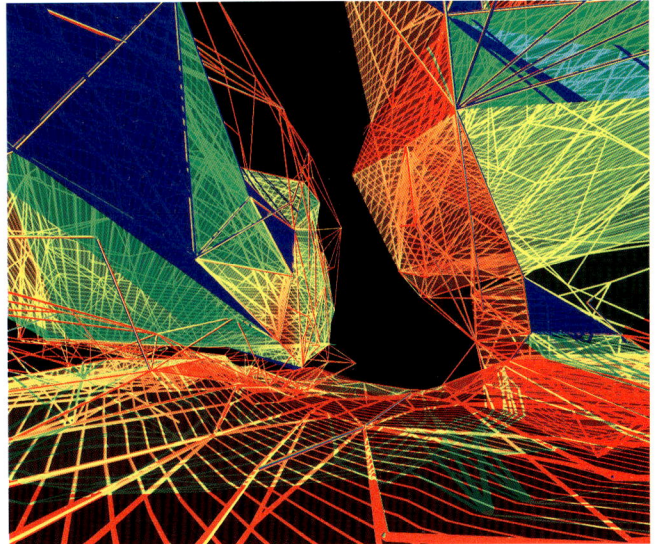

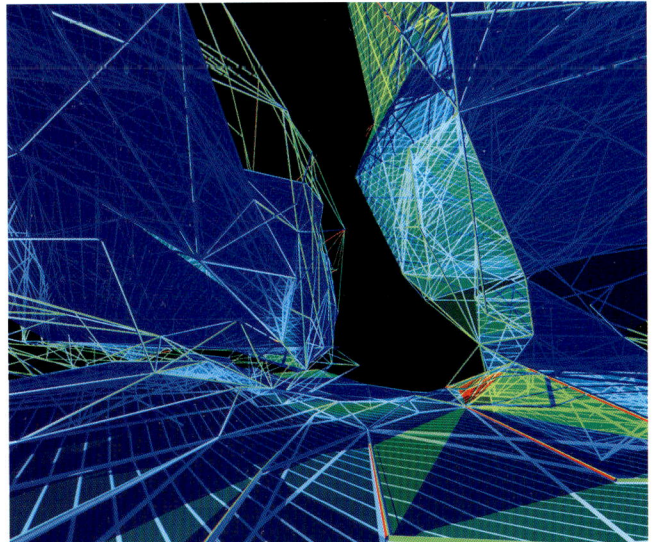

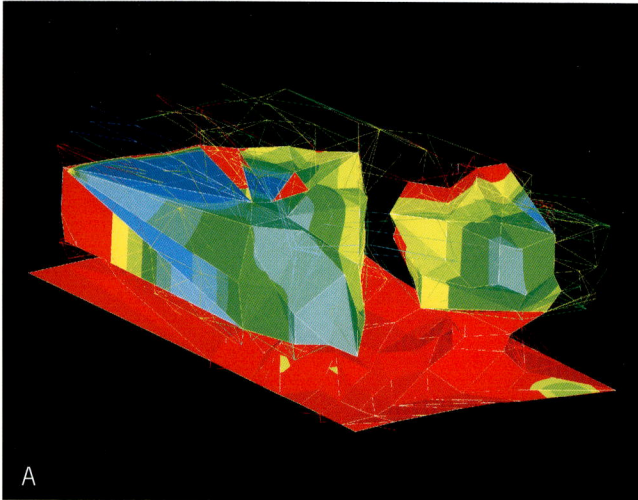

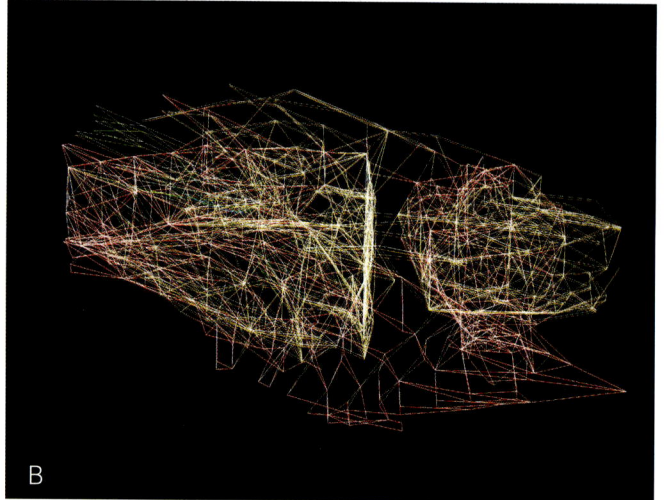

the material). The understanding and deployment of gradient thresholds in materiality and environmental conditions can yield the potential for complex performance capacities of material systems. This will require a detailed understanding of the relation between material make-up and resultant behavioral characteristics.

Instrumentalizing the design of material systems as a way of deploying behavioral characteristics and tendencies requires analytical methods, skills and tools with respect to the performative capacity of the overall system under investigation, and the narrower capacities of local elements that enable the global system to unfold its wider capacities.[4] The aim is to develop an approach to design that integrates analytical and generative methods. Analysis is of central importance to the entire generative process, not only in revealing behavioral and self-organizational tendencies, but also for assessing and designing spatial-environmental modulation capacity. In this way, feedback between stimuli and responses and the conditioning relation between constraint and capacity will become the operative elements of heterogeneous spatial organization. This suggests an architecture that modulates specified ranges and gradient conditions across space and over time, and that is based on strategically nested capacities within the material systems that make up the built environment.

Such an approach to architectural design consolidates and merges the tradition of substantial structures with the one of ephemeral spaces and gradient thresholds towards an enhanced performance capacity of the built environment and, in extension, promotes choice-based social formations and inhabitational patterns. The latter are of great consequence for a built environment that becomes increasingly dense and begins to preclude common strategies of spatial transitions to provide for environmental diversity. For human dignity, health, choice and excitement to be preserved and provided for, differentiated multi-performative architectures may well be the most promising intervention. One begins to image Robin Evans's matrix of interconnected spaces animated by Banham's gradient thresholds and enabled and articulated by the differentiated performance-oriented material systems that could make up the built environment, pushing towards an architecture that is ecological in its endeavor of addressing the relation between environment and organisms, habitat and inhabitants.

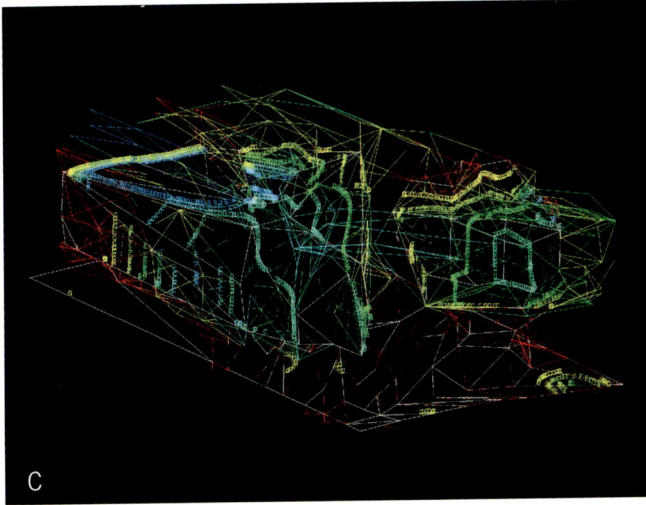

C

5.11: Digital structural analysis (red indicates highest deformation, blue indicates lowest deformation), left to right: (A) vertical displacement contours for deformation produced by gravity loading; (B) and (C) vertical displacement vector plots for deformation produced by gravity loading; (D) plot showing the deformed shape of the structure produced by gravity loading.

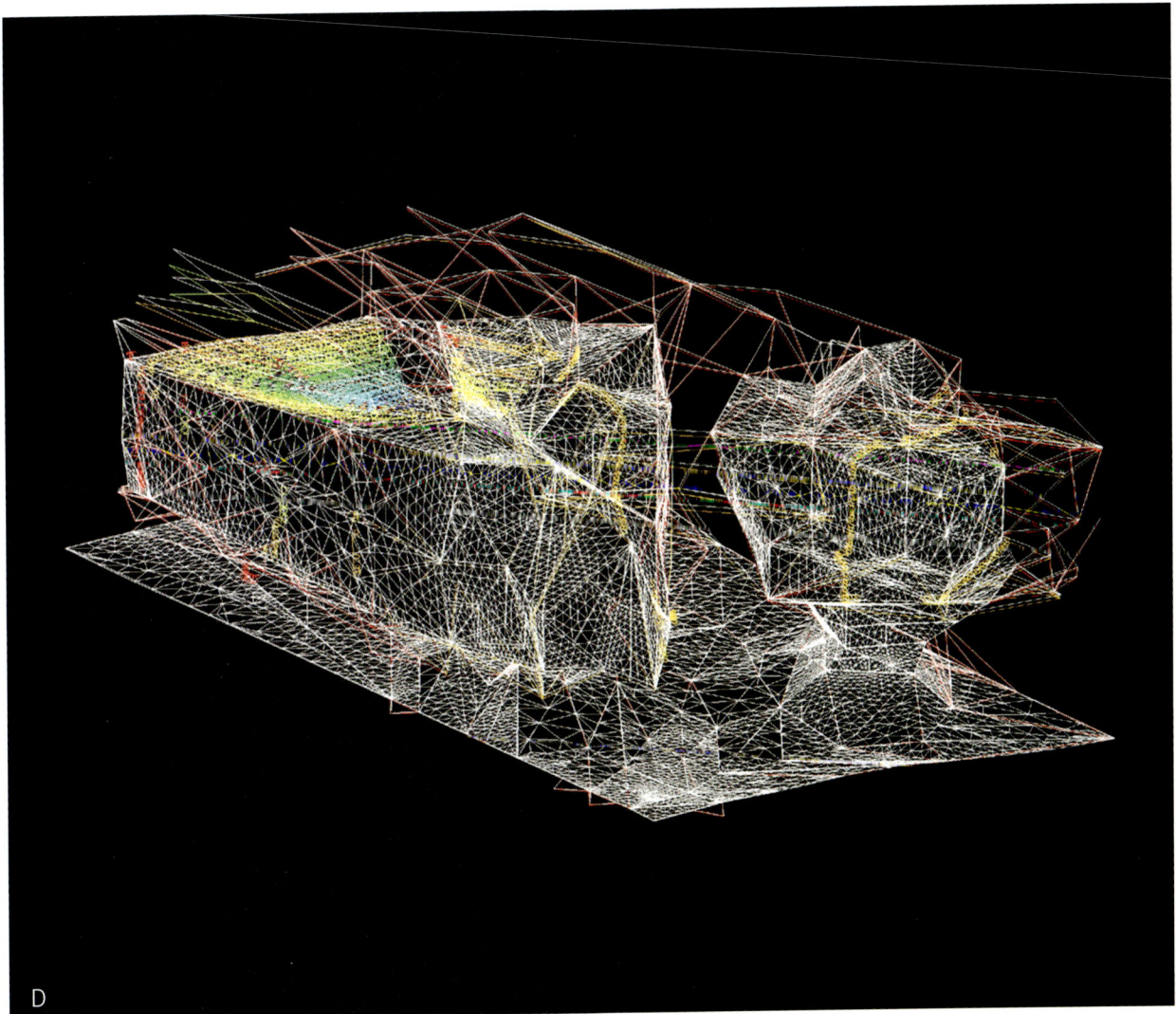

D

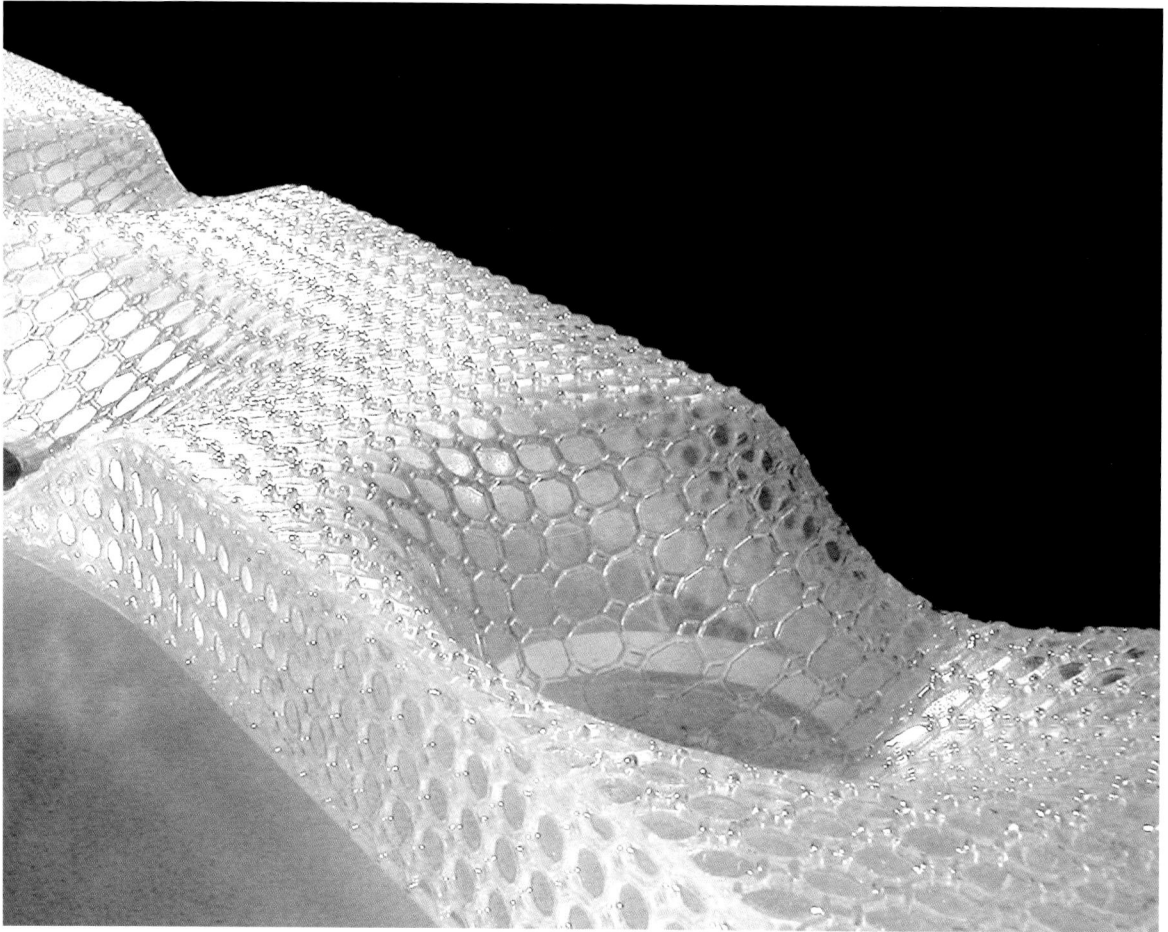

6.1: Ecoscape physical model, 2002.

Dissipative procedures:
Optimization through 'phenomenonization'
Open Source Architecture
Chandler Ahrens, Eran Neuman and Aaron Sprecher

The Baroque world, in fact, may be characterized as a great theatre where everybody was assigned a particular role. Such participation, however, presupposes imagination, a faculty that is educated by the means of art. Art, therefore, was a central importance in the Baroque Age … the art of the Baroque concentrates on vivid images of situations, real and surreal, rather than on 'history' and absolute form. Descartes says: 'The charm of fables awakens the mind.' The integral aim was a way of life in conformity with the system … the character of Baroque art brought forth a 'phenomenization' of experience, which made man more conscious of his own existence. Baroque participation, which had secured the system, in the end therefore brought about its disintegration.[1]

In the last century, form-finding procedures in computer-based-design architecture focused on both optimization and generative design. Capitalizing on new tools as means to interpret design and production, methods of optimization sought ways to efficiently correlate formal and functional aspects of the architectural project while considering organizational systems, and spatial division and distribution. Procedures of generative design were based on form evolution as a consequence of evolutionary design. Nevertheless, even when integrated these procedures were centered mainly on relatively limited parameters. In this essay we return to an analogous historical case in order to examine the possibility of including more parameters both in optimized and generative designs.

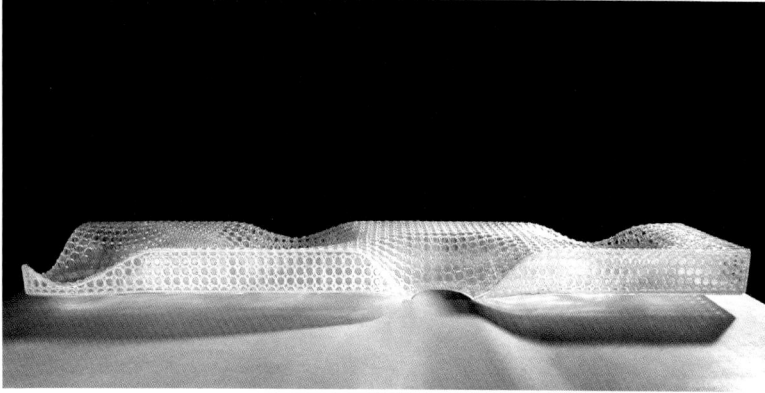

LEFT, 6.2 Ecoscape model, elevation view, 2002. OPPOSITE TOP, 6.3: Ecoscape Project Protocol. BOTTOM, 6.4: Surface displacement sequence on 21/09 between 6 a.m. and 2 p.m.

In the early 1970s, while analyzing the Baroque period, the Scandinavian architectural theoretician Christian Norberg-Schulz returned to an examination of central architectural typologies, concentrating on their tactile, spatial, material and visual properties. Norberg-Schulz's interpretation addressed these properties as part of his arguments about the inclusiveness that characterized the period. As a phenomenologist, Norberg-Schulz did not accept the interpretations that viewed the period solely as a time of visual manipulations, deviating from the Renaissance linear perspective; for him, the Baroque was a matter of creating a totalizing greater system. In that respect, Norberg-Schulz's model of the Baroque conceptualization can, in many ways, function as the foundation for the interpretation of recent considerations of the Baroque, or what has been termed 'digital Baroque'.[2]

When returning to the Baroque today, many architectural historians and theoreticians find similarities between the seventeenth-century period and contemporary architectural manifestations, and also indicate the differences between the two. Those historians and theoreticians rely mostly on visual and historiographical claims to argue that contemporary architecture is an advanced interpretation of the Baroque period. This view considers the visual effect created by the convoluted, folded and twisted morphology, the formalistic approaches and the geometrical articulations expressed in architecture since the 1990s to be links to the Baroque. On the other hand, the two periods are perceived as different interpretations of similar ideas, not only because of the transformations in the cultural conditions that brought about the different architectures, but also because of the technological means that assist in the articulation of the respective ideas. With digitization and computation, contemporary Baroque is considered to be an empirical praxis that evolves out of and goes beyond visual manipulation into the optimization of form, function and matter based in information streams. As such, contemporary Baroque refers to and integrates Modernist ideas in its discourse.

As a historical causality, the Baroque and the digital Baroque are compared for their similar mode of operations. Like Baroque architecture, contemporary architectural manifestations are claimed to implement geometry and morphology that criticize previous practices: the Baroque reacted against Renaissance spatial idealism, while contemporary twisted morphology refers to Modernist idealism as expressed most evidently in the early Corbusian Euclidean geometry and space. Nevertheless, digital Baroque, it is argued, does not run counter to this Modernist perception of architecture, but tries to advance the early twentieth-century preoccupations with more sophisticated technological tools by referring to Baroque formalism. The digital Baroque is perceived through Modernism in such a way that the Baroque contributes the formal articulation, while Modernism suggests the technological discourse.

Thinking of the Baroque as a neo-Modernist practice through optimization and efficiency raises some difficulties. Indeed, parts of the contemporary architectural discourse on digital and computational articulations try to go beyond the question of the image as the carrier of architectural significance by referring to the architecture's

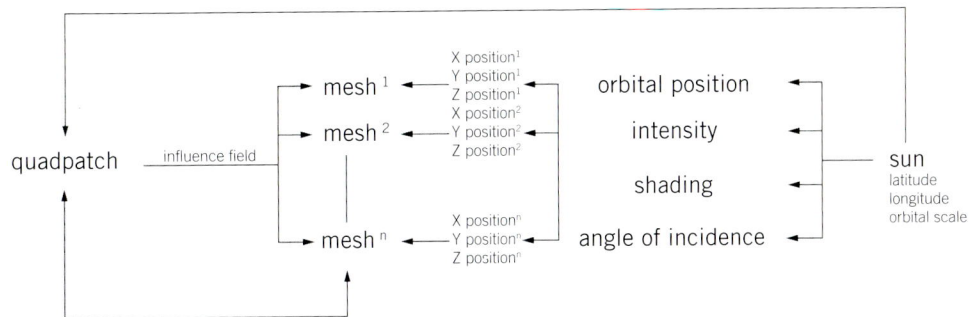

quadpatch — influence field — mesh ^{1} ← X position^1 / Y position^1 / Z position^1 ← orbital position ← sun (latitude, longitude, orbital scale)

mesh ^{2} ← X position^2 / Y position^2 / Z position^2 ← intensity

shading

mesh ^{n} ← X position^n / Y position^n / Z position^n ← angle of incidence

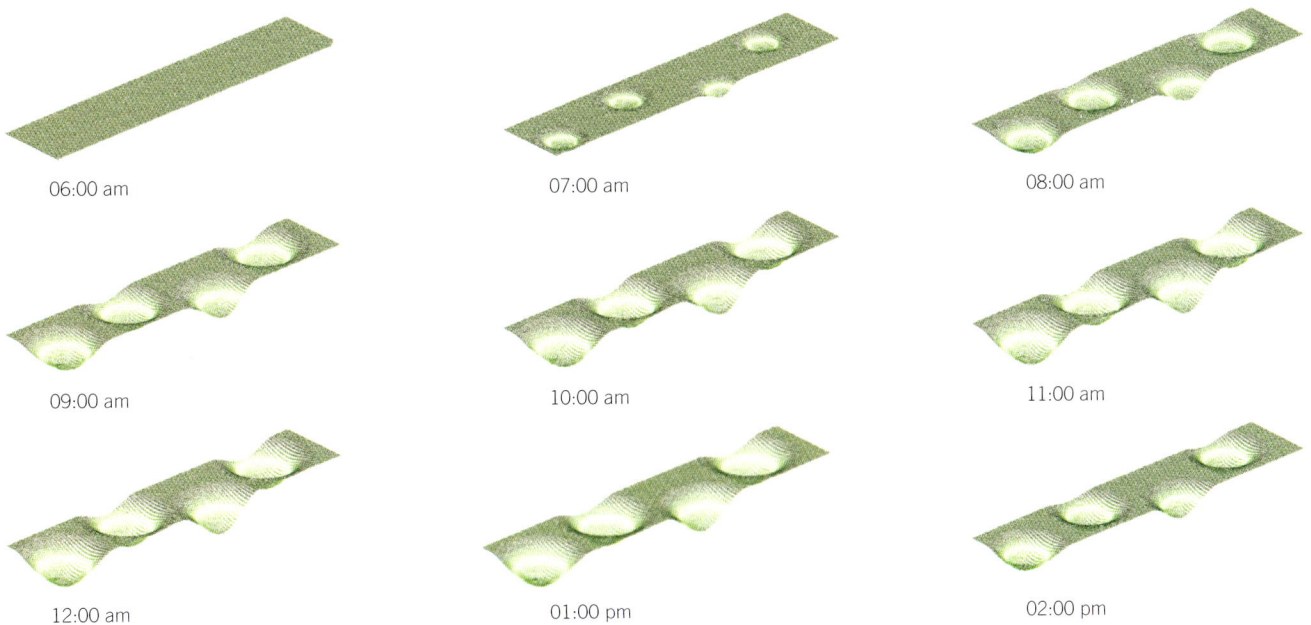

06:00 am   07:00 am   08:00 am

09:00 am   10:00 am   11:00 am

12:00 am   01:00 pm   02:00 pm

Project: ECOSCAPE

Phenomenon 1: Optimization of natural architecture

In a hyper-technological and cultivated world, Ecoscape proposes a structure that would be located discursively midway between culture and nature. It does not propose to distinguish architecture from nature, nor does it suggest implementing post-Modernist operations of imitating nature by creating it artificially. Instead, Ecoscape proposes to treat the project as a phenomenon that integrates nature and architecture, and to create architecture as nature, based on naturalistic mechanisms, methodologies and processes. That is accomplished by treating the extreme conditions of the site as the means for the formal and conceptual evolution of the project.

Customized according to the principles of non-Euclidean geometry, the structure is a contemporary system led by a technological convergence of properties that generates its own natural paradigm. Its hypothesis seeks a modality that would engender architecture as nature by the use of cladding that generates both internal climatic and external architectural conditions such as skin and landscape. Consequently, the structure does not concentrate on the performance of the architectural entity as only a matter of climatic conditions, but asks to treat the environment as an inclusive situation in which climate, surface and landscape are integrated to propose the evolution of events. Applying this methodology, the structure

RIGHT, 6.5: Differential
intensive surface formation.
OPPOSITE, 6.6: Ecoscape
optimized surface.

06:00 am > 0 lx

06:15 am > 1765 lx

06:30 am > 15082 lx

06:45 am > 30609 lx

07:00 am > 43499 lx

07:15 am > 53631 lx

07:30 am > 61595 lx

07:45 am > 67935 lx

08:00 am > 73054 lx

08:15 am > 77243 lx

08:30 am > 80710 lx

08:45 am > 83607 lx

09:00 am > 86045 lx

09:15 am > 88109 lx

09:30 am > 89862 lx

09:45 am > 91354 lx

10:00 am > 92623 lx

10:15 am > 93698 lx

10:30 am > 94605 lx

10:45 am > 95360 lx

11:00 am > 95980 lx

11:15 am > 96475 lx

11:30 am > 96855 lx

11:45 am > 97126 lx

12:00 pm > 97293 lx

12:15 pm > 97358 lx

12:30 pm > 97323 lx

12:45 pm > 97187 lx

01:00 pm > 96948 lx

01:15 pm > 96602 lx

01:30 pm > 96142 lx

01:45 pm > 95561 lx

02:00 pm > 94848 lx

02:15 pm > 93988 lx

02:30 pm > 92966 lx

02:45 pm > 91748 lx

03:00 pm > 90336 lx

03:15 pm > 88665 lx

03:30 pm > 86699 lx

03:45 pm > 84379 lx

04:00 pm > 81628 lx

04:15 pm > 78342 lx

04:30 pm > 74383 lx

04:45 pm > 69561 lx

05:00 pm > 63613 lx

05:15 pm > 46727 lx

05:30 pm > 34678 lx

05:45 pm > 19752 lx

06:00 pm > 4633 lx

functional part as a means of liberation from the constraints of the image; yet at the same time, this reference converts the discourse mainly into techno-scientific considerations, much like the Modernist one. This discourse deals with production in a similar fashion to Modernist accounts of functionalism and expands it into the information technology era as a matter of optimized articulations and performance architecture. Similar to cases executed at the beginning of the twentieth century, contemporary production refers to the Modernist paradigm and tries to overcome its flaws, revealed in concepts such as standardization and universal architecture.

The difficulties in such a discourse and references are that, much as in Modernism, contemporary architecture is at risk of ending up the architectural act by concentrating on the activation of information as a matter of functional articulation of efficiency without addressing architecture as a phenomenon of inclusiveness. Much as in Modernism, the concentration on production by new tools – digital and others – may result in the employment of technological procedures for their own sake and as a mechanism for investigating the tools' performance. This process would not necessarily lead to the development of another type of evaluation mechanism as part of the design procedure. Consequently, the instrumentalization of the *techne* would result in an autonomous condition in which the evaluation of the architectural product would address only the fulfillment of the technological procedure as a self-referential condition.[3]

The difficulties in this condition arise not as a result of a lack of signification other than the technological

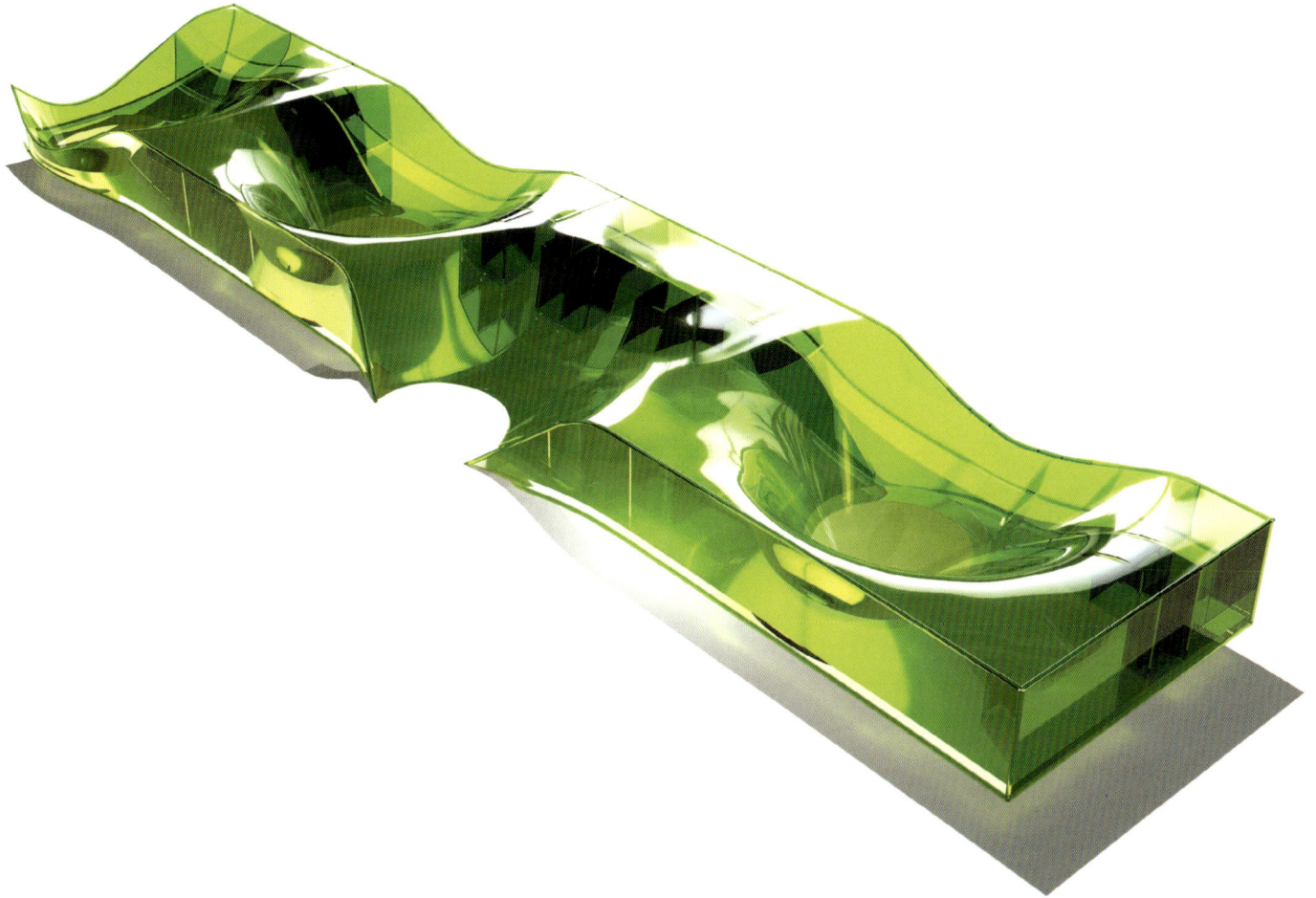

advances the architectural discourse concerning architecture and nature a step further. It functions as an interface between architecture and nature, both literally and conceptually.

Prioritizing the reaction as a means of acquiring environmental data in a responsive manner above merely informing the environment, Ecoscape is based in a single unit (photovoltaic cell), which follows biotechnological methodologies and genetic codification growing out of the phenomenology of the site. It evolves into an autonomous structure according to an exponential serial development.

Ecoscape, based on a horizontal meshed surface, is a dynamic engine that develops a phototactic behavioral pattern. By considering the intricate ele-

ments of its geometry (vertex), a parametric algorithm links each vertex with data related to the sun's position over the course of a year. Each parameter (the sun's intensity [lux], orbital positioning and angles of incidence) is registered on the surface, which deforms accordingly while assuring a consistent exposure to solar energy. The resulting model is exemplified by a geometry that integrates all movements of the vertexes registered by the algorithm at work. Because Ecoscape's skin is made out of in-print photovoltaic cells, the computational parametric interface (CPI) assures stability of the ratio between the PV-cells' energy reception and the sun's intensity. Beyond its bio-mimetic topology, Ecoscape acts as an integrated engine intimately linked to the ecological system.

6.7: Ecoscape Ecological System. Legend: (01) Building integrated photovoltaic panel (BIPV)-PV cells laminated between fluoroplastic film. (02) South façade: operable unitized structural silicone; 2.5 cm insulated low-E glazing on aluminum frame. (03) Fresh air heating element integrated into the sill of the aluminum frame of the glazing system. (04) North façade: formed insulated metal panel on 15 cm metal stud; with batt insulation in cavity; operable windows in aperture extensions. (05) Existing potable water well. (06) Existing 50kW hydro-electric plant. (07) Pond. (08) Geothermal heat pump with closed loop exchange coil in pond; contingent on feasibility study of utilizing existing pond; substitute: vertical closed loop exchange. (09) Hydronic radiant heating tubes in unitized floor panels. (10) Waste water plumbing. (11) Supply water plumbing. (12) Electric water heater for kitchen and bathroom facilities; excess heat from the geothermal heat pump to be utilized. (13) Existing septic tank with added filtration and oil separator.

in contemporary digital architecture, but as a result of the intentionality in the tools' implementation in design methodologies and their consideration as solely scientific instruments. When addressing the question of tools, some contemporary scholars refer to the Baroque period and its scientific attributes, criticizing the ways in which it was implemented as a mode, resulting in a visual manipulation of the human subject that did not fully consider the specific operation's scientific aspects. While employing mathematical processes to determine the oval forms and sculpted surfaces, for example, the Baroque architectural occupation concluded in visual and ornamental representations, which were not about the scientific procedure but rather about the image.

Today, with the introduction of new tools based on digital and computational processes, design considerations based on performance and parametric procedures go beyond the consideration of form, space and matter as the articulation of visual regimes. This is due to scientific procedure that yields visual and ornamental effects by introducing an empirical scientification of the architectural act. Form is considered a matter of evolutionary processes, simulating those in nature. Following the evolution of complex morphologies, the evolution of contemporary architectural form is achieved through digital articulation and computational configurations. Almost identical to Modernist precepts, contemporary digital form-making seeks form that will follow function, or more precisely function as a matter of informational systems.[4]

Yet, unlike in Modernist architecture, the definitions of the desired functions are not universal. On the contrary, digital processes allow the specification of functions' definitions in each individual case, facilitating the production of particularized forms that are precisely suited to specific needs. That is achieved by treating the functional aspect of the architectural project as an informational matter. In that respect, the contemporary architectural discourse on digital design refers, yet does not subscribe, to the Modernist paradigm. It also attempts to invigorate aspects of architectural production; the nature of production in terms of logic and design is pushed into specification of the produced object.

The implementation of tools as a means of reaching optimized production, indeed, gives rise to new definitions of the relations between form, function, information and production. Through parametric design, the application of genetic algorithms and performative design, new formal manifestations are mostly optimized in relation to their predefined use. Nevertheless, and similar to Norberg-Schulz's criticism of the interpretations of the Baroque as a solely visual practice of deception, it seems that contemporary digital processes employ the architectural tool – digital or otherwise – as a means of speculating about form without addressing broad aspects of architectural design. The optimization of the architectural tool as a means of informational configuration of differentiated functions reduces the architectural procedure to an isolated scientific process based on rationalization of the performing object. It optimizes through science, without articulating broader aspects of architecture.

Furthermore, the extent to which the scientific procedures consider architectural aspects other than

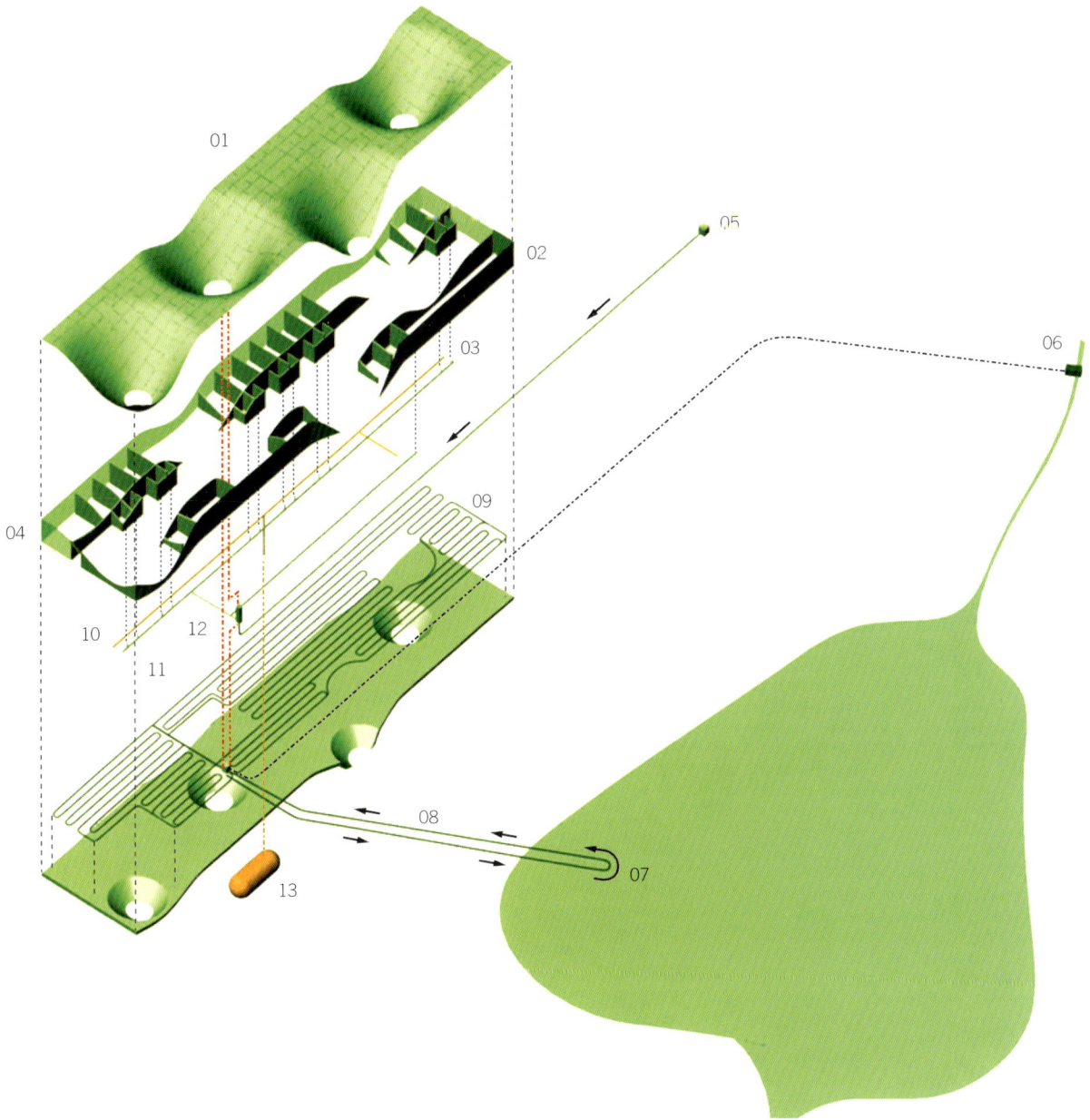

OPPOSITE TOP, 6.8: Iso-Morph
Project Protocol. BELOW, 6.9:
CNC milling of five iterated
isomorphic polysurfaces.

the technological reflects a self-referential condition. Indeed, the predetermination of the scientific process conducted by a human agency already includes decisions other than the scientific considerations in and of themselves. The choice of a scientific procedure, the definition of an experiment or the selection of tools, for example, does not exist in an isolated condition outside of human agency. As such, the scientific procedure is conditioned by cultural, social and even political aspects. Nevertheless, the architectural-scientific process is conducted as an autonomous process and becomes self-referential, in such a way that it applies the scientific procedure to prove its validity without addressing the ethical nature of the process itself. Consequently, in these cases other architectural aspects are only by-products of the architectural act and do not evolve as internal properties.

As a counter-model, the phenomenization of the scientific procedure, or what can be termed scientific phenomenology, requires the consideration of methods of optimization that negotiate between form and information as a politicized procedure. Throughout the design process, the politics of information as the parameter that determines the potentialities of the end product should be considered in order to achieve what Gilles Deleuze referred to as multiplicity resulting from dynamic essentialism.[5] The significance of the data that determines the content of the process has to be considered in conjunction with the digital procedure as the structure that brings about the evolution of the architectural entity. Together, they should be reconsidered constantly and dynamically. This is necessary to avoid

a rigid essentialist approach that tries to expose a supposed inner truth that exists in the scientific procedure. The reciprocal reconsideration and the process that evaluates the digital procedure and the significance of the inserted data will conclude in the evolution of new tools suitable to the architectural task at hand. The tools will dynamically evolve as the means to articulate the architectural procedure. As such, the specifications of the tools and their dynamic reconstitution will optimize the architectural processes as a critical procedure relying on data.

The reciprocal procedure would almost inevitably result in the rejection of the dichotomies between science and culture, object and subject, computer and man, matter and space, environment and architecture. It would lead to the consideration of multi-layered aspects of the architectural entity, beyond the features of production that determine form as a consequence of function or information. And it would insert into the process of morphogenesis neglected parameters of the explored phenomena by rejecting an idealist approach and by incorporating as many vertexes and aspects as possible in the evolutionary process.[6]

As a result, the design processes would embody an approach that initially examines the phenomenological traits of the design problem. While considering the programmatic and functional aspects of a certain architectural project, the design process would integrate several parameters through processes of negotiation between information systems that generate the project and the architectural features, and through the introduction of event-based temporal structures that are not derived

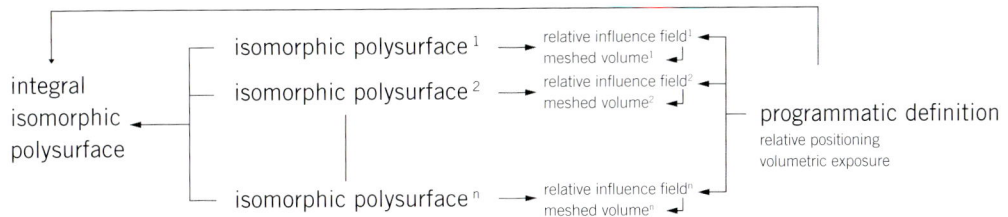

isomorphic polysurface [1] → relative influence field[1] / meshed volume[1]

isomorphic polysurface [2] → relative influence field[2] / meshed volume[2]

integral isomorphic polysurface

isomorphic polysurface [n] → relative influence field[n] / meshed volume[n]

programmatic definition
relative positioning
volumetric exposure

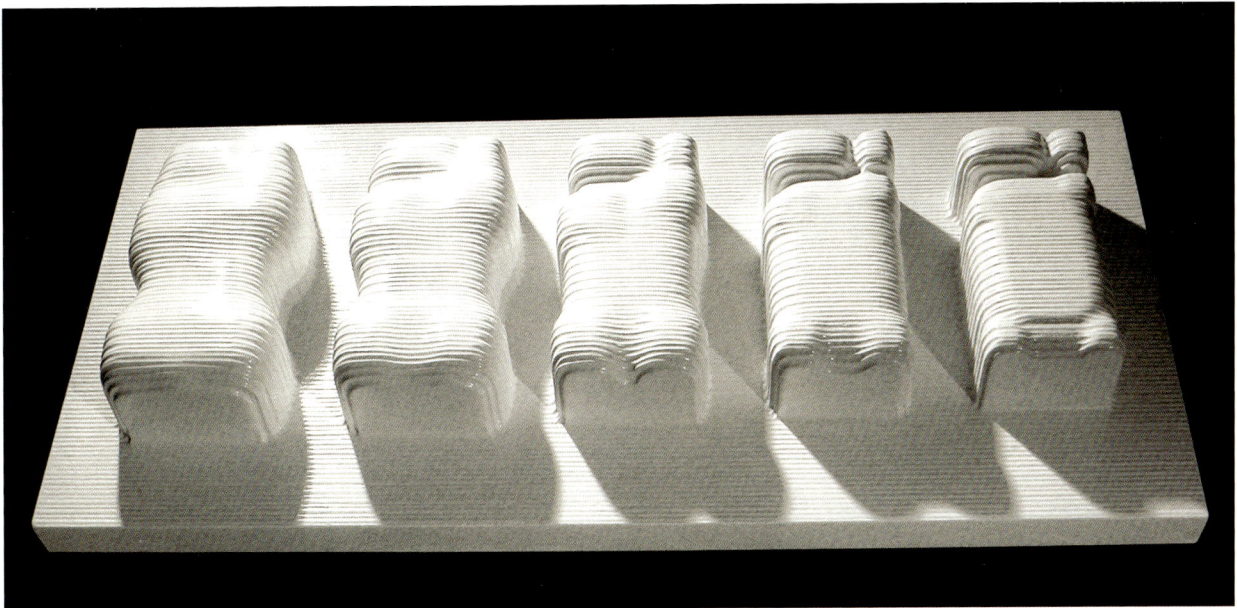

Project: ISO-MORPH

Phenomenon 2: Optimization of the singular The Iso-Morph fiberglass structures were developed for an invited competition sponsored by the Israel Gas Company. As the country shifts from coal- to gas-fired power stations, the company is building a gas pipeline from Egypt to the north of Israel. The competition sought prototypes of small structures, or booths, to be built along the pipeline to serve as maintenance, gas delivery and inspection sites.

Given that the booths were not required to address issues of program, space or function, the OSA entry proposed to develop a 'smart skin' structure. The booth was conceived as a phenomenon of singular reaction resulting in complex structure. It applied a diachronic process of emergence, attempting to integrate data derived from the immediate surroundings into the programmatic component of the evolutionary procedure. As such, referring to the observation of the macro-phenomenon in its vital form, the proposal employed the processes of an evolution of gas composites as a reference for creating the booth's skin. Accordingly, its form was determined by following a calculation procedure presented in the evolution of the structure of metaclay.

The outer skin was conceived as an inclusive system enfolding and creating a monolithic structure; thus, the design process stemmed from scripting methodologies in which the different parts of the booth were converged into a singular entity. Accordingly, the structure sought means by which one

LEFT, 6.10: From top to bottom:
Iso-Morph delivery station, valve
station, delivery station. OPPO-
SITE, 6.11: Morphological tracking of isomorphic polysurfaces.

from the architectural object as an efficient entity. Treating the design process as a phenomenon would require
finding common ground among the different aspects of
the design problem. This is done to avoid creating a single feature that would lead the design process, because
the phenomenology of optimization does not prioritize
one architectural aspect over another. On the contrary, it
seeks to activate as many aspects of the design problem
as possible, while maintaining specific features of each
individual aspect. In this way, this methodology avoids
distinguishing between the several aspects, which would
lead to the creation of a hierarchal structure.

At the end, the optimal means of performance is achieved by the engagement of the phenomenon throughout
the design process itself. The design process becomes a
reflective process enabling a greater level of accuracy, yet
it stays open-ended. Optimization through phenomenization thus results in a higher performance of architecture, not only as an object but also as an event.

time > 1 sec
influence field > 0.00

time > 2 sec
influence field > 0.03

time > 3 sec
influence field > 0.06

time > 4 sec
influence field > 0.09

time > 5 sec
influence field > 0.12

time > 6 sec
influence field > 0.15

time > 7 sec
influence field > 0.18

time > 8 sec
influence field > 0.21

time > 9 sec
influence field > 0.24

time > 10 sec
influence field > 0.27

time > 11 sec
influence field > 0.30

time > 12 sec
influence field > 0.33

time > 13 sec
influence field > 0.36

time > 14 sec
influence field > 0.39

time > 15 sec
influence field > 0.42

time > 16 sec
influence field > 0.45

time > 17 sec
influence field > 0.48

time > 18 sec
influence field > 0.51

time > 19 sec
influence field > 0.54

time > 20 sec
influence field > 0.57

time > 21 sec
influence field > 0.60

time > 22 sec
influence field > 0.63

time > 23 sec
influence field > 0.66

time > 24 sec
influence field > 0.69

time > 25 sec
influence field > 0.72

time > 26 sec
influence field > 0.75

time > 27 sec
influence field > 0.78

time > 28 sec
influence field > 0.81

time > 29 sec
influence field > 0.84

time > 30 sec
influence field > 0.87

time > 31 sec
influence field > 0.90

time > 32 sec
influence field > 0.93

time > 33 sec
influence field > 0.96

time > 34 sec
influence field > 0.99

time > 35 sec
influence field > 1.02

time > 36 sec
influence field > 1.05

time > 37 sec
influence field > 1.08

time > 38 sec
influence field > 1.11

time > 39 sec
influence field > 1.14

time > 40 sec
influence field > 1.17

time > 41 sec
influence field > 1.20

time > 42 sec
influence field > 1.23

time > 43 sec
influence field > 1.26

time > 44 sec
influence field > 1.29

time > 45 sec
influence field > 1.32

time > 46 sec
influence field > 1.35

time > 47 sec
influence field > 1.38

time > 48 sec
influence field > 1.41

time > 49 sec
influence field > 1.44

time > 50 sec
influence field > 1.47

BELOW, 6.12: Iso-Morph
GRP profile detail. (01) Glass
reinforced plastic (GRP) panel;
polyester resin with fire-re-
tardant. (02) GRP structural
panel. (03) Slip-joint bolted
connection. (04) Ventilation
hole in panel. (05) 1.5 cm rigid

insulation. (06) Operable filter
door. (07) Steel reinforcing.
(08) GRP structural panel
overlapping plate. (09) GRP
panel overlapping plate at
panel joint.

OPPOSITE TOP, 6.13: Perpetuating Particles Project Protocol.
BOTTOM, 6.14: Perpetuating
Particles stereolithography
model.

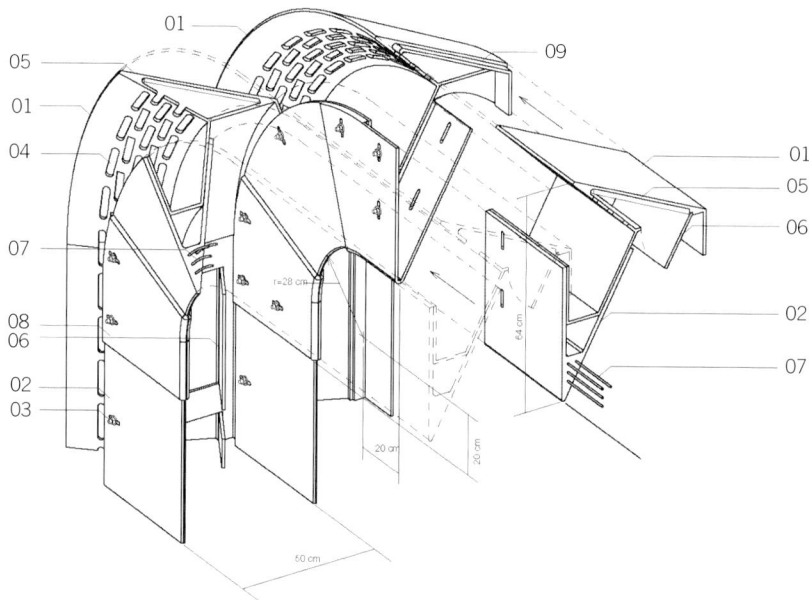

procedure or gesture would result in a differentiated
entity. This would maximize the single procedure into
an optimal performance of a skin that is simultaneously a structure, a cladding, a sign, and an envelope.
Given the opportunity to create a single and continuous skin, the assigned programmatic entities are modeled as a singular isomorphic polysurface bearing an
influence field parameter. Following this configured
system, a proportional increase of each surface's in-
fluential force ultimately produces a single continuous
surface that is striated in order to create a series of
GRP composite ribs based on a single extrusion profile.

Whereas each isomorphic polysurface is formed
by non-differentiated yet singular entities (vertex), the
influence field has the ability to connect each intricate element with neighboring geometries in order to
react to their presence, and their forces of repulsion
and attraction. Iso-Morph's singular surface results
from a registration of external forces carried by each
programmatic component rather than the empirical
appropriation of a more specific arrangement set.
The isomorphic polysurfacing model is comparable
to Leibniz's monadic system: each geometry includes
a set of parameters that is dynamically animated by
external forces – literally networked with surrounding
influence fields of environment – to act upon itself
and the others by means of geometrical deformations,
volumetric transformations and topological mutations.

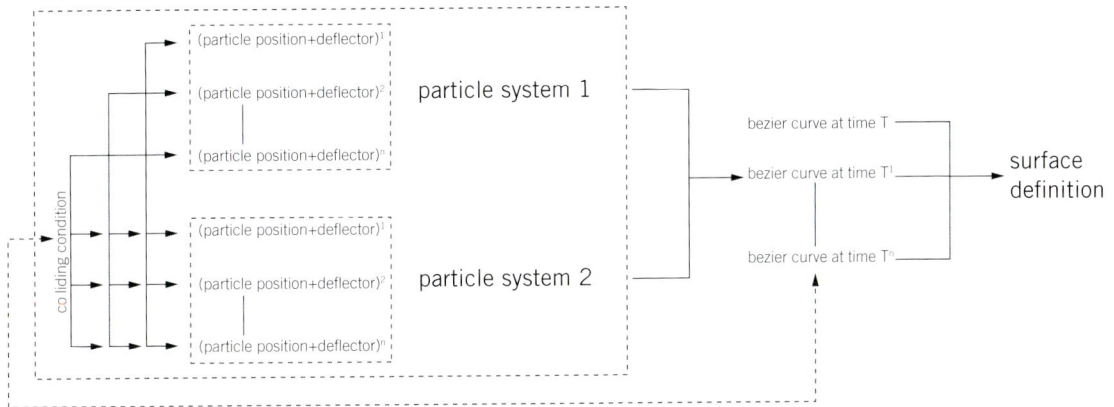

Project: PERPETUATING PARTICLES

Phenomenon 3: Phenomenal commemorations Reflecting on how to represent the Holocaust in order to advance the discourse on this topic to its next stage, Perpetuating Particles suggested individualizing commemoration while maintaining a continuous and comprehensive systematic discourse. Addressing the question of the inability of representing commemoration in a phenomenological fashion, the form-making and architectural conceptualization proposed blurring the differences between life and commemoration, knowledge and experience, and architecture and nature. Hence, the project is determined by endless trajectories that create the final intricate structure and form, which initially remain indeterminate. A number of particles were injected into the open space, where

Perpetuating Particles.
6.15: Sequence of surfaces
generated out of two colliding
particle systems.

Particle Stream [plan view]

time > 12 sec

time > 18 sec

time > 24 sec

time > 30 sec

time > 36 sec

time > 42 sec

time > 48 sec

time > 54 sec

time > 60 sec

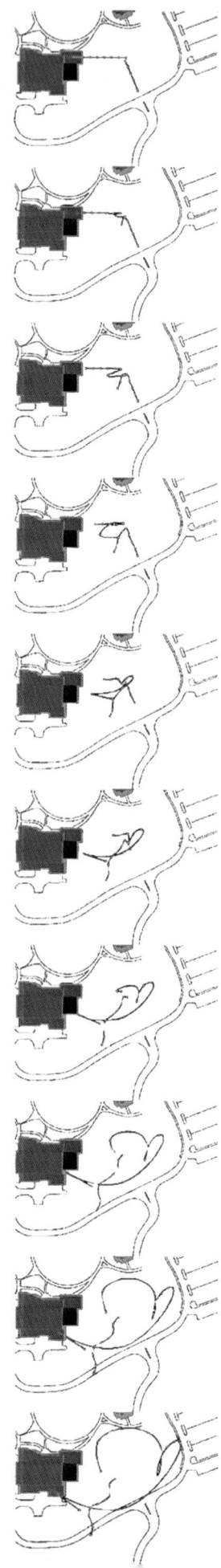

they traveled freely and created a holistic phenomenon. The direction of their release was controlled; nevertheless, their collision was chaotic. The negotiation
between the various particles created a crystallization
of a continuous surface. In that way, each individual
contributed to the development of comprehensive narrative.

While particle systems are increasingly the subject of studies on behavioral patterns (among others,
numerous studies on swarm behavior as a means of
interpreting natural systems), one limitation lies in the
calculation ability to implement a set of parameters
identified with each particle. Such a condition is es-
sential to the achievement of a far-reaching simulation
of phenomena present in nature. Consequently, the

Particle Stream [elevation view]

Surface Generated with Particle Stream

Splines Stream [elevation view]

produced surface of Perpetuating Particles is generated by tracking the movement of two sets of ten particles navigating along two force vectors identified on the operating field. The collision point disrupts the continuous movement where each particle reacts to its neighboring entities while being diverted to an alternate navigation path.

Based on the logic of a movement from particle to path to field, Perpetuating Particles employs a set of logarithmic space warps applied to each entity while embedding all data information concerning the presence and the prescribed reaction to a collision condition. The resulting surface embodies the special positioning of each particle during the experiment's sixty-second time lapse. This surface results from

a network strategy that 'forces' each particle to be conscious of its surrounding influences. Rather than navigating on a set of two continuous trajectories, the particles possess a level of autonomy (internal data) that is activated by an external, logarithmic yet chaotic set of forces, producing an event-surface.

Applying this specific methodology, the evolution of the event-surface positions the human subject outside systems of significations. It suggests an infinite evolution of events in terms of the creation of form and use of platform. And if for Deleuze the event is a pre-verbal condition, then Perpetuating Particles is a pre-formal evolution. It sets the formation of matter at a point when it still remains undecided, just a moment before it evolves from information to matter.

Perpetuating Particles. OPPO-
SITE, 6.16 and BELOW, 6.17:
Two versions of cloud surfaces.

7.1: Wen-Ying Tsai –
Cybernetic Sculpture, 1968.

Cybernetic anything...
Marcelyn Gow (servo)

[W]hat is also ultimately disturbing and fascinating about the whole cybernation scene when you get down to its nitty gritty, is precisely that it isn't 'neutral' and safe, but that it constantly poses threatening opportunities that invite us to do some basic human thinking, and not make culturally automated yes/no binary responses.[1]
– Reyner Banham

From an architectural perspective, the work of the Art and Technology practices, notable for their integration of cybernetic principles, electronics, and computational technology into artistic practice during the 1960s, is informative for a broader understanding of the cultural role that technology played in the shift from a mechanized to a mediatized society and the ramifications this has for contemporary obsessions with responsivity in architectural practice and discourse. The 'proto-interactive' environments that emerged from this art and technology nexus operated in many instances as performing *media* rather than iconic representations of technological processes.

Low-definition effects

Dynamic systems were the order of the day in London's Institute of Contemporary Arts in August of 1968. The seminal exhibition Cybernetic Serendipity: The Computer and the Arts had just opened. Curated by Jasia Reichardt, it was one of the first exhibitions to bring together an extensive résumé of developments in computational technology and electronically motivated projects in the context of an art venue. It included a myriad of contributions from such diverse disciplines as music, engineering, computer science, medicine, and philosophy, and was instrumental in establishing the category of 'cybernetic art'.

Cybernetic Serendipity was also notable for the direct involvement of corporate contributors in the exhibition. The Boeing Computer Graphics organization included a display on pilot visibility simulation, General Motors research laboratories included a section on computer diagnostic graphics and Bell Laboratories contributed a series of computer-animated films. The optimistic pitch of the show was hard to miss. Its title was suggestive; the definition of 'serendipity' as 'the faculty of making happy chance discoveries' featured prominently next to the definition of 'cybernetics' as 'a science of control and communication in complex electronic machines like computers and the human nervous system' in the catalogue's table of contents.[2]

Serendipity was organized in three sections: one was dedicated to computer-generated material including graphics, film, electronic music, and poetry; the second featured interactive or cybernetic installations including robotic devices and drawing machines; while the third acted as a kind of educational section with demonstrations of various applications of computers and information on the development and history of cybernetics. The Machines and Environments section, which fell into the second category, included the work of Wen-Ying Tsai in collaboration with Frank Turner, one of a then emerging category of engineer/artist practices.

Their aptly titled *Cybernetic Sculpture* combined the low-inertia qualities of oscillating servomotors with high-frequency strobe lighting to produce an 'electronically activated environment' in which a cluster of vibrating steel rods traced luminous patterns that ranged from linear bands to fluid sinusoidal curves.[3] The individual

steel elements, arrayed in a hexagonal matrix, appeared to dissolve into a fluid, undulating field of light as they moved. Ambient sound levels in the gallery were used as inputs that modulated the frequency of the strobe flash through a voltage control system. In this way the actions of people in the surrounding space would have a direct effect on the frequency of the pulsing strobe illuminating the vibrating steel rods. The oscillation of the light was varied a-periodically against the constant rhythm of the vibrating rods and interference between the two frequencies generated variegated effects ranging from stasis to undulation. Tsai and Turner's work was also awarded a prize that year in a competition for artists and engineers sponsored by the Experiments in Art and Technology organization, gaining it inclusion in Pontus Hultén's seminal exhibition The Machine as Seen at the End of the Mechanical Age, which opened at New York's Museum of Modern Art in November of 1968.

The *Cybernetic Sculpture* was pertinent to the artistic debate at the time, and to contemporary architectural discourse, as it strove to generate a relational *environment* through connections between a series of objects, as opposed to reifying objects in and of themselves as content. The tendency for objects to elude their materiality or corporeality through literal motion was characteristic of the majority of kinetic projects but *Cybernetic Sculpture* was also *responsive*. The piece absorbed inputs from external stimuli in the environment and was affected by them, changing the environment in turn through the effects that it generated. This system of inputs and outputs acted as a self-regulating phenomenon that incorporated feedback into its logic of development and adaptation. This phenomenon of self-regulation is tied to the cybernetic theories of Norbert Wiener who defined it in the following terms:

> The control of a machine on the basis of its actual performance rather than its expected performance is known as feedback, and involves sensory members which are actuated by motor members and perform the function of tell-tales or monitors – that is, of elements which indicate a performance.[4]

Cybernetic Sculpture connected physical presence, sound emission, and vibration and light frequencies, enabling these variables to produce an environment that was not in stasis and to generate low-definition effects of oscillating matter.

When the machine becomes ambient...

Outlining some of the discursive dilemmas of Art and Technology practices of the 1960s, Edward Shanken, in his dissertation 'Art in the Information Age: Cybernetics, Software, Telematics, and the Conceptual Contributions of Art and Technology to Art History and Theory', proposes that there have historically been three approaches to Art and Technology: the

> aesthetic examination of the visual forms of science and technology, the application of science and technology in order to create visual forms, and the use of scientific concepts and technological media both to question their proscribed applications and to create new aesthetic models.[5]

Cybernetic Sculpture exemplifies the last approach – creating a more nuanced form of performance or responsiveness, which seems to have otherwise been a missed opportunity in the exhibition. This shortcoming is, in all probability, tied to the failure of many of the exhibited devices to generate spatial effects that would have the potency to subsume their conventional roles in the context of industrial production, their 'proscribed applications'. The devices in Cybernetic Serendipity were largely 'on display', calling attention to themselves as machines rather than eroding their conventional identities through the production of more extensive spatial and environmental qualities. Tsai and Turner's contribution was one of the few to approach the territory where the machine itself was secondary to the effects it generated. The machine in a sense became ambient.

Cybernetic Serendipity was hailed in the popular press as a nearly undisputed success. The event's detractors were few in number, but notably they included Reyner Banham, whose skeptical review appeared in the journal New Society shortly after the show had opened. Banham critiqued the array of 'electronic gismology' assembled in Nash House for a lack of artistic concepts:

> cybernation is all too often being used as a front ... The general lack of aesthetic originality or creativity that paralyses so much of the show is neatly (and inadvertently) underlined by a statement on the wall in the cybernetic music section which says (and I quote verbatim) where ideas are relevant to the development of computer-generated music, material is included which antedates cybernetic music. That just about sums it up; most of the ideas around antedate cybernetic anything.[6]

It is revealing that Banham's critique centers on what he refers to as the 'lack of ideas' that characterized the work shown at the ICA. This points to a central theme that was being played out at the time (quite *advertently* in many instances) where the relations between things were deemed more important as phenomena than the content of the things themselves or the capacity of some*thing* to express an idea. Banham's reservations are symptomatic of a larger issue at stake in the art of the time, and to some extent in contemporary architectural practice, notably the concern with foregrounding relations instead of objects. In many Art and Technology projects, aleatory processes were embraced; eschewing an overt message behind the work, significance emerged instead in the connections between various entities. John Cage's performance *Variations VII* at the intermedia event 9 Evenings: Theater and Engineering in 1966 is a good example of this approach, where the artist appropriated a number of telephone lines as a sound detection system to pick up ambient sounds from outside of the performance space and import them into the arena's loudspeakers. Banham's skepticism regarding Cybernetic Serendipity permeates his closing remarks in the article, where he asserts that there can be no binary response to technology: technology is multifaceted and nuanced. His critique centers on the failure of the artists to address the complex nature of the medium. A more considered approach to technological performance would possibly have produced the 'new aesthetic models' to which Shanken alludes.

The integration of electronic and digital media into a popular cultural context addressed by exhibitions like Cybernetic Serendipity; the Software, Information Technology show at the Jewish Museum in New York in 1970; and Information at the Museum of Modern Art in New York in 1970 had obvious ramifications for the status of the object in artistic practice, and was played out somewhat differently in Conceptual Art and Art and Technology practices. This phenomenon coincided with the tendency towards the machinic mass production of articles, using newly available industrial techniques for proliferating objects in a serial fashion, thereby raising questions of value, authorship, and ownership. Equipment that had previously been the exclusive purview of industrial fabricators for commercial applications or was being developed in the context of defense-related research – including infrared lasers, electronic telecommunications devices, and computer and holographic equipment – was increasingly becoming integrated into the production of art. As evidenced by the Experiments in Art and Technology (EAT) organization and the Art and Technology initiative – a corporate artist residency program established by the Los Angeles County Museum of Art (LACMA) between 1966 and 1970, which placed artists in close collaboration with industrial firms – the appropriation of high-end technology for artistic ends was not always possible without the intervention of a cultural institution. The absorption of these technologies was due not only to reduced costs and increased availability but perhaps more significantly to a shift in attitudes toward the production of 'high art', which made the precision and efficiency of industrial processes attractive.

Art and Technology projects, among them earlier events like the EAT organization's 9 Evenings: Theater and Engineering from 1966, usually took a literal approach (as opposed to Conceptual Art's more semi-otic approach) to 'dematerializing' the object by creating responsive 'environments' with programmed light, sound, and kinetic systems in which various sensory stimuli would be connected, as opposed to producing physical objects.[7] Marshall McLuhan, in his 1967 book *The Medium is the Massage*, defines environments as 'invisible. Their ground rules, pervasive structure, and overall patterns elude easy perception.'[8] These practices went beyond the literal use of devices with which to communicate between diverse inputs and outputs internal to the artwork, and often performed such communication in the form of collaborative working processes. For example, 9 Evenings was a collaborative attempt among ten artists and thirty scientists and engineers from Bell Laboratories to harness the latent performative qualities of technology in the interest of cultural production rather than for commercial consumption or defense-oriented military applications. Collaboration was required in the production as well as in the reception of the work. The viewer's participation, advertently or inadvertently, was often used as a trigger to motivate these kinetic pieces: staging connections between the motion of bodies and the oscillation of objects, for instance. These projects relied heavily on technological processes to act as transducers between the inputs and outputs that they connected, causing detractors to dismiss the work as simply reifying the technological apparatus.

Relational materialities

A copy of Banham's Cybernetic Serendipity review eventually found its way into the archives of LACMA's then Senior Curator of Modern Art, Maurice Tuchman, which is hardly surprising given Tuchman's own interest in the integration of contemporary art and technology. Tuchman, who had launched his ambitious Art and Technology program two years earlier than Cybernetic Serendipity, was susceptible to the same critique that Banham had leveled at the ICA exhibition. His initiative, which was ongoing at the time and would culminate in a 1970 exhibition at LACMA, included a series of projects ultimately concerned with foregrounding *relations* between various entities, in some cases connections internal to the work and the viewer and in others establishing meta-connections between institutions, corporations and the individual artist.

By the time Cybernetic Serendipity had been exposed to thousands of visitors and Tuchman was well under way with his Art and Technology program, attitudes towards the role of technology in artistic practice were becoming increasingly polarized. In contrast to the proponents of technological art like Reichardt, Tuchman, and the EAT organization, the shared interests of hi-tech corporate sponsors and the US defense industry had generated substantial skepticism in other sectors of the art world regarding the use of new technologies in art. It is significant that the alliance between art and technology was promoted through these corporate sponsors and given public exposure by governmental institutions like the United States Information Agency, who managed the US pavilion for the Osaka World Expo in 1970. The war in Vietnam had clearly demonstrated the destructive capabilities of technology and the underwriting of technological developments by corporations involved in hi-tech defense contracts. In the Osaka Expo technologies being developed for the space program were displayed prominently in a section of the US pavilion dedicated to the Apollo 11 moon landing while other technologies with potential military, aerospace, scientific, medical, and broadcasting applications were integrated more discreetly into a section on LACMA's Art and Technology program.

The Art and Technology program is ultimately of significance for the collaborations it enacted through one-year artist residencies in industrial manufacturing firms and research facilities, producing a contact point between commercial, political and cultural interests, and for the agents that it engaged in a dialogue. The interaction between industry and artists under the aegis of these collaborations led to a new form of multiple authorship, emphasizing developmental processes and exposing the intricate systems of negotiation and communication that operate in the production of an art work. LACMA's collaborators included forty industrial partners and sponsors ranging from specialists in electronics, radar, and aerospace, such as Hewlett-Packard, IBM, Lockheed Aircraft Corporation and NASA, to a government-contracted strategic-planning agency – The Rand Corporation. The entertainment industry was represented by Universal City Studios, Inc., and Twentieth Century Fox Film Corporation, and the Bank of America was also a major sponsor.

The art produced in the LACMA program, for the most part, fell short of producing the more nuanced forms of performance that Banham had alluded to in his review of Cybernetic Serendipity. One exception was Robert Rauschenberg's contribution, *Mud-Muse*, designed in collaboration with the Teledyne Corporation for display at Osaka but not realized until the LACMA exhibition in 1971.[9] *Mud-Muse*, in its final instantiation, comprised a 9 ft × 12 ft glass tank filled with high-viscosity driller's mud. Some thirty-six compressed-air inlets, maintained at three different pressure levels, were placed on the sides and bottom of the tank. These inlets could be electronically activated to produce various intensities of disturbance in a distributed and constantly changing pattern as the compressed air traveled through the mud. An electronic selector system that controlled the pneumatic valves was activated by sound signals picked up from microphones in the surrounding exhibition space. These audio inputs were processed to both influence the eruption of the mud and relay the selection of additional soundtracks to be emitted from underneath the tank.

Mud-Muse as a system of inputs and outputs that incorporated local feedback could be understood as a responsive 'software' in which mechanical 'hardware' was used to produce atmospheric effects. *Mud-Muse* in some ways epitomized the merging of 'the mechanical and organic in a world of undulating forms', which for McLuhan characterized the movie as a medium, but through its real-time pervasiveness and irreversibility the piece extended outside of the linear movement that characterizes film.[10] Instrumentalizing this real-time potential in a dynamic system was crucial to Rauschenberg and the

7.2: Robert Rauschenberg
– Mud-Muse, 1968–1971.
Art © Robert Rauschenberg /
Licensed by VAGA, New York,
NY. Photo: Moderna Museet,
Stockholm.

Teledyne team, as indicated in documents summarizing brainstorming sessions between the artist and the Teledyne engineers. Lewis Ellmore, then Director of Special Programs at Teledyne and Rauschenberg's primary collaborator, reflected on the potentials of specific technologies as an impetus in defining the viewer's experience of the piece:

> We considered many types of three-dimensional displays ... closed loop machining systems where the output of the machine was subsequently modified and fed back into the input ... We thought about the types and forms of energy, which could be sensed and used to activate and regulate the dynamics of the work. Again, everything from deliberate and direct observer control to purely random processes. We included sound, light, motion, odor, etc. ... We went on to explore ways of stimulating the observer, not only visually, but with both audible and non-audible sounds, pressure differentials and so on.[11]

In a letter to Rauschenberg from 1968, Ellmore outlines some of the specific potentials for *Mud-Muse* in reference to an earlier interactive piece by Rauschenberg, *Soundings*.

> It seems to me that what you and I have been discussing is essentially a way of creating a bilateral interaction between art and an observer as opposed to the predominantly unilateral reaction one currently finds. Soundings is revolutionary (or perhaps evolutionary is a more appropriate term) in that there does exist this bilateral relationship, using three basic elements: sensing, processing,

> and reaction ... we have been tending towards ... increasing the number of structural elements; for example, the number of phenomena sensed, the sophistication of the processing, etc., utilizing the elements where possible as components of the work; for example, the use of fluid computational devices which would visually form part of the work, directing the response to trigger known psychological and physiological characteristics in the observer and perhaps, to the extent possible, using the reaction of the observer to further modify the composition of the art.[12]

It becomes clear in Ellmore's detailing of the technical possibilities how the piece could be conceived as an operating system in which the hardware could be subsumed by the atmospheric effects of the software:

> We have, first, the input or motivating influence ... The output of these sensing devices may be ... combined or used to modify one another in many ways ... The processing, that is altering the form and/or nature of the sensor output signals, can be a direct modulation of one signal with another, or the use of computational techniques, or the use of a signal to operate upon itself, or the selective distortion of a signal according to some external functions, or any combination of these ... There is also the interesting possibility of not only causing the signal processing to be in itself sensed by the observer, but also to derive the nature of the processing through the observer's behavior.[13]

Low-definition effects on hi-tech time

If we look at *Cybernetic Sculpture* and *Mud-Muse* as media, their decorporealizing effects align with McLuhan's description of low-resolution or 'cool' media like TV, which encourage increased involvement on the part of the viewer who has to work to fill in the gaps that are not presented.[14] In *Cybernetic Sculpture* the substance of the piece itself ultimately dissolved into a barrage of pure media, turned into electrostatic by the pulsating strobe, implicating its viewers in real time through connections between sounds they emitted and emergent light patterns that issued from the piece. The substance of the hardware was evacuated, creating an overriding 'mosaic mesh', demanding the viewer's involvement and subsuming content. In *Mud-Muse*, the audience was also implicated in a feedback loop in which gaps between observer influence and spatial effects were intended. In Rauschenberg's words:

> Mud-Muse *starts from sound. An impulse is turned into electrical signal and then spreads out into three other breakdowns, depending on its dynamics. Then each one of those splits off in three ways. I don't want it to have a one-to-one relationship to the spectator.*[15]

The audience's immersion into a cycle of captured sound and emitted sound was implied; they were simultaneously being recorded and receiving recorded information in a feedback loop.

Feedback, according to McLuhan, is the end of lineality that came into the western world with the alphabet and the continuous forms of Euclidean space: 'feedback [is a] dialogue between the mechanism and its environment'.[16] McLuhan's understanding of media as 'any and all technological extensions of body and mind' suggests that electronic media are inseparable from the people who engage with them. In *low-definition* technology, these 'proto-interactive' environments can be understood as performing *media* rather than iconic representations of technological processes. *Cybernetic Sculpture* and *Mud-Muse* performed as ambient machines – anticipating, perhaps, contemporary ideas of architectural *operating systems* in which hardware is subsumed by the atmospheric effects of software, and materiality de-instantiates itself into responsive networks.

8.1: Detail, Vestigii Ticker Chair.

The archoid chimera:
Electric space as social machine
Tobi Schneidler (maoworks)

Networked and pervasive technologies are increasingly designed to talk to each other, to take decisions for people, citizens and individuals. Technical systems are becoming increasingly autonomous and 'artificially intelligent'; they start to act, behave, and occasionally misbehave. But where do these new conditions leave human identity and the way we expect to interact with our physical environs? The question is not if, but how, they affect our space, and how we as architects can tackle these issues as a new aspect to include in design strategies. Designing emotional affordance into our built environments has the potential to create an entirely new quality of dialogue between the building and its occupant, creating relationships with buildings that feel and respond.

The border between natural and artificial is rapidly dissolving, not least with the introduction of bionic research that merges natural body and mind with man-made technology in a new symbiosis. It is proposed here that space is becoming a form of artificial life, a bionic hybrid of sorts that can take on new roles and qualities that have not been possible in architecture previously through the creation of a spatial chimera – a hybrid between physical architecture and artificial life forms – involving physical spaces, people and emotional interaction. The investigations discussed here are thought of as scaled-down prototypes of a new type of space that emotes, converses and responds: the *feeling building* is instrumentalizing emotions to connect to the soul, not just the intellect, of its master.

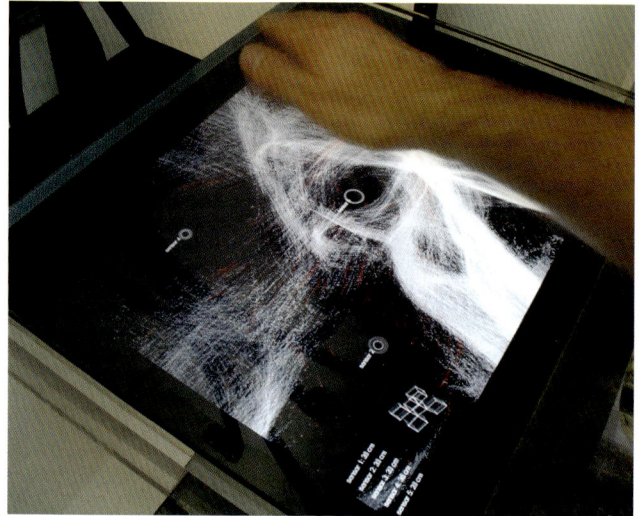

The archoid chimera: taming the beast called technology

Architecture has a tradition for absorbing and reapplying new technologies, but rarely have architects been able to allow their buildings a degree of autonomy in the sense of artificial intelligence, robotic behavior and emotional responsiveness.

We are living in a time of cultural and technological convergence. This process of rapid evolution, adaptation and rejection of ideas is also helped by the fast dissemination of knowledge and memes around the planet. Our habitat as human and social beings has been extended into a previously unknown domain, where space, time and synchronicity are to be redefined and redesigned. Crucially, emerging technologies are introducing new relational qualities that are connecting people in new ways to one another through inanimate or artificial surroundings. Fellow humans and tame animals have until recently been the only responsive creatures that people can interact or converse with. This is all changing now that machines start filling certain roles, such as utility, entertainment and emotional comfort.

The emotional affordance of bionic hybrids

The architectural utopia I want to propose here is one of space becoming a form of artificial life, a bionic hybrid of sorts that can take on new roles and qualities that have not been possible in architecture before. An assistive space, equipped with artificial intelligence and modalities for multi-sensual expression, would be an example in the scope of this proposal. Squeezing the interaction and relational qualities between man, machine and

8.2: Playing with the digital
agents to cause variation in the
interactive architectural scale
model.

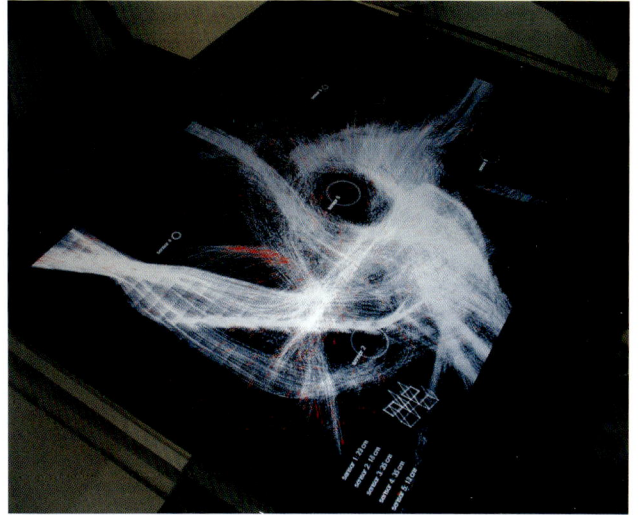

The three projects discussed here are architectural
in their intention, probing interaction modalities that
could be scaled up to become larger projects or parts
of architectural schemes: the Responsive Fields is a
scale model for a reactive space of digital agents; Remote Home is a full-scale prototype for an apartment
that exists in two cities at the same time; and the Vestigii Ticker Chair is projective furniture that forms part
of a converged internet and real-world experience.

Project 1: RESPONSIVE FIELDS

Responsive Fields, the digital beehive The Responsive Fields provide a space in which people can play
with an artificial 'livestock' of 5,000 digital agents.
The idea behind this project is to test a degree of
autonomy and self-rule within a digital system that exemplifies an abstracted architectural space. Responsive Fields was produced together with Pablo Miranda
and the Smart Studio at the Interactive Institute.
The piece was commissioned by Peter Weibel, for the
Algorithmic Revolutions show at ZKM in Germany in
2004, a show that traced the history of digital projects in art and architecture.

The project was scaled down to become a fully
interactive architectural model that invites observers
to occupy its responsive space. It is demonstrating a
new kind of typology of representation, between the
classic architectural model and the full-scale, interactive, functional prototype. This should give the emerging notion of interactive architecture an expression,
before it is realized in full scale.

The Responsive Fields are acting like a digital fish
tank, a sensual void. Visitors are finding their reflections in the animated surface beneath their hands, as
they are reaching inside the model space. It senses
and interprets the occupation of its inhabitants and
the users of this scaled three-dimensional space. A
semi-autonomous algorithm is continuously fed by an
embedded sensory field, which influences the

8.3: Reaching inside the data-cloud.

space through the experiential bottleneck of handheld computers or clip-on microphones will not help to create engaging examples within this area of thought. It will be necessary to hybridize the sensual qualities that people demand from other living creatures with those of buildings and technical systems that can engage users on a human level. Achieving these new qualities is about learning from successful interaction design, and evolving new concepts of interfaces that reach beyond the audio-visual paradigm of the media industry.

A key term in interaction design is the notion of *affordance*, the visual clue to the function of an object. Digital and interactive technologies have brought forward many new application scenarios of use, but many concepts failed to break through because the design of the interactive product did not make its benefit or attraction explicit. This is mainly a question of designing successful affordance into a project. Affordance in interactive design is as much a key ingredient as the thinking about circulation and guidance is in architecture. But eventually it provokes a much deeper emotional level of engagement.

I would argue that the moment of truth has come, when some of these new relational qualities are merging into built space and smart furniture, creating hybrid entities that are absorbing some of the spirit previously reserved for living beings. Affordance will be to interactive architecture what attitude is to human beings – a mental gateway to new types of relationships.

About sociable machines and electric affections

Nature is unpredictable, and that seems to be the core to our interaction with fellow humans: moments of the unexpected, uncertainty and surprise would need to be designed into our artificially alive buildings to make them emotionally acceptable to people. Researchers at MIT have already started dedicated groups that are dealing with questions of sociable machines. One of their most prominent results has been Kismet. Kismet is a robot, designed by the MIT Media Lab, which physically mimics facial expressions – similar to 'infant-caretaker interaction' – as well as using voice and hearing to facilitate a 'social' contact. It shows how robots can move from the purely functional to more personal domains.

There would be many reasons to attempt creating such a spatial chimera, a hybrid between physical architecture and artificial life forms. This could produce totally new concepts about relationships through mediating spaces and artifacts, between people as well as between people and information. Changing the character of a building could soon mean something very different. Ubiquitous computing, social networking sites and artificial intelligence, to name the most prominent concepts in the contemporary technology debate, have concrete effects on our 'meat world', the physical environments that we inhabit. The question is not if, but how, they affect our space, and how we as designers can take part in shaping the future. Since the design space (engineering lingo) is largely undefined, designers of all kinds are currently writing their own briefs, and inventing their own projects in collaboration with engineers and scientists. Now is the time to conceive these hybrid spaces, which

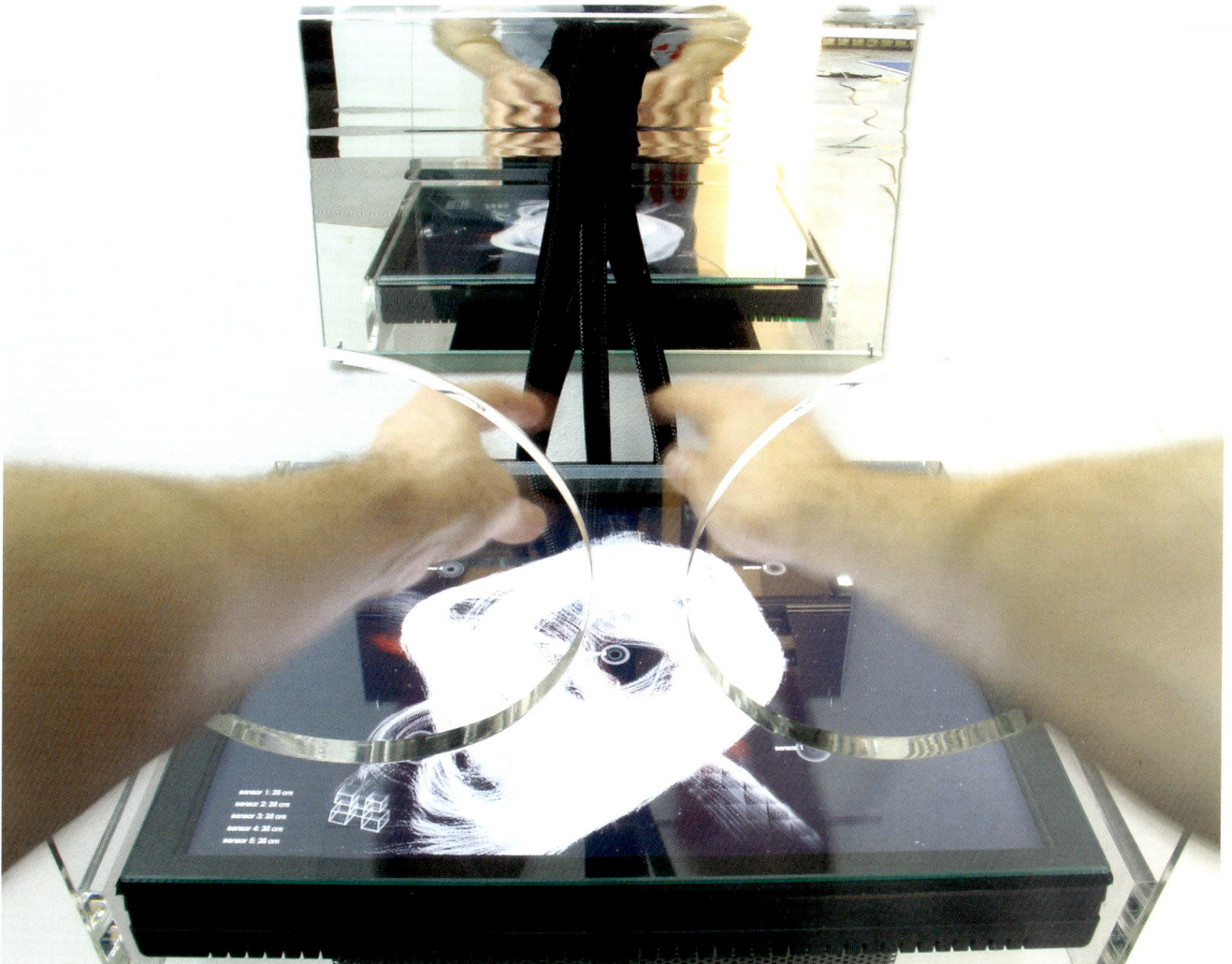

behavior of 5,000 red agents roaming the digital space. The process is irreversible, but ephemeral. The visualization shows a continuous reference to recent events, but the current is in ongoing flux. The visible memory is programmed to decay over time. An invisible sediment of recent digital impressions is stored, and influences future behavior in this responsive space. The space learns over time, building sediments of sensed experiences that are casually surfacing at idle times of low activity.

The space thus develops an *autonomous behavior* that depends on the context and location, and the kind of interest it receives from 'visitors'. A new kind of mental relationship could therefore be formed with the environment, when space is in flux and the surrounding is reacting in a way that can have unexpected outcomes, just like playing with a pet or wild animal. Imagining this idea scaled up to building level could very much transform buildings into a truly living architecture: a utopia not of artificial intelligence but of behavior.

Robotic pets are already in the shops, emulating the real-life species in an astonishing way. Could these qualities be translated into the larger and more distributed scale of architectural organizations?

occupy the physical domain as we do as humans, but
also stretch into the ephemeral, yet real, universe of
digital potentials.

Man meets machine meets mind

Buildings that think? Spaces having feelings, environments that talk aloud and rooms that respond? These
ideas have been around for a while, from Archigram's
walking cities to Kubrick's HAL in *2001*. While science
fiction and architecture have concluded their earlier
liaison, reality has caught up fast. In a very clandestine
way, technologies, networks and digital services have
infiltrated in a manner our parents could not even have
dreamt about. Many of these effects aren't visible, but
are hiding within the ubiquitous, world-spanning laby-
rinth called the internet, facilitating communication
protocols, controlling postal logistics and monitoring
innumerable sensors, listening out for secret nuclear
tests and whale songs. The brutalist vision of a gigantic
city turning into an animal of sorts has today become a
ridiculous technological dino-vision. HAL, on the other
hand, is a much more familiar concept, as the pervasive
voice of clever cars and smart phones that invites us
to converse – albeit this is usually still limited to less
emotional and engaging issues, concerned with control
and functionality.

But the next step in development is something much
more sinister, and yet fascinating: pervasive computing. This area is so comprehensive and lacking in clear
borders that even seasoned computer scientists have
trouble explaining it coherently. Pervasive computing is
the possibility for computers to dissolve into the fabric

of everyday life; it is where networked systems start to
have autonomous character and, crucially, talk to each
other. Examples include cars that instantly communicate icy roads over mobile mesh networks, warning
other cars in the vicinity or even telling these cars to hit
the brake without the intervention of the driver.

Is this about overriding human instincts or aug-
menting human potentials? We all seem to be increasingly surrendering autonomy and decision-making to
complex and highly abstract systems. But far from feeling victimized, most people seem to be accepting these
new relationships almost as a second nature. The next
level of development will be that of evolving emotional
affordance in visual, audible and haptic interactive
engagements with such systems, a design space that will
be quite alien to architecture but will require initiative
and collaboration from many other disciplines such as
game designers, sociologists and psychologists.

Two other areas that have greatly influenced how we
share social spaces are the internet and mobile phones.
Those spaces are hard to express in the traditional language of built architecture, but they are hardly virtual.
In fact, technologies like internet dating sites, social
networks and instant messaging have collapsed space
and time, to provide synchronous social experiences
that were unthinkable before. Interaction with friends,
peers, individuals and groups are taking place through
numerous modalities now, defining new conversation etiquettes and happening on different levels of
synchronicity. And the human consciousness seems to
be adapting at a blazing speed – or does it? While as
recently as fifteen years ago personal messages could

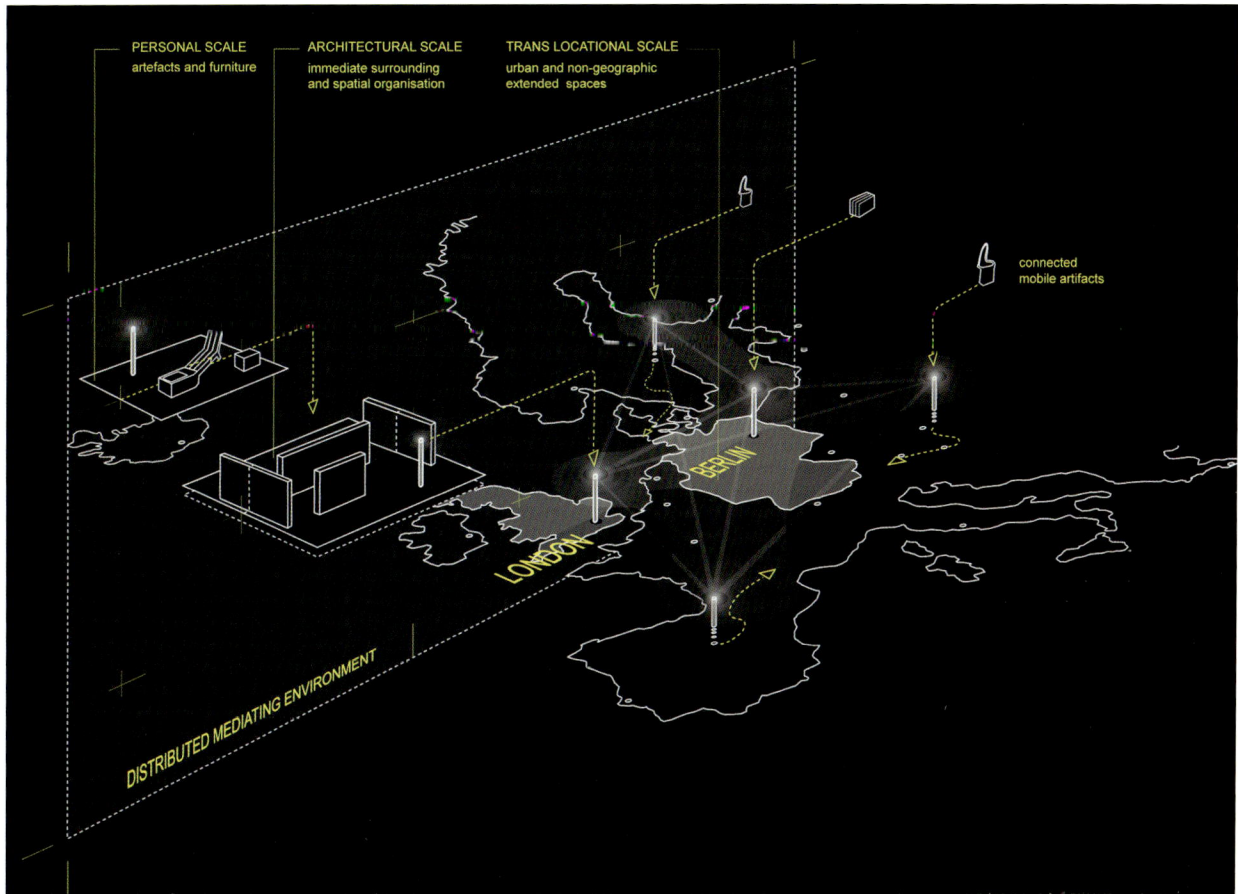

PERSONAL SCALE
artefacts and furniture

ARCHITECTURAL SCALE
immediate surrounding
and spatial organisation

TRANS LOCATIONAL SCALE
urban and non-geographic
extended spaces

connected
mobile artifacts

BERLIN

LONDON

DISTRIBUTED MEDIATING ENVIRONMENT

Project 2: THE REMOTE HOME

The Remote Home, mediating space as a social proxy
Architecure's most potent motive is that of a social
space, a hull filled with life and exchange. The Remote Home was started with the observation that people are increasingly traveling, sharing friendship over
distance or working in a different country from the
one they are living in. This also happened to be the
author's very personal situation at the time. The brief
was to design an environment that could play a role
in encouraging togetherness between close friends
or couples over distance, to create one shared space
that exists in two different cities, without resorting to
typical communication tools like video conferencing.
Instead, the apartment should be experienced with

tactile sensibility and visual alternations relating to
the physicality of the place, rather than a projection
or screen interface. While most technological advances are functionality and engineering driven, the
Remote Home is introducing emotions as a driver for
development. 'Softspace' in this case relates more to
social values than to computational software.

Reactive furniture and spatial elements provide
a physical setting, to relay presence over distance.
Bodily actions are translated into TCP/IP data packets, and sent on their 30 millisecond journey to the
connected home. The original exhibition demonstrated the prototypes between London's Science
Museum and the Raumlabor Gallery in Berlin. Visitors

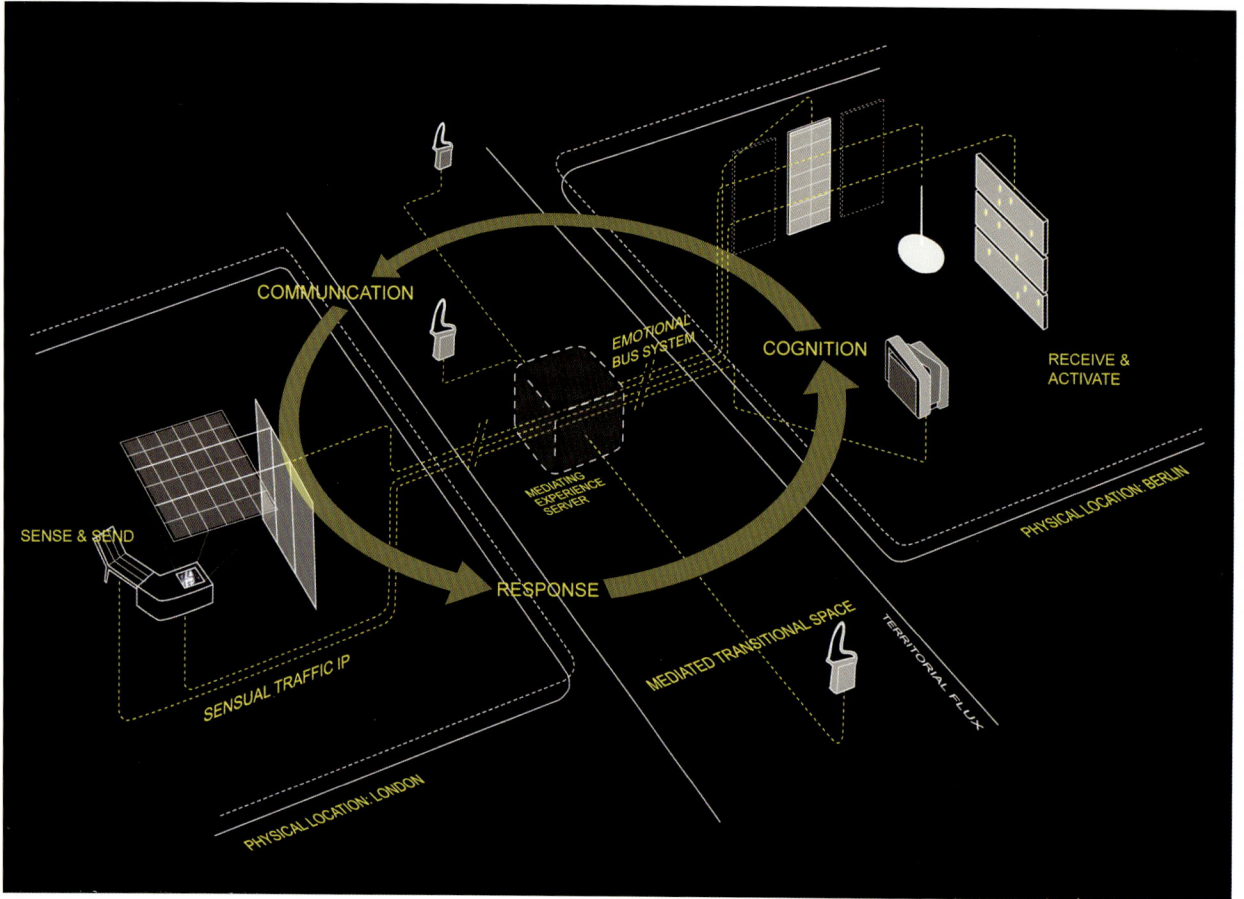

ABOVE, 8.5: System diagram of the trans-locational spatial entity. BELOW, 8.6: The two spaces, in two cities.

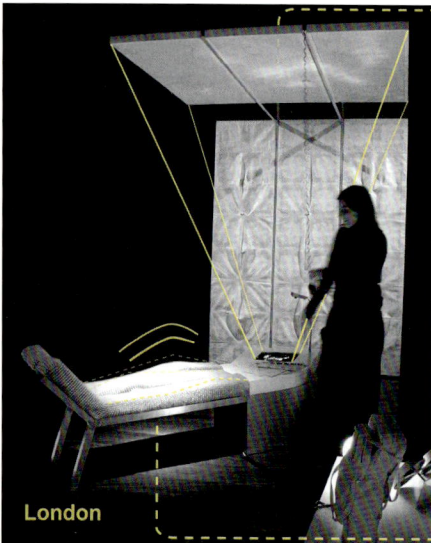

London

Berlin

ABOVE, 8.7 and BELOW,
8.8: The Lonley Home bench
and lamp are part domestic
furniture and part robotic pet,
coming alive unexpectedly.

were encouraged to get into contact with their remote counterparts. Spoken language and generation gaps faded into the background when people felt the digitally mediated, physical touch through the tangible environment.

Two of several elements are presented here: the Busy Bench and the Lonely Lamp. These furniture installations are reactive to the occupant through embedded sensors that sense movement and presence to report them to a central server, which is continuously mediating the experience between the spaces that make up the Remote Home. The Bench is dealing with issues of personal territory in a shared space, while the Lamp is mediating remote presence in a more ambient form through locative gesturing and dimmable light levels, which give it the lively appearance of a random wood fire. When the objects are in use, their physicality becomes a place holder, a mediating proxy in the social interaction between the two friends sharing the space remotely.

However, the individual qualities of those physically animated pieces only became apparent as objects of simulated autonomy when the prototype was ready to use. The quality of engaging people on a similar level to the Responsive Fields positively surprised the team and led to a set of relatives being created – called the Lonely Home. The ability to induce curiosity and affection in the visitors actually exceeded the original design intention and led to a new strain of thought that is more about behavioral aspects themselves in relation to the user.

OPPOSITE, 8.9: Variations on the Vestigii Chair's interactive mirror. BELOW, 8.10: Detail of the electromechanical character set projection device.

only be transported via phone, fax or snail mail, people are suddenly inhabiting the ubiquitous information universe. One number connects to (almost) any place on the planet; instant messaging, at the workplace, at home and on the move, is blurring private and work time, personal and public space. Social networking and dating sites are redefining the concept of meeting people. Our flesh-and-blood reality seems to be increasingly extending into the virtual, non-locational realm. So do we accept these conditions as a secondary given, or can we as designers propose objects and spaces that are occupying a threshold position between the physical and the digital worlds?

Another field of growing maturity is that of android robots, especially in Japan. The latest generation is occupying an interesting field between practical utility and emerging social intelligence. Those creatures are already blessed with limited autonomy to navigating nursing homes with food trays, patrol after-hours industrial sites or comfort home-alone children (the AIBO robo-dog, for example). Emotions have already become a design material, in a very active way. Automated call centers are not just artificially intelligent, but increasingly become artificially emotional, just to make us mortals feel more natural and understood. We are increasingly entering into subtle relationship with systems, as well as systems with us.

If buildings are becoming more intelligent, connected and connecting, how could those spaces appear and behave? And could we afford a degree of affection to our designed spaces? One could see the shift in architectural design paradigms coming from the sculptural,

going through the filmic, time-based phase and arriving at the relational narrative of interactivity and emotional engagement. Interactive installations are often associated with effect and spectacle, but in the end they may have much greater value in driving the emotional qualities of a space to facilitate dialogue between a sentient building and its master.

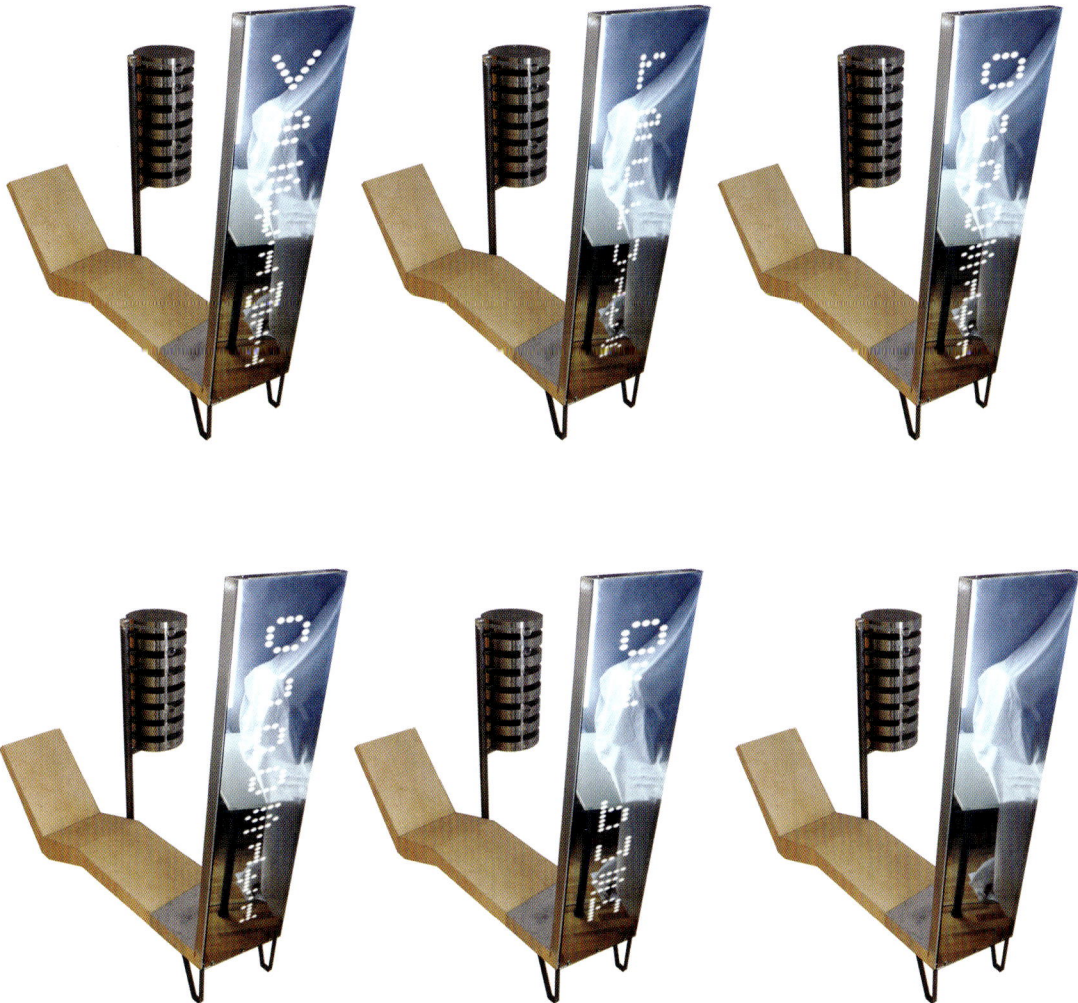

Project 3: THE VESTIGII TICKER CHAIR

The Vestigii Ticker Chair, an interactive spatial modifier

The Vestigii Ticker Chair is an object that derives its behavior from human activity on a global scale: world events, communicated through internet news feeds, are provoking this installation to initiate its projective spectacle. It is being developed as a living tool for the Vestigiii fashion studio in Berlin. It is not just being placed in the centre of the designer's activity, but also inhabits an ephemeral and invisible information space that continuously streams information, news and data through the airwaves and copper cables of our modern cities. The chair is designed to catch those ephemeral digital fragments, derived from on-going world affairs and events, and relay them back into the physical space of the designer's studio to let them condensate on the creative environment.

In reference to physical reality, the projection is using electromechanical character sets that project words and short sentences onto a special mirror. The immaterial information bits are transformed into the very physical rotation of eight metal drums that act as electromechanical projection devices. Each drum can project one letter at a time onto a special screen-mirror, so a word of eight characters can be displayed at once. As a side effect, an ambient, randomized data-veil is thrown around the surrounding interior, giving animated reference to its constant flux.

The piece is designed less as a digital instrument and more as a spatial modifier, to be inserted into the creative space of the studio and to become a

LEFT, 8.11: The Vestigii Chair
and projection device.
OPPOSITE, 8.12: Detail of the
projection device.

familiar part in the life of the designer. The news information is thrown onto the back of a mirror that is a semi-transparent projection surface; hence people can mirror themselves in the live world events as they unfold. The news fragments become body language. This mirror transforms the light spectacle again into an intangible image, which magically overlays with the image of the observer. The rhythm of the incoming data packets can be influenced by visitors resting on the chair. The project receives its input from a special 'news spider', which also works towards the fashion company's website, designed by Marcus Kirsch.

The project converges public information space, internal inspiration tool and part of the studio furnishing into one project. In fact the Ticker Chair acts as a responsive environmental attributor – a reactive element that can be inserted into an architectural space and change its entire presence.

9.1: Olafur Eliasson – *Weather Project*, 2001, Tate Modern.

In the simplest terms, the radicalization of matter requires three recognitions: that matter is from the beginning irreducibly sensate and responsive; that at every scale sensate, responsive matter organizes itself hierarchically into discrete, irreproducible configurations with specific emergent behaviors; and that all discrete material configurations at any and every moment and any and every scale further arrange into complex ecologies.
– Jeffrey Kipnis, 'On the Wild Side' (1999)

Eco_logics Helene Furján

Deleuze and Guattari, in their explanation of the 'abstract machine', proclaim the operation of the 'diagrammatic' as pure 'Matter-Function' – a performativity that implies function over form, matter over substance, effects over meaning. Diagrammatic techniques do not map or represent existing objects, systems and data sets so much as project or speculate – they are central to the paradigm of architecture-as-research, a practice in which graphic strategies, techniques and technologies are integral not only to the mapping of the contemporary world, but to its generation. In architecture such 'diagrammatic' thinking is involved as much in the structuring of the process, the tools, the experiment or the research parameters, as in that of a 'product'. As Manuel De Landa notes: 'true thinking consists in problem-posing, that is, in framing the right problems rather than solving them. It is only through skillful problem-posing that we can begin to think diagrammatically'.[1] Architecture becomes a process of tooling the design as well as the instrumentalization of highly specific tools. In diagrammatics, nonlinearity – the emergence of unpredictable effects or orders – and dynamics – behavior over time, flow and flux – are operationalized.

This essay will track the influence of a 'diagrammatic' logic in architecture in two differing but related directions, equally dependent on advanced visualization techniques and simulation modeling: the development in contemporary architecture of an interest in architecture-as-environment leading towards a science of effects on the one hand, and towards architecture understood in ecological terms – architecture as ecosystem – on the other.

9.2: EAT (Experiments in Art and Technology) – *Pepsi-Cola Pavilion*, World Expo, Osaka, 1970. Courtesy of: Research Library, The Getty Research Institute, Los Angeles, California. Photo: Moderna Museet, Stockholm.

A science of effects could be understood as the liberation of atmospherics, 'a transition from imagining space as an abstract thing, which is framed, to imagining space as matter itself',[2] a shift in which atmosphere becomes the very *matter* of architecture. Banham's science of effects, posited all those decades ago in *The Architecture of the Well-Tempered Environment*, saw a shift from architecture as building system (cladding, structure, program, form) to architecture as conditioner-of-effects (heat, light, moisture, color). In this conception, architecture is no longer confined to surfaces, whether thick or thin, but opens to a notion of 'matter' in which the air itself is latent with design potential, in which architecture is able to script and modulate a 'thick atmosphere'.

The corollary of effects is behaviors. If architecture today is finally beginning to draw the realm of the ambient into its territory, no longer through a phenomenological interest in the perception of environments, that territory was already marked out in the possibilities Banham saw for the environment: as a system of control that modifies, conditions, and regulates. In this sense, 'building' gives way to 'ecosystem', to a built organization that operates at the level of vivisystems – dynamic and complex systems that learn, adapt, evolve, and mutate in response to the feedback of environmental conditions. Architecture today is no longer interested in the primacy of shelter, or even the dominance of form-generation, but in researching smart materials, adaptive envelopes, and responsive environments.

[Effects] do not operate in a pure and undiluted form, but, at best, take part in a kaleidoscope of enactments, in which the vividness of each individual effect is moderated by the simultaneous presence of other effects. Effects are actions and they emanate from relations. The best effects that architecture can produce in the contemporary world are those that are proliferating and moving, effects that are anticipatory, unexpected, climactic, cinematic, time-related, non-linear, surprising, mysterious, compelling and engaging.

– Ben van Berkel and Caroline Bos, 'Effects: Radiant Synthetic' (1992)

Thick atmospheres

In the last decade or so the proliferation of digital media has had an explosive impact on the pervasiveness of what Debord termed 'the society of the spectacle'. Within this culture of spectacle, the dominance of occularity and image, recent architectural discourse has begun to map out a resistance, shifting the question of visual culture away from spectatorship (questions of the gaze, of the primacy of viewing, and so on), and towards an immersive, interactive engagement that breaks down the authority of the viewing subject and engages other senses – an experiential understanding of space interested in atmosphere and effect. As a result, significant shifts are opening in the relation of the object to its wider environment; the boundary between building and its environment blurs. This occurs at two levels at least: architecture-as-object giving way to architecture-as-environment; and the thickening of the skin to include a 'sandwich' of envelope and air (including heat, light, moisture), or of different forms of matter. Both paradigms might be understood as a 'thick atmosphere' – architecture as a system of control that modifies, conditions and regulates.[3]

Architecture-as-environment exploits technology to develop new vibes and atmospherics – what I have elsewhere called 'hyper-lounge'.[4] The spaces that result are ambient and moody, wrapping the visitor (who is no longer strictly speaking an observer, and therefore no longer passive) in the affective and interactive possibilities of special effects. Jeff Kipnis has developed the concept of 'cosmetics', which operates as a field condition – diffuse, ephemeral, atmospheric thinness[5]

– lifting free of the surface in projects like Servo's *Lattice Archipelogics* to produce a diffusion of effects through a thickened region of space. This configuration of environment could be understood as a 'smooth mixture', an emulsion of atmospherics, matter, form, technology, event.

The return of a sensory understanding of architecture has its links to the interest in 'effect' and sensation manifested in Baroque and Enlightenment architecture and architectural theory (and belatedly rediscovered in Gothic cathedrals), from mysterious lights and atmospheres to the kinetic effects of light and shade on three-dimensionalized surfaces – effects tied both to temporal changes and the mobility of the spectator. The primary theories of mood and atmosphere remain Edmund Burke's essay on the sublime (1757), Le Camus de Mézière's treatise on sensation (1780), and Richard Payne-Knight's essay on the associational and affective properties of the picturesque (1806). Phenomenological readings of space, from Hilderband and Fielder to Merlot-Ponty or Bachelard, must also be counted as important precursors.

But perhaps the most direct genealogical linkage lies between contemporary experimentations with immersive sensory space and the interactive and immersive artworks (the 'happenings', multimedia pavilions or shows, and so on) of the post-war period. In particular, the vibrating color fields of Verner Panton's interiors or the flux of affectively charged atmospheres of Constant's unrealized New Babylon stand out, as do the many interactive multimedia environments designed for expos – Saarinen and the Eames's IBM pavilion at the New

York World's Fair, Le Corbusier's Poème Électronique for the Philips Company pavilion at the Brussels World Expo, or EAT's Pepsi-Cola pavilion at the Osaka World's Fair.

The Pepsi-Cola pavilion, for instance, was 'an early and important example of research on the integration of an electronic, programmable environment into a habitable structure': cloud machine, multimedia performance space, simulation generator, responsive environment, interactive and immersive.[6] No longer a static object, it was a protocol that generated an adaptive environment through feedback mechanisms, one allowing visitors to be fully participatory – to construct their own experiences, to merge with the environment, to become protagonists in a laboratory of creation and experimentation – rather than the passive recipients of a pre-programmed narrative. In this project lies the concept of environment we have been tracking – architecture as conditioner-of-effects, as ecology. For EAT, the concept of environment provided a means to allow programming to mediate 'human interaction with technology'.[7] Contemporary with Marhsall McLuhan, the pavilion invokes his 'acoustic man', the multi-directed immersiveness of sound, light and color scapes creating an acoustic-optical simulation that challenges the primacy of the purely optical.

The Pepsi-Cola pavilion neatly captures the twin interests in contemporary atmospherics: affect/effect, and technology. As an affective space, it generated a kind of 'delirious immersion' by activating air, media technologies, light and color (a color that becomes light and a light that becomes color) alongside more traditional architec-

tonic elements. Space becomes luminescent, colorized, iridescent, saturated, dense, intense, emulsified. Central to this conception is the participation of the user:

> *The ambiance of an environment possessing certain specific plastic and acoustic characteristics depends on the individuals who find themselves there ... The quality of the environment and its ambiance no longer depends on material factors alone, but on the manner in which they will have been perceived, appreciated and used – on the 'new way of looking' at them.*[8]

Ben van Berkel and Caroline Bos describe a particular category of architectural effect that they liken to walking through a painting: 'your gaze swerves and orients you through color, shininess, light, figuration, and sensation'.[9] Taken from Gilles Deleuze, this effect is derived from 'a haptic vision of color, as opposed to the optical vision of light'. Such a 'sense' of color is tactile-optical: it 'implies a type of seeing that is distinct from the optical, a close-up viewing in which 'the sense of sight behaves just like touch'.[10] This tactile-optical experiencing of space is one in which the real and virtual collapse – a space in which imagination, fantasy, hallucination, effect mingle with the material, the visual, the sensory; like the club or rave, an environment in which the synaesthetic merging of light, sound, motion, and chemicals combine with the propriosensory processes of the body as it turns and moves. The world opened up for the participant is one of flux and flows, a dynamic field of provisional, contingent and distractive effects.

Atmosphere as environment, effect (with a concomitant interest in 'materials', such as light, shade, or sound,

9.3: Francois Roche / R&Sie
Architects – Lausanne Gallery,
competition entry, 2004.

that might enhance the construction of sensory atmospheres), and vibe (affect or mood) posit a resistance to the dominance of ocularity in Modernism. Working either to remap vision within a bodily, fully sensory terrain, or to obfuscate it, filling the air with special effects (glooms, mists, colors) that prevent a totalizing gaze, atmospheric architecture (or architectures of atmosphere) return the 'spectator' to a bodily awareness, and to a kinetic, tactile field in which they are fully immersed. The question here is no longer one of spectacle, the understanding of contemporary culture through a privileging both of spectatorship and of visuality, nor is it a problem of the registration of visual culture and its impact upon architecture. In the blurring and dissolution of both the matter of building and the notion of 'spectacle' itself (here the view, intended to be occluded by the very immaterial 'matter' of the building's fabric), the reign of visuality is resisted, submerged by the ambient effects.

Also critical, of course, is the role of technolgy. Immersive and interactive architectures require sophisticated digital control systems to conjure their effects. These algorithmic controls, or rather regulators and generators, transform the logic of built space into a dynamic network organization – an ecosystem – sensing and responding to the feedback of visitors' movements. The 'thick atmosphere' is produced by the complex interaction between visitor, architectonics, a bundle of sensors, computers, and light and sound emitters. Co-evolving components are networked into a dynamic assemblage, the clustering relations formed by interacting behaviors. New clusters form and dissolve as the network learns, remembers, and evolves. Thick atmospheres today generate their effects from a hybrid emulsion of digital and physical constructions, smoothly admixed into new interactive and immersive systems, new fields of intoxication and sensation.

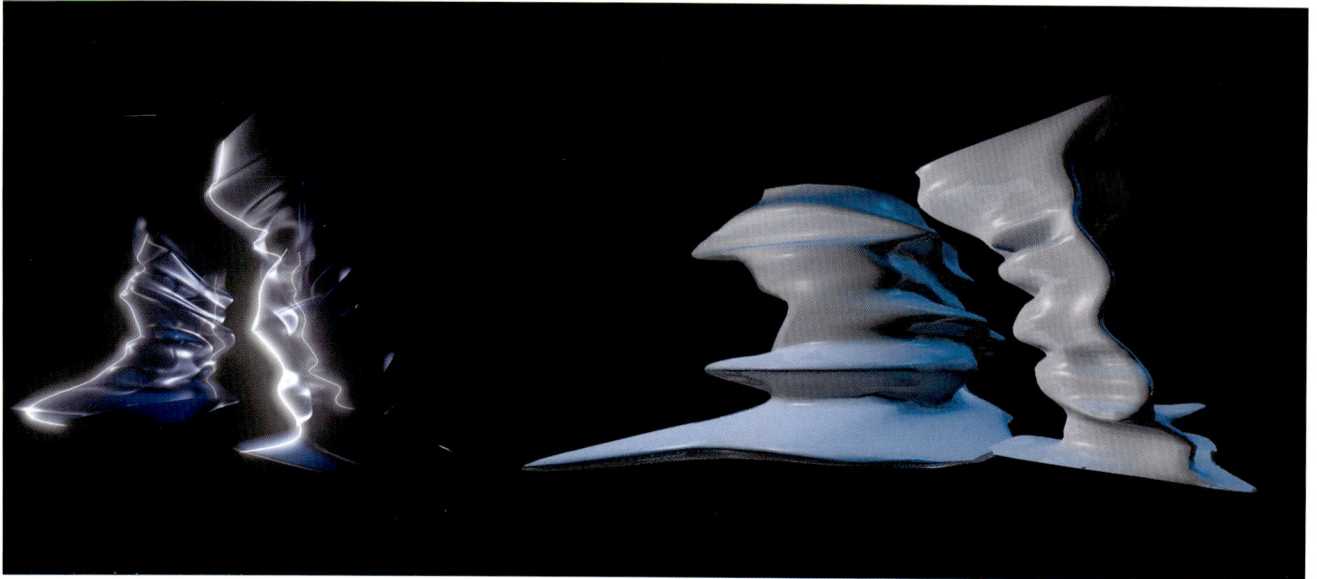

9.4: Winka Dubbeldam /
Archi-tectonics – Sound-
scapes, installation at the
National Building Museum,
2004.

For complex adaptive systems to maintain
themselves, they must remain open to their
environment and change when conditions
require it. Complex adaptive systems, there-
fore, inevitably evolve, or, more accurately,
coevolve.

– Mark C. Taylor, *The Moment of Complexity: Emerg-*
ing Network Culture (2001)

Responsive environments

'Thick atmosphere' also refers to the redefinition of 'skin' to include not just layers of matter and structure but also the air that abuts and permeates these layers. Added to this new sensitivity to ambience and its operationalization is a question of performance – the instrumentalization of this thickened atmosphere as a means of tooling the envelope in response to shifting parameters of heat, light, moisture, sound, the structural properties of materials, and so on. This 'smart' envelope is reconfigured as an 'environment' in its own right.

In *Out of Control*, Kevin Kelly contrasts two morphologies of organization: the 'linear' structure of sequential operations that governs top-down hierarchical systems like factory assembly lines or traditional corporate structures, and the 'nonlinear' structure of assemblies of parallel operations that governs networks. As he writes, 'action in these systems proceeds in a messy cascade of interdependent events'. Complex organizations are collectivities of 'autonomous members', which means a bottom-up system of highly connected agents who are not individually responding to centralized commands but *independently* and individually reacting to 'internal rules and the state of their local environment'.[11] Characteristic of networks, swarms and vivisystems alike, 'what emerges from the collective is not a series of critical individual actions but a multitude of simultaneous actions whose collective pattern is far more important'.[12]

Linear systems are closed systems – they can only exchange work and heat with their exterior – and are characterized by a single global stable state – equilibrium. Until relatively recently, science focused on closed systems, largely because they were easily modeled, while environmental systems engineering preferred buildings as closed systems, maintaining their internal environments in steady equilibrium condition. But linear systems rarely exist in the world, just as it is virtually impossible to prevent energy exchange between a building and its environment. Nonlinear systems are open systems that can exchange work, heat, and matter with their exterior, and they are complex – that is, more than the sum of their parts.

The modern city is today understood as a complex, self-organizing system akin to an ecosystem. It is a messy assemblage of networks, systems, ecologies, all competing with, and contaminating, each other. It is inherently nonlinear: a site of expansions; tactical and strategic interventions; confrontations between localization and globalization (including shifting cultural identities based on migration patterns); a terrain of constructed space (architectonic and urbanistic); and a map of flows, networks, transfers, and transits (the immaterial images, messages, and vectors of communications and transportations). As Mike Weinstock notes,

> We are within the horizon of a systemic change, from the design and production of individual "signature" buildings to an ecology in which evolutionary designs have sufficient intelligence to adopt and to communicate, and from which intelligent cities will emerge.[13]

Ecosystems are characterized by bottom-up logics and networked flexible organizations. Structure and evolution are linked, both a function of environmental pressure and 'fitness': adaptive feedback loops that are not simply reactive but a combination of learning and creativity, processing information about the environment into a model that uses interpolation and extrapolation to make predictions and develop modifications. Evolution relies on a combination of order, flexibility or dynamics, and unpredictability; in other words, on a process of replication and mutation as much as design and control.[13] Such systems generate 'stable instability' through the interplay of noise and information generated by environmental feedback mechanisms.[14] Ecosystems are coevolutionary, coadaptive, codependent: 'since all organisms adapt that means all organisms in an ecosystem partake in a continuum of coevolution, from direct symbiosis to indirect mutual influence'.[15] The development of such systems is dependent less on degrees of complexity or noise than on the *pattern* – the *topologies* – of interrelations that characterizes the system.

Crucial, then, to an ecosystems approach to architecture is the blurring of boundaries between building and environment – both merge into one continuous ecology – and the generative capacity of that environment – an instrumental engagement with the dynamic forces and flows that condition the environment: the flows of matter, air, heat, light, moisture (geological, seismic, geothermal, climatic), but also infrastructural flows of energy, information, capital, transportation, and so on. In order to achieve these levels of feedback, the architectural system must model its 'fitness landscape', a mapping of the internal constraints of the system with the parameters of its external environment, to produce potential pathways of development. Used by René Thom (biology), Stuart Kauffman (physics) and Conrad

Waddington (developmental biology), fitness landscapes are models of coadaptation, since each ecology or even organism will have its own competing fitness landscape.

Formal or infrastructural development, in such a model, is always contingent, and always evolving. Practices at the leading edge of architectural research today are increasingly turning to the use of sophisticated digital visualization and generation tools – borrowed from the sciences of weather simulation, materials and systems research, and from the multiple engineering disciplines – to push architectural generation simultaneously into the micro-scale of matter and the macro-scale of the environment. Such design practices search for adaptation and variation, scripting simulation modeling to genetically breed envelopes as enhanced environmental systems. Parametrics here couples form-finding and energy systems into advanced processing systems, linking the changing intensity and directionality of variables such as sunlight or rainfall to handle inundation as a localized flood response as well as a hedge against drought or heat, modifying the skin to reflect or maximize heat absorption, or to optimize the ability of photovoltaics to generate energy, for instance, all with profound morphological implications.

Responsiveness reformulates digital production in the direction of contextuality – no longer the old meaning-laden form but one in which feedback mechanisms are not simply internal to the algorithms generating the project but linked to specific environmental parameters that the architectural project is now able to fully instrumentalize. Looped into ecosystems, architecture

9.5: Future Cities Lab: Jason Johnson / Nataly Gattegno – Seoul Opera House, competition entry, 2005. Top: Sectional perspective view of hanging opera house. Bottom: Interior perspective.

in this model becomes ecosystemic itself. The building envelope becomes part of a 'thick 2-D' in which environmental *control* gives way to environmental *modulation* – dynamic modulations of territories and micro-climates – creating a building responsive to both its internal and its external environments, through a control system based on the centrality of variation in behavior rather than an optimized and statically maintained condition. The building in this model is a cybernetic system, capable of self-regulation – an integrated, complex system possessing its own intelligence – and is stable in the non-linear, disequilibrium manner in which vivisystems are 'stable': a 'stable instability'.

We might understand the tight coupling of building and environment though Lynne Margulis's model of 'fused assemblages': micro-organisms evolve their own complexity by incorporating simpler organisms into larger multiplicities that become capable of reproduction as a singularity. A single body and an ecology of organisms are similar – both exploit one another's functions and machinic behaviors through feedback and exchange. A body is the fused assemblage of an ecosystem operating with a high degree of continuity and stability. Ecosystems, however, are generally less tightly coupled – not so much superorganisms as loose 'federations'. Organisms are tightly bound and strict, ecosystems are loosely bound and lax; evolution is a tight web, ecology a loose one. The fused assemblage of building – environment is such a loose network, a 'soft system'. Soft systems are 'fluid, pliant, adaptive fields that are responsive and evolving', and that have 'the capacity to absorb, transform, and exchange information with [their] surroundings'.[16]

Félix Guattari identifies three ecologies, in an essay of the same title, as the environment, social relations and human subjectivity. He argues for the need for an ethico-political relation between the three, which must be at once global and molecular, and which he terms 'ecosophy'.[17] 'Eco-logics' is a generalized ecology that does not strive for resolution and that moves between collective action and individual creativity. In other words, it allows for emergent orders and practices: the drift or bifurcation of a project from its initial path by the introduction of an unpredicted 'event-incident'. 'Eco-logics' is therefore a practice and a process; it is applied *and* theoretical, ethico-political *and* aesthetic; it is a process of 'continuous resingularization' – continual mutation, reinvention, becoming.[18]

Nonlinear dynamic processes have been central to the development of digital practices for some time, as indeed have advanced computational logics that allow the generation of form to become 'genetic', a process of growth and evolution that breeds prototypical solutions. Less so has been the question of responsiveness. The work collected together in this volume – and that of other key emergent digital innovators – is moving in an important direction, adding to the genetic mix a concept of performativity rigorously tied to material dynamics, climactic and environmental parameters, urban and social organizations (as infrastructural parameters rather than socio-political representations), and ambient conditions.

9.6: Olafur Eliasson – *Weather Project*, 2001, Tate Modern.

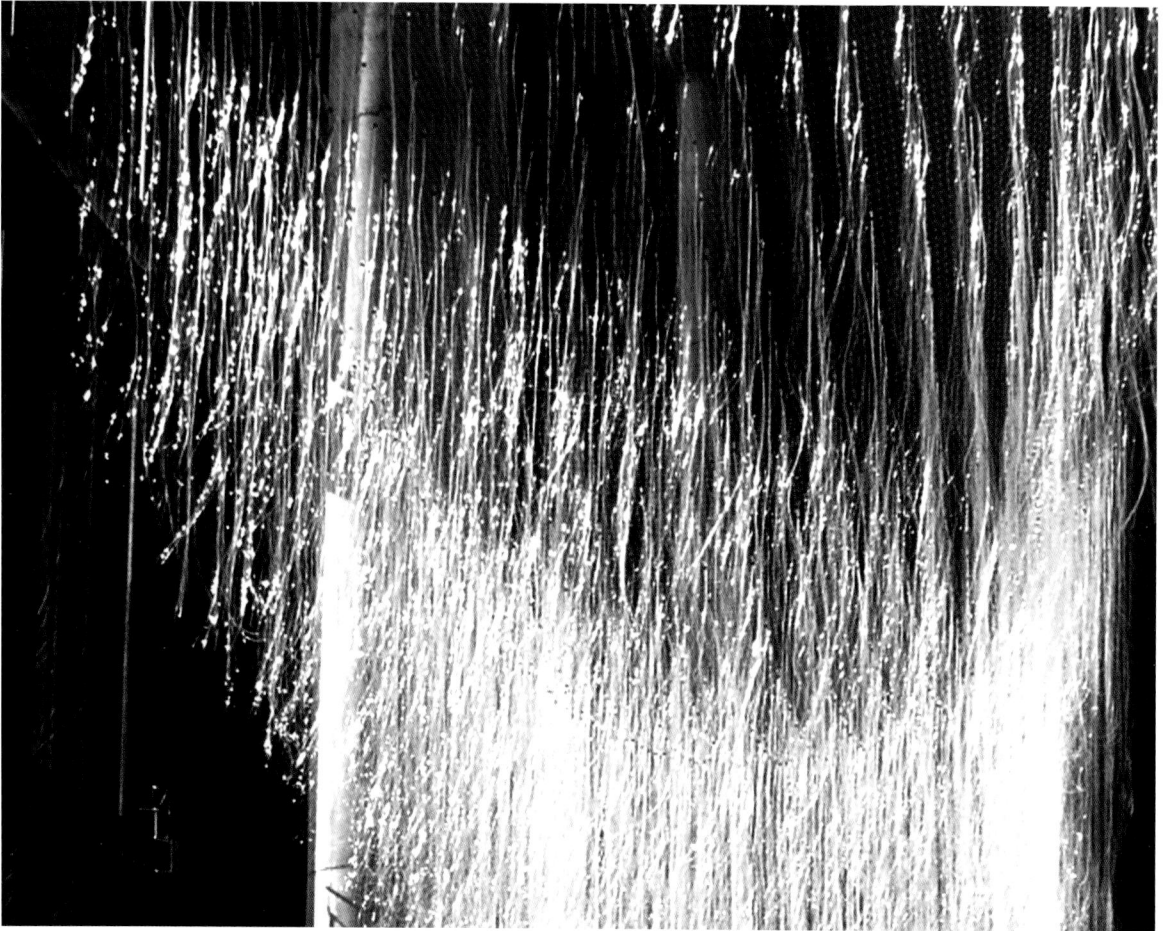

10.1: Man-O-War detail.

Matter and sense
Jason Payne and Heather Roberge
(Gnuform)

'Matter' is the new 'space'.
– Sanford Kwinter, 2005

What matters

Manuel De Landa has suggested that built form exists as the highest level of geological articulation of the earth's crust. Assuming this to be the case, the continually shifting methodological terrains of architectural practice are enmeshed within the much slower but no less inexorable flows of soil, rocks, water, biomass, and all of the various other 'natural' elements. This suggests that these elements in their most primordial states may not be so foreign to architecture as is typically assumed. This is to say that *matter as it is understood within the disciplines of biology and the natural sciences is relevant for architecture as well.*

Historically, the role of matter in architecture has been secondary to that of organization. This is true at both the methodological and the morphological levels. Matter, more conventionally termed 'material' or 'building material', typically did not enter into the design process until an organization had been generated to which it could then respond. An organization existed on the higher plane of ideas, disengaged from the base condition of matter. This relationship between matter and the organizations it expresses holds true for most approaches to the generation of architectural form, including various modes of classical, modernist, and postmodern composition.

Recently we have begun to see a shift away from this model, toward one in which matter is liberated. This new model results from the co-mingling of three separate areas of thought. The

10.2: Detail of Man-O-War's
weighted points and mono-
filament.

first comes from the realm of the natural sciences, in
which complexity is increasingly understood as the
engine of creation. Here, matter and the flows of energy
it regulates is the foundation for larger organizations
that, prior to their emergence in actual time and space,
did not exist in some prior space of ideation. The second
comes from the realm of philosophy, as an appreciation for the post-structuralist challenge to signification
increasingly dismantles architecture's reliance upon
signs and references. The third comes from the realm of
technology, in which the expanding role of computation
in all phases of design inevitably changes the way we
conceive and construct architecture. Advanced modeling and visualization applications allow for increasingly
realistic simulation and exploration of the dynamics of
material behavior. It is now possible to create entirely
new materialities no longer confined by the limited set
of behavioral characteristics embodied in traditional
building materials. The pace quickens as new developments in fabrication feed back into software design in
an accelerating process of evolution. Matter becomes
increasingly *informed*.

This new model posits matter as organizer: matter
first, organization second. Interestingly, it is within
the discipline of architecture that this model has taken
shape. Perhaps this is due to our discipline's capacity
for the incorporation and re-organization of the external, or perhaps we are simply in the right place at the
right time. Whatever the case, a methodological model
in which material dynamics generates architectural
form promises an age of proliferation and abundance,
for the organizations of matter never cease to unfold.

Matter senses

This model for architectural composition requires a different mindset of the designer. Instead of understanding the basic ingredients of architectural composition
– points, lines, and planes – as empty vessels for extrinsic values, affiliations, and meanings, this material
is conceptually reframed as *intrinsically motivated* and
full. Points, lines, and planes come laden with distinct
qualities in measurable quantities such as density, pull,
drag, tension, compression, acceleration, and poros-
ity. These qualities and quantities, or *properties*, allow
geometry to become behavioral and active rather than
representational and passive. In this alternative practice
the designer no longer develops geometry for what it
draws but for what it does.

This kind of geometry is intimately tied to the material it forms.[1] Vector geometry is a well-known example.
Vector and other similar geometries are designed to car-
ry certain techniques within them. They describe flows,
effects, and atmospheres that are close to their own con-
stitution. These geometries are actually like what they
describe, and because of this they move beyond passive
description toward a condition that is partially real.
Further, they are literally tied to the body they describe
in both space and time, moving as it moves. These more
dynamic, material geometries allow us to work in the
elusive zone between diagram and building. As a result,
the methodological gulf between where a diagram ends
and a building begins is narrowed.

This geometry is only useful for the description, formation, and manipulation of matter that senses. Indeed,
sensate matter inevitably requires such geometry, unlike

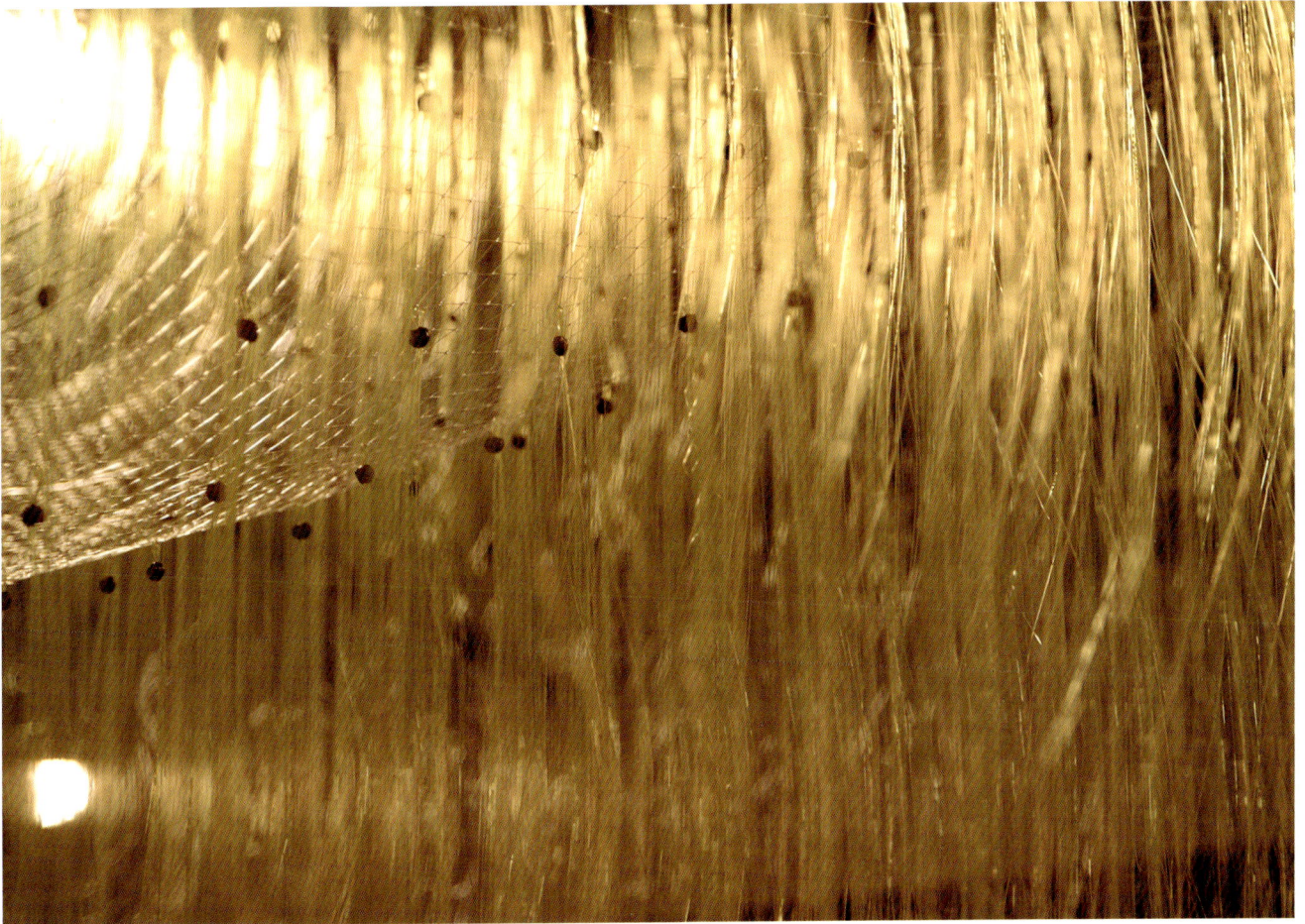

Sensing matter

We present the end-game: the sensing of matter. The sensations created by this work cannot be adequately conveyed through the format of a written essay. Therefore we invite you to examine the accompanying images and their associated captions. They describe some of the operative properties in recent Gnuform projects in direct terms so that you may get a sense of how they feel.

Project: MAN-O-WAR

Man-O-War (2004): Tactility Named for the sea creature it resembles, the Man-O-War is a gallery installation meant to produce a thickened atmosphere of matter and light. Designed for a show of architectural design and research involving hirsute (hairy) morphology, the piece hovers midway between floor and ceiling like a heavy storm front. Its global shape emerges from the accumulated material dynamics of 15,300 green, yellow, and blue monofilament lines of various weights, lengths, and curl parameters suspended from 1,352 weighted points. Construction of the Man-O-War follows from a research article we wrote entitled 'On The Uses and Advantages of Hirsutery for

more conventional architectural material formations
mentioned above that require types of geometry more
suited to pictorial representation. These geometries
have come to be known by the general term 'indexical'
in contemporary architectural discourse and practice.
Masses of sensate matter respond to one another through
mechanisms embedded within their constituent properties. Designers working with this material access these
mechanisms through the sensitive, indexical geometries
designed for their description and manipulation.
Again, imagine the vector geometries commonly used
to describe weather systems. While far simpler than
the material system itself, vector notation does contain the rudimentary controls, or 'senses', required to
manipulate properties. Direction, magnitude, speed,
acceleration, and time are all modeled into the geometry
at both the local and global scales. This makes possible
the manipulation and prediction of the material system
through simulation.

Sensing and indexing

Theorist and designer Robert Somol has argued that
practices using these kinds of geometries are actually
only pursuing a different kind of representation and are
not nearly as projective as the arguments above would
suggest. This argument resides within his larger critique
of indexical practice,[2] a critique that bears addressing in
this context. Somol observes that as these geometries index some underlying condition, they simply represent
that condition despite their non-pictorial approach.
For example, while a vector map of a weather system
may describe the behavior of the clouds rather than their

shape, it still involves description. As such, the shift to
the representation of behavior evidenced in indexical
practice is not, in his view, a move away from a representational project.

He characterizes these geometries and their methodological deployment as 'hot' and 'difficult', adjectives
meant to convey a kind of hyper-articulation that, because
it cannot escape being representational, is needlessly
overworked.[3] Also implied is a kind of pointlessness akin
to navel-gazing: why, after all, would one pursue relatively difficult, often obscure methods for the production
of form and argue for their generative potential when in
fact they are simply a different sort of representational
practice? Are they really generative at all?

To answer this question we must first dispel an assumption and then distinguish between two approaches
to indexing in contemporary practice, for, as it turns
out, Somol's argument illustrates a divide between two
kinds of indexical practice and is thus an important ba-
rometer for their distinction. But first the assumption:
geometry should be non-representational to be properly
generative.[4] This is not true, as no geometry could at-
tain such a rarified status. Even intensively behavioral
geometrical systems used in artificial life in some sense
'represent' the rules driving their disposition in space
and time. A more nuanced view of representation accepts its inevitability while promoting a tendency away
from its more static, conventional manifestations (e.g.
pictorial) toward more invigorated, sensate models. This
assumption is in fact a straw man, not set up by Somol
but resulting from the problematic conceptual ether
surrounding indexical practice itself. Constant repetition

Architecture', involving the materialization of linework in architectural representation.

Moving within the Man-O-War produces a gentle tickling sensation all over your body, especially on exposed skin. This sensation is most intense in the 'curly zone', an approximately six-inch band of material at the bottom of the overall mass. Within this region the monofilament strands curl the most and cling to each other, creating a more dense layer. The curly zone moves up and down your body as you move because it has a convex section. At the same time the motion of the strands around your face creates differentially shifting optical effects: quick moves close up, with slower undulations further away.

Man-O-War: Opticality From afar the Man-O-War often appears to congeal into a gently swaying, gel-like mass. It stirs at the slightest disturbance in the surrounding air. Usually its glowing greens and yellows predominate, though in some direct sunlighted conditions it reflects a bright golden-white color. In dim indirect light it can nearly disappear. The proportion of green, yellow, and blue monofilament shifts across its body to create a great variety of colors that change continually with movement.

of the term 'generative' in concert with geometries and projects more concerned with process than product has created this false premise – easy fodder for a critic with an alternative agenda.

This then leads to the distinction between two types of indexical practice: those whose interest lies in the process as an end unto itself and those whose interest in process is as a means to an end. The first type Somol effectively dismantles. Practices of this kind are characterized by a heavy emphasis on 'hot' process in both argument and methodology, the latter usually being more ingenious than the former. These are highly technical practices and their number has multiplied in recent years as younger, digitally expert designers engage this material. While much can be said in favor of the proliferation of the expert techniques this group generates, their seeming lack of awareness of or interest in higher-level control over the end product threatens their long-term survival. Further, their general myopia alienates various larger contexts and discourses they might otherwise engage (from the polemical to the technical) and exposes them to the poaching of their 'trade secrets' by practitioners in the second camp.

The second tendency is characterized by a more sparing and directed use of indexing in which the geometries and techniques are always immersed in a larger agenda. Such practices combine bottom-up generative methods with top-down awareness to carefully modulate the degree of unpredictability and control at play at any given time during the design process. This kind of directorial insight demands wide-ranging knowledge of a variety of compositional approaches and leads to more heterogeneous mixtures of systems.

In fact, perhaps the easiest way to distinguish between the first and second tendency (assuming the two practices being compared are equally facile in the modulation of matter and geometry) is to look for the number of systems at play in a given design problem. Practitioners in the first group usually work with a single, dominant geometrical system and attempt to draw the inevitable host of other systems involved in the project into alignment with the 'mother system'. In the best cases invention occurs through the rethinking of conventions that this way of working demands. Less positive results occur when the inherently reductive nature of the approach produces ill-formed parts and features or when, in the worst case, elements are ignored altogether and removed from the project. In contrast, designers working within the second tendency generally deploy several systems at once. Coherence and cohesion are understood to rely more upon multiple, interwoven economies than on the differentiated modulation of a singular geometry. Sometimes the number and variety of agencies involved creates difficulty. Such conditions

Man-O-War: Structure and form The Man-O-War takes its shape largely from its upper catenary surface formed of monofilament netting and a grid of lead weights. The curvature of this surface can be adjusted to create any number of natural forms. Thus, this surface and its manipulation is no different from classic catenary structural models (though its grid of weights is much more dense than usual). From this surface down, however, the Man-O-War swerves from the norm through the increasing internal dynamics of the free-hanging monofilament strands. Their light weight, natural curl, and tendency to cling to one another frees the lower region from gravity and, consequently, the logic, mechanics, and history of catenary modeling.

Man-O-War: Temporality and motion The monofilament lines are not bottom-weighted, allowing their curl and cling to reshape the lower region of the overall mass. The shape of this zone changes over time as these two properties respond to temperature, humidity, and surrounding air movement.

RIGHT, 10.6: Front elevation
of bar. BELOW, 10.7: Plan
of reception bar at (from top
to bottom) +48", +36", and
+24". OPPOSITE, 10.8: View
of entire bar.

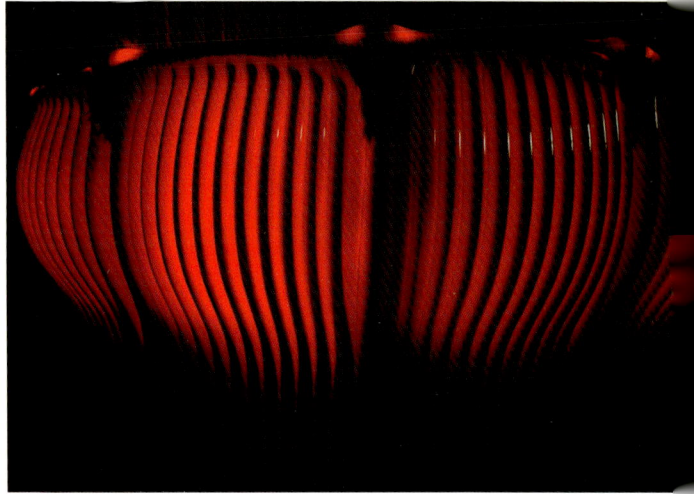

are not only understood as inevitable but in fact are
sought out for their potential productivity. However,
their successful exploitation demands of the designer a
certain amount of agility and courage: discontinuities
of surface, orthogonal interruptions of curves, conventional pressures on the exotic, and, most importantly,
material restrictions on geometry must be handled with
discipline and grace. It is the willingness to accept these
difficult realities that separates the latter group from
the former and makes their work, refined as it is, more
rough than smooth.

Ultimately indexing is a subset of sensing, a way
to describe matter as sensate – and one particularly
well-suited to architectural notation. It will likely
soon become clear that the present rise in criticism of
indexical practice targets only one form of indexicality:
that which delights in the overt expression of the index
for its own sake. Whether the force of the critique slows
the development of this kind of work or not is of no
import here, for the tendency is not really involved in an
increasingly matter-oriented field anyway. That mode of
practice is immaterial.

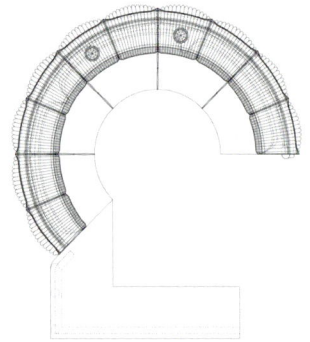

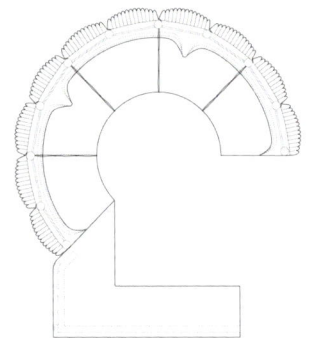

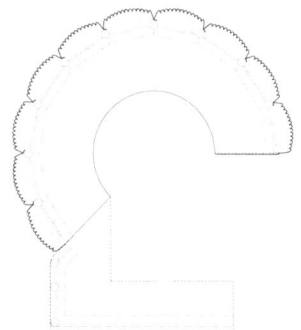

Project: NO GOOD TELEVISION RECEPTION BAR AND FILM SET

No Good Television™ reception bar and film set Designed as part of a larger project for the new No Good Television™ Headquarters in Beverly Hills, the private bar is the heart of a heavy, sensual atmosphere created throughout the building using rich color and light. Materials, effects, and techniques used more sparingly in other areas of the project come together in the bar to form an enriched core. The bar is used as a reception area for guests, a set for celebrity interviews, and as a standard bar for frequent company parties. It works well because everyone is drawn to it: atmosphere as infrastructure. In fact, the strikingly voluptuous bar exudes the risqué sensuality that

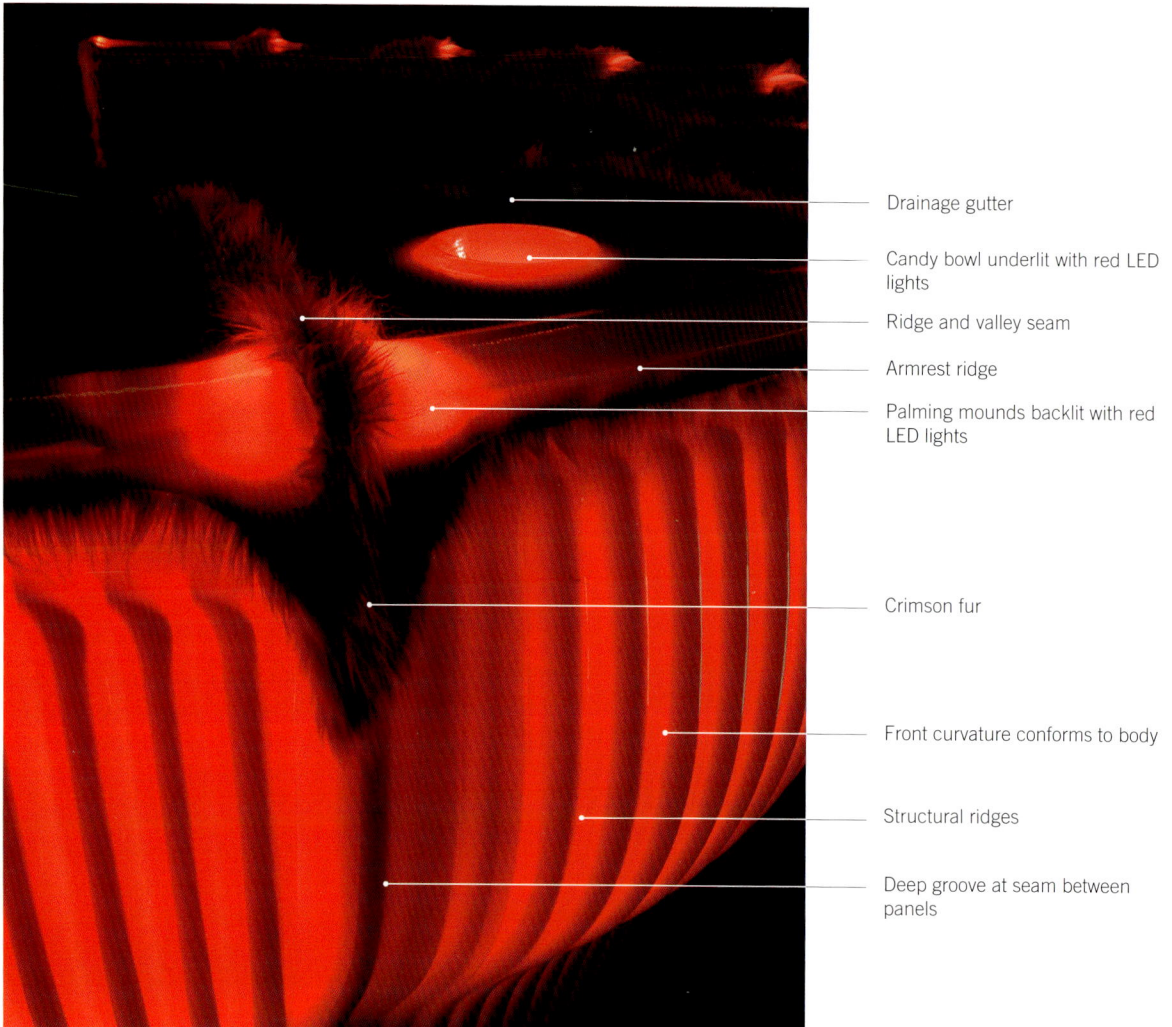

- Drainage gutter
- Candy bowl underlit with red LED lights
- Ridge and valley seam
- Armrest ridge
- Palming mounds backlit with red LED lights
- Crimson fur
- Front curvature conforms to body
- Structural ridges
- Deep groove at seam between panels

forms the core image of NGTV™, with the result that the channel has since relocated most of its interviews from the green room to this space.

Our earlier work involving hirsute (hairy) morphology led to, among other things, an interest in the construction of fuzzy edges between and within individual panels and between the bar and the curtains beyond. Hazy edges are produced within a panel when light passes through acutely curved surfaces. Because of intense curvatures, the light falls off before it illuminates the actual edge of the material. This falloff is shaped by the surfaces in such a way that the light appears more coherent than ambient illumination yet less defined than the plastic edges themselves.

Topographical stimulation Our growing commitment to an ever more direct appeal to the senses combined with NGTV's erotic content provides us the opportunity to explore more literal exchanges of form and feel. While the smaller ridges in each front panel provide structural integrity, their ribbed repetition across a larger bulge engages the torso of the bar patron. The user's intimacy with the form increases with the passing of time and consumption of drink. Palming mounds surrounded by soft, red fur at each panel's intersection facilitate the gentle pulling of the body into the bar and stir the sensitive nerve endings of the hands and fingers. Of course, each of these features is also visually provocative, creating a heady mixture of sensory stimulation.

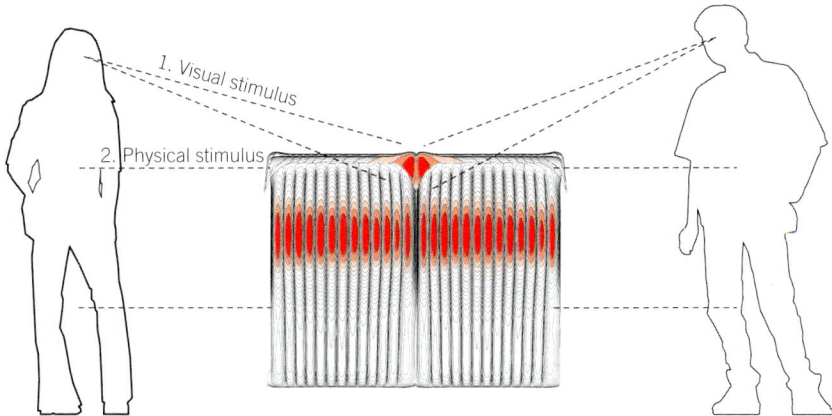

1. Visual stimulus

2. Physical stimulus

LEFT, 10.9: Topographical stimulation. BELOW, 10.10: Typical fur tufting details. OPPOSITE, 10.11: Top and front panel features.

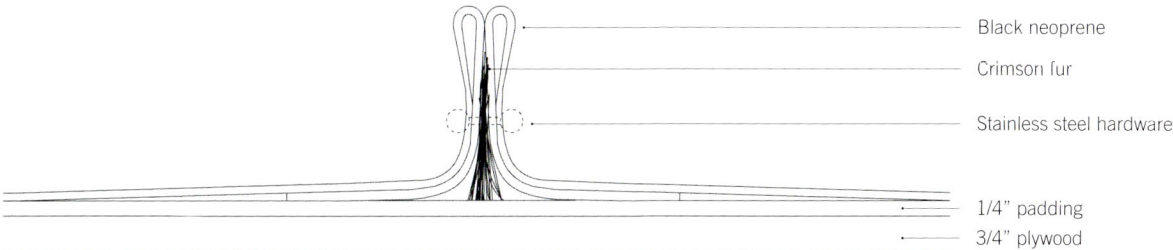

Black neoprene

Crimson fur

Stainless steel hardware

1/4" padding

3/4" plywood

No Bloom

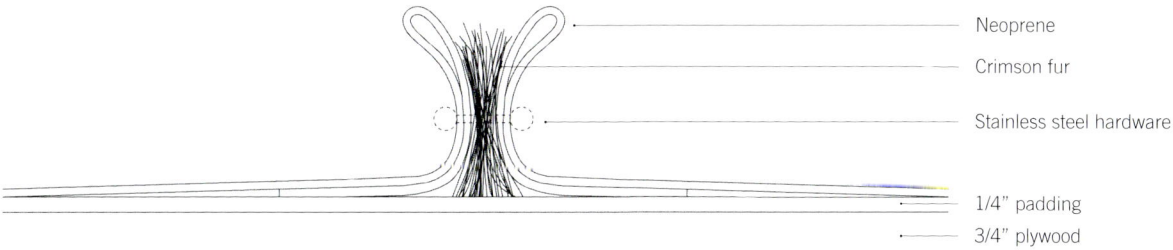

Neoprene

Crimson fur

Stainless steel hardware

1/4" padding

3/4" plywood

Half Bloom

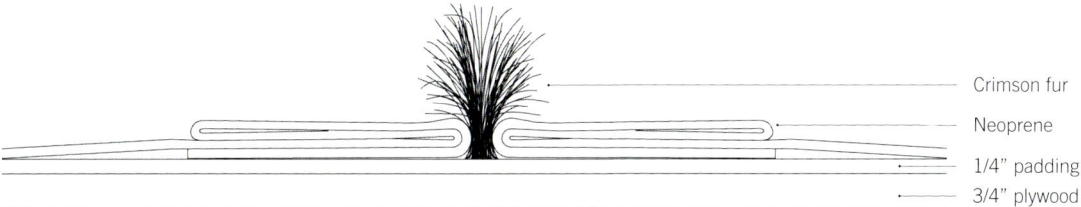

Crimson fur

Neoprene

1/4" padding

3/4" plywood

Full Bloom

RIGHT, 10.12: Detail photograph of front panel. BELOW, 10.13: Detail section through top and front panel seam.

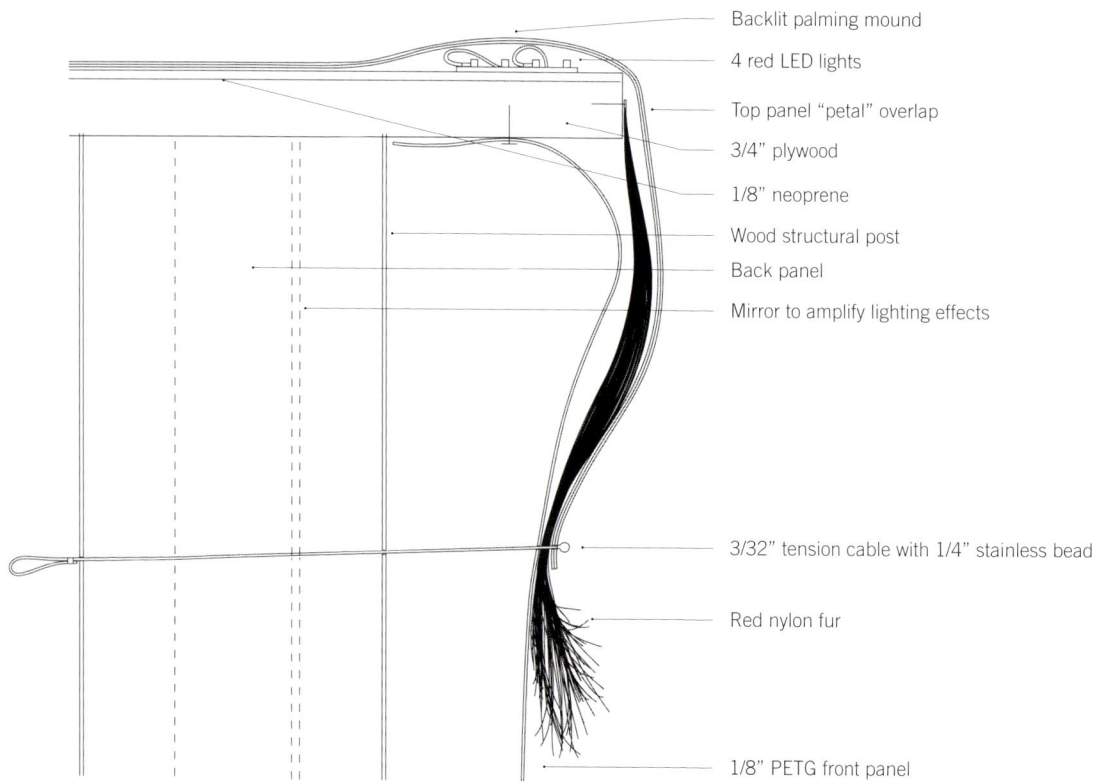

Backlit palming mound

4 red LED lights

Top panel "petal" overlap

3/4" plywood

1/8" neoprene

Wood structural post

Back panel

Mirror to amplify lighting effects

3/32" tension cable with 1/4" stainless bead

Red nylon fur

1/8" PETG front panel

10.14: Detail photograph of top
and front panel seam.

*We shall not cease from exploring. And at the
end of exploration we will return to where we
started and know the place for the first time.*
– T.S. Elliot.

To assume innovation exists only through developing
the new is almost as naive as questioning the validity
of such innovation when it begins with appropriating
and advancing the work of our predecessors. As architects, designers and writers, I can only imagine that
one would strive to engage the nuances of the present
that make our contributions unique while simultaneously projecting through our imagination the possible
futures of tomorrow. Anything less wouldn't be so much
irresponsible as it would be just a missed opportunity.

POSTSCRIPT

This pipe is not a pipe dream

Lars Lerup

Architects notorious for their straying off the field (Gehry in paintings, Eisenman in deep structure, the blobbers in biology and generative mathematics) have recently stumbled back into Umberto Eco's semiotic cave only to find a roaring fire.

The prospects are tantalizing: imagine an architecture where the bricks and mortar have been replaced by the very heat that helped them both to petrify. Ephemeralization has been on my radar since Karl Popper wrote 'Of Clouds and Clocks' published in 1972. But the leap across the chasm between the built and the living (in this case the burning fire) appears to be a more radical departure from the ancient stability.

I suggested in my book *Building the Unfinished: Architecture and Human Action* (1977) that architects have available a menu of walls ranging from the behavioral to the built, using the Japanese Hand Wall as an example of the former. Here a Japanese person can cross a space unnoticed by holding up a hand shielding the eyes. But again this 'wall' remains within the built field, since the hand serves as the token. The fire emanating comforting heat and centering behavior is a different matter. Here we may have to take another tack.

When Sean Lally reminded me of Yves Klein's idea for a house sporting a blast of hot air as its roof, blown from what looks a bit like Magritte's pipe, it struck me – that it was. (This was made more clear in the confusion resulting from a recent visit to Gehry's Guggenheim Museum Bilbao where at first the building shone like a lamp, but somehow lost its glow once I was inside, when I encountered for the first time the original drawings of Klein's air-architecture. Was Klein's conceptual art keeping Gerhy's cave inflated?) With this mind-bender I turn back to the pipe, because there is a cautionary tale in Magritte's painting that although a painted pipe is not a-smoking (gun) it is in our days of intense streams of images close enough, in turn making Klein's airflow house a house – the truth here is that all the money has been put into the heating system, turning the architect into a heating–cooling engineer. So in the end, I suggest that it is not wise to blow out the briar with the smoke.

Not entirely for contrarian reasons, I will suggest that my pipe dreams are of some relevance in the current climate of ephemeralization and Kleinian replacement therapies. It is not that I don't like the soft, or the warm for that matter, and that the architects in pursuit of the fire will eventually replace the smoker, but I don't think that we have quite yet exhausted the enigmatic firmness of the distinctly visible that in its otherness is also olfactory and haptic – aside from keeping out the chill. One of my favorite poets, Joseph Brodsky, puts my concern like this in 'Axiom' (1990):

> ... *space itself, alias the backdrop of life, rendered blind by a surfeit of plots, heads towards pure time, where no one applauds.*

And let's admit it, the roaring fire is much closer to time and stim (as in stimulation, always bound intimately to duration) than the stability and ever-lasting quality of the cave – the mere dross in the deer-in-the-headlight pursuit of our everyday plots. I cannot help but have a suspicion that architects in pursuit of the fire are also in the pursuit of fame – as a profession, we have not only been pursuing the 'backdrop of life' but have simultaneously become the backdrop in an ever-changing building industry that still produces 8 percent of the GNP. Don't get me wrong, I understand the sentiment, and I am all in favor of the pursuit. Having spent, in my youth, many winter days ice-fishing with a roaring fire next to me ready to cook the 'pin-bread' and the trout, while the sun rolls on the horizon, I love the heat too, but I can't help that I am not willing to abandon the hunt for the most ephemeral surface between the hot and cold that you feel on your face and neck – respectively and simultaneously – that most fickle of walls waving like a sloppy organ in the winter light.

In the end we cannot abandoned the pipe for the smoke – the alchemist's errand is also the fool's – the road to a *perpetuum mobile* is forever broken. Klein's pipe-cum-hairdryer will not blow without its furnace, without its oil. In building as in life, everything is circular.

Lars Lerup is the Dean and William Ward Watkin Professor at the Rice School of Architecture in Houston, Texas.

I, the scent cube and CSI; or, the controlled soft interior

Bart Lootsma

Beginning a new job and waiting for my own spaces to be renovated, I was offered by my university a temporary room. Filled with bookshelves containing old books and students' theses, it smelled terribly. Some good friends pitied me – and rightly so – and after a few days they brought me a Scent Cube. That is, a handsomely designed black box, which, after one connects it to electricity, produces wonderful scents, depending on the kind of wax one fills it with. The amount of scent the cube produces is adjustable with two sliders, so that one can just cover up other smells while hardly noticing the new one. Now I could work without being distracted. With the help of loudspeakers on my laptop I could listen to music, and occasionally even immerse into a movie – completely forgetting about my surroundings, in the evening forming my own space in the dark. After that, I left for the small guestroom the university had offered me as well for the time being, and watched all the different versions of CSI and other forensics series that dominate television these days on the small TV next to my bed. After a while I even got used to the stiff acting, nerdiness, showing-off and almost complete lack of humor and emotions, realizing that these series are about something else, something new that is almost there. They breathe the desire and prepare us for a culture to come.

Reading *Softspace*, I was reminded of this episode in my life. Because before anything else, the phenomena described in this book are already omnipresent and completely normal – so normal that we hardly notice them any longer. It is the secret longing of architecture to produce an environment that speaks to all senses; I wrote once, 'secret because it is pursued only surreptitiously, for commercial purposes like shopping malls and theme parks, or for underground happenings like techno-parties'.[1] These are what Lars Lerup once called 'stims', places that largely depend on infrastructure like air conditioning, refrigerators and media to attract crowds of people.[2]

As a restrained position, we find the emphasis on producing spaces rather than the enveloping walls already with Adolf Loos in his essay 'Das Prinzip der Bekleidung', in which he takes us back to the textile origins of architecture – and thereby to Gottfried Semper who, just like Reyner Banham more than a century later, lets architecture originate from the campfire.[3] And at least over the last century, and probably much longer than that, it has also been the outspoken desire of ambitious architects to create such a sensuous architecture. Think of the Expressionists with their extensive use of colored glass, allowing the light of sun, moon and stars to penetrate deep into the interior of the architecture. In some drawings of the Gläserne Kette, we can see people dancing around a fire in the middle of these strange cathedrals. Think of Theo van Doesburg's 'Aubette', where colored walls, film production and dance music created a new, artificial atmosphere in which no visitor could remain unmoved. And think of the experiments by such diverse talents as Konstantin Melnikov or Samuel 'Roxy' Rothafel of Radio City Music Hall in New York, who wanted to produce an accelerated experience of day and night in their buildings by blowing additional ozone into the air. It is architecture of the kind realized by Coop Himmel(b)lau in the 1960s, with the 'Flammenflügel', 'Hard Space' and 'Soft Space', as well as a series of helmets, glasses, boxes and inflatable constructions. For Coop Himmelb(l)au, it was not just the campfire but the whole architecture that must burn. The 1960s was also the period of Haus Rucker Co.'s experiments with similar multimedia environments, experiments that culminated in Hans Hollein's manifesto 'Everything is Architecture' and his (provisional) all-surpassing architecture pill.[4]

It is, however, not necessarily this kind of hallucinatory excess that the authors of *Softspace* are looking for. They seem convinced that today an architecture that addresses all senses can be achieved with, among other things, the help of the computer. But they do not, as far as I am concerned, refer to the only two buildings that successfully created completely immersive environments with the help of computers: the 'Poème Électronique' by Le Corbusier, Iannis Xenakis and Edgard Varese on the 1958 Brussels Expo (characterized by Le Corbusier as 'Entirely an interior job') and the H20 Pavilion by NOX and Kas Oosterhuis in

the Netherlands from 1997. They seem to avoid any of these ambitious theme park attractions. Instead, in their preface, Sean Lally and Jessica Young ask whether emotions, sensations, temperature, humidity and scent, for example, can be quantified, simulated and deployed as definitively as structural forces and descriptive architectural geometries.[5] So, the interest in 'softspace' seems to be an interest in controlling and disciplining all these factors.

Again, this fits in a long tradition that started with Modern architecture. The Expressionists were just as interested as Le Corbusier in scientific experiments with the components, for example. Already in the first issue of *Esprit Nouveau*, Le Corbusier and Ozenfant confess they believe in scientific research. 'We are aesthetes who believe art has laws, just as psychology and physics ... We want to apply the same methods to aesthetics that are used for experimental psychology.'[6] In the same issue, Victor Basch, the founder of experimental aesthetics, explained what he understood as 'New Aesthetics and the Science of Art'. He distinguished three different factors in the appreciation of a work of art: direct factors, formal factors and associative factors. According to Basch, traditional aesthetics had neglected the direct factors whereas these were very well suited to experimental study because of their psychophysical influences. The aesthetic experience should therefore be separated into its elementary parts; color, form, rhythm and tone should each be analyzed individually.[7] Naturally, he was also persuaded of the converse, that works of art could be created through the use of 'scientific' data.

The theories of Victor Basch exerted a great influence on Le Corbusier and Ozenfant. Under the title 'Discipline of the Arts and Sight', the latter wrote: 'We do not know exactly how the eye works (but what do we know exactly?). Yet it is evident, that independent of each comprehensible treatment or evaluation, forms and colors are intense enough to influence our primary feelings.' Using a series of examples, he goes on to show how color produces reactions in humans and animals that are intense enough to influence behavior, as for example in the bullfight. Or again: 'In the Lumière factories in Lyon, the laboratories where photographic plates were produced were lit ruby red: the result was that the male workers were constantly in a state of arousal, and became importunate. As for the female workers, they began having more children, as many as possible. Horrible! A calming green replaced the red and suddenly their birthing rate dropped to around average.'[8] According to Ozenfant, people were machines requiring care and 'special instructions for use'.[9]

Still, remarkably, *Softspace* does not contain any empirical research or even examples of it, or quotes similar to those Ozenfant used. It contains work of different artists and architects; art and architecture history; and particularly theoretical reflections, putting both the work of the artists and architects and that of the architectural theoreticians in a larger scientific, methodological and philosophical context – but not to use it literally. The goal of the book seems rather to produce a cosmological context that would justify or legitimate that the way of dealing with space and architecture in the way the authors propose is culturally correct and important. It is a rhetoric that has become increasingly dominant in architectural theory over the last decades. Philosophy and science seem to have replaced religion in this constellation, but their legitimizing role is exactly the same. The language used may not be Latin, but therefore often mimics the language used in scientific articles.

It is this procedure that seems essential in (re)-appropriating a field that already exists in many ways on a more (or even less) banal level to the level of high art or architecture with a big A. This elitist level is small and therefore the amount of examples is rather small in relation to the interpretative text. Architecture here seems no longer the production of buildings or spaces or phenomena themselves, but to be about the conscious reflection on and interpretation of some of them. Architectural theory becomes like forensics: the traces are minimal, but if we take the cotton tab to a laboratory and put it into one of those wonderfully mysterious machines, we may construct the Truth. And we can only construct the Truth if we know a multitude of the most unbelievable stories and miracles. Then we have authority. But whereas the truth in criminology is a more or less clear goal to achieve, what is the truth in architecture?

As Greg Lynn likes to demonstrate, Pete Townsend's guitar playing in the1970s anticipated synthesizer music. It prepared us, so to say, for a new culture. There is something similar with CSI that not coincidentally opens with 'Who are you?' by The Who. CSI prepares us for the next series of movies and television series in which actors have been replaced by virtual characters. The fantastic simulations of bullets, knives, poisons, insects, electricity and other stuff that does not belong there penetrating human bodies and showing from the inside how they come to an end can only work because we look at these bodies already as machines. The meanest torture is reduced to a malfunctioning and thus the culprit accepts his unmasking, resigned and without complaining.

In the future, CSI and the Controlled Soft Interior will merge into one thing: a kind of stim – but that really of the William Gibson kind, in *Mona Lisa Overdrive*, and virtual-reality soaps, in which we will completely immerse, play our role and forget about anything else. I am almost ready to resign. 'Who wants to be human anyway? Only machines do.'

Bart Lootsma is an architectural historian, critic and curator. He has published numerous articles on architecture, design and the visual arts, and was the curator of Archilab 2004 (The Naked City).

Notes

Introduction: Energies, Matter & the Gradients of Space, pages 1-7

1 Ole Bouman, 'Architecture, Liquid, Gas', *Architectural Design*, 75(1): 14–22.

2 Robin Evans, 'Translations from Drawing to Building', in *Translations from Drawing to Building and Other Essays* (London: MIT Press, 1997), 156.

3 Hugh Whitehead, 'Laws of Form', in *Architecture in the Digital Age, Design and Manufacturing*, ed. Branko Kolarevic (London: Spon Press, 2003).

Putting Out the Fire with Gasoline, pages 10-23

1 This would presumably amuse Banham, who remarked in the second edition that the book often fell through the categorical cracks of the discipline, finding its home in libraries next to technical manuals. He added a final sentence pleading that it no longer be housed there, but to little avail.

2 Reyner Banham, *Theory and Design in the First Machine Age* (London: The Architectural Press, 1960).

3 Reyner Banham, *The Architecture of the Well-Tempered Environment* (London: The Architectural Press, 1969), 14–16.

4 Foucault's explanation for the importance of a distant origin in the discourses of modernity is still useful in understanding such tales; Michel Foucault, *The Order of Things* (New York: Random House, 1970).

5 Banham (1969), 18.

6 Banham (1969), 19.

7 Banham (1969), 277–8.

8 Banham (1969), 227.

9 Erwin Schrödinger, *What is Life?* (Cambridge: Cambridge University Press, 1944).

10 Ilya Prigogine and Isabelle Stengers, *Order Out of Chaos* (New York: Bantam,1984),140.

11 Mae-Wan Ho, 'What is (Schrödinger's) Negentropy?', *Modern Trends in BioThermoKinetics* 3 (1994), 50–61.

12 Ho (1994), 60. If all this sounds a bit quaint, one should recall the interest in hypotheses mooted by 'new

materialists' such as Manuel De Landa or, in a rather different register, Jared Diamond's *Guns, Germs and Steel: The Fates of Human Societies*.

13 Again, this is of more than historical interest; it is echoed in the story of the emergence of cities that Manuel Delanda provided in *A Thousand Years of Non-Linear History* and which today is a touchstone within contemporary architectural discourses of complexity.

14 Banham (1969), 19–20.

15 Arendt's reading of the Greek polis and oikois would be useful in analyzing the implicit political spacing within Banham's text: Hanna Arendt, *The Human Condition* (Chicago: University of Chicago Press, 1998 [1958]), 28–78.

16 Banham (1969), 19.

17 The seeming similarity of Banham's material thermodynamics of wood's energy-to-artifact transformation to Deleuze and Guattari's discussion of material singularities and their varied assemblages to produce different actualizations as technologies deserves some examination, which I lack the space for here. See 'Treatise on Nomadology: A War Machine', in *A Thousand Plateaus* (Minneapolis: University of Minnesota Press, 1987).

18 Banham (1969), 20.

19 For an extended analysis of the historicity and nature of Banham's concept of 'machine age', refer to Panayotis Tournikiotis, *The Historiography of Modern Architecture* (Cambridge, MA: MIT Press, 1999), 154–62: PN.

20 Reyner Banham, *The Architecture of the Well-Tempered Environment*, 2nd edn. (London and Chicago: The Architectural Press and The University of Chicago, 1984), 287–8.

21 Banham does not seem to recall that this understanding of the post-war suburban housewife was, in part, produced through the same social and technical regimes that were responsible for these appliances.

22 Banham (1969), 100.

23 Indeed, in cities like Houston, air conditioning

allowed small populations to become vast interior sub-urban conglomerations in the way sewage systems had allowed cities like Paris to become nineteenth-century metropolises.

24 Banham (1969), 209–28.

25 Banham (1969), 228.

26 As Brett Steele has argued, in Lever House the technologies of cleaning are presented as brand for the company's cleaning products, a spectacle of taut soap-film-like glazing, which gleams transparently and is itself endlessly cleaned.

27 As quoted in Banham (1969), 249; originally in *World Architecture I* (London, 1964), 35.

28 In a strange way, the anxiety of building services' overwhelming structure may anticipate our current con-dition, when modern office towers and research build-ings use the same percentage of the total construction budget on various IT cablings as on foundations and structures. Even the all-important FAR can be made less efficient if it increases IT infrastructure permeability. An example occurred in Pelli Associates' Enron Tower in Houston, Texas, where a second IT riser punches through the middle of the leasable typical office floors of the entire tower simply because not all the neces-sary wire could fit into the already massive central core. Indeed, the entire building is fed with redundant IT, electrical and plumbing systems, and gated with nested levels of smart-card-regulated access and surveillance fields to resist any disruption to its operations. Though made out of mercury-like shimmering glass curtain wall, as if it were pure electricity, the Enron Tower complex is at once a fortress and an organism detached from its immediate locale and instead existing in the de-territorialized nomadism of global energy economies, offshore companies and non-existent entities. Architec-ture is not conserved, and nor is the civic social order that it requires via the structural solution maintained. In fact, Kahn's domestication here becomes a cynical desublimation of the sort that the megastructualists and Brutalism sought to resist.

29 Tournikiotis (1999), 165.

30 It is important to note that one can employ Ban-ham's theses to investigate why the post-modern criti-cisms of 'Beaubourg-Effect' seemed to utterly misap-prehend what is at stake in the work; they claim the civil society made possible by the 'structural solution' has entered maximum entropy but criticize the architecture as failing to provide a civic infrastructure, when in fact it is attempting to engage and project a social organiza-tion as detestable to the French cultural establishment as ducts seemed to be to Louis Kahn.

31 Hadas Steiner, 'The Forces of Matter', *Journal of Architecture*, 10(1): 101.

32 Indeed, as Kittler argues, the distinction between software and hardware is rather more complex than con-ventionally understood. Kittler, 'There is no software', *CTheory*, October 1995.

33 Georges Canguilhem, 'The Knowledge and the Living', in *A Vital Rationalist* (New York: Zone Books, 1994).

34 Steiner: 104–6. I have also discussed the Suitaloon in reference to televisual production of domesticity and subjects: Christopher Hight, 'Inertia and interiority: 24 as a case study of the televisual metropolis', *Journal of Architecture*, 9(3) (Aug 2004): 369–84.

35 Banham notes that even a masterpiece of environ-mental design, Wright's Robie House, has been so neglected in regard to this aspect of its architecture, that no historical document existed that described that es-sential aspect of the architecture, so he had to commis-sion one. Banham (1969), 11.

Potential Energies, pages 24-37

1 Greg Lynn, *Animate Form* (New York: Princeton Architectural Press, 1999), 10.

2 Michelle Addington, 'New Perspectives on CFD Simulation', in *Advanced Building Simulation*, eds Ali M. Malkawi and Godfried Augenbroe (London: Spon Press, 2003), 147.

3 NCSA <http://access.ncsa.uiuc.edu/Stories/super-twister/index.htm> 12 March, 2005.

Nested Capacities, Gradient Thresholds and Modulated Environments, pages 52-65
1 Reyner Banham, *The Architecture of the Well-Tempered Environment* (University of Chicago Press, 1973).
2 John Pile, *Open Office Planning* (London: The Architectural Press, 1978); see also Brandon Hookway, *Pandemonium: The Rise of Predatory Locales in the Postwar World* (New York: Princeton Architectural Press, 1999).
3 Werner Nachtigall, *Bionik – Grundlagen und Beispiele für Ingenieure und Naturwissenschaftler*, 2nd edn (Berlin: Springer, 2002).
4 Evolutionary biology can provide some useful analytical methods for this purpose. See Robert Cummings, 'Functional Analysis', *Journal of Philosophy*, 72 (1975): 741–65.

Dissipative Procedures, pages 68-85
1 Christian Norberg-Schulz, 'The Baroque Age', in *Baroque Architecture* (Milan: Electra Architecture, 1971), 10.
2 Among others, Francesco Dal Co, Kurt Forster and Antione Picon claimed that contemporary digital architecture is a praxis that refers to the Baroque. Kurt W. Forster, 'Architectural Choreography', in *Frank O. Gehry: The Complete Work* (New York: The Monacelli Press, 1988), 9–38; Francesco Dal Co, 'The World Turned Upside-down: The Tortoise Flies and the Hare Threatens the Lion', in *Frank O. Gehry: The Complete Work* (New York: The Monacelli Press, 1988): 39–61; Antoine Picon, 'Digital Architecture and the Poetics of Computation', in *Metamorph* (Fondazione La Biennale di Venezia, Italy, 2004), 58–69.
3 In one of his seminal essays, 'Die Technik und die Kehre', Martin Heidegger connects the poetic action to the application of instruments. The instrumentalization of tools, he argues, not as techniques of replication and simulation but as instruments of *techne*, would result in a poetic revelation that would go beyond the significance of the technological application into the essence of the artistic action. Martin Heidegger, 'The Question Concerning Technology', in *Martin Heidegger: Basic Writings*, ed. David Farrell Kerll (San Francisco: Harper Publications, 1993), 307–42 (first published in German in 1962).
4 In his two recently published books, Branko Kolarevic elaborated on this condition: Branko Kolarevic, ed. *Architecture in the Digital Age: Design and Manufacturing* (New York: Spon Press, 2003); Branko Kolarevic and Ali M. Malkawi, eds. *Performative Architecture: Beyond Instrumentality* (New York: Spon Press, 2005).
5 Gilles Deleuze, *Difference and Repetition* (New York: Columbia University Press, 1994), 182–4.
6 For reference see Manuel Delanda, 'Deleuze and the Use of the Genetic Algorithm in Architecture', in *AD: Contemporary Techniques in Architecture*, ed. Helen Castle (London: Wiley-Academy, 2002), 9–12.

Cybernetic Anything... pages 88-97
1 Reyner Banham, 'Arts in Society: Cap'n Kustow's Toolshed', *New Society*, 22 August 1968: 275–6.
2 Jasia Reichardt, 'Cybernetic Serendipity: The Computer and the Arts', special issue, *Studio International* 1968: 3.
3 Catalogue description of *Cybernetic Sculpture* in Reichardt, 'Cybernetic Serendipity', 41.
4 Norbert Wiener, *The Human Use of Human Beings: Cybernetics and Society* (London: Eyre and Spottiswoode, 1950), 12.
5 Edward Shanken, 'Art in the Information Age: Cybernetics, Software, Telematics, and the Conceptual Contributions of Art and Technology to Art History and Theory', Ph.D. Dissertation (Duke University, Durham, 2001), 126.
6 Banham, 'Arts in Society', 275.
7 For examples of Conceptual Art and dematerializa-

tion see Lucy Lippard, *Six Years: The Dematerialization of the Art Object from 1966–1972* (Berkeley: University of California, 1973).

8 Marshall McLuhan and Quentin Fiore, *The Medium is the Massage: An Inventory of Effects* (New York: Bantam Books, 1967), 84–5.

9 The 9 ft x 12 ft dimensions of the glass tank were ultimately reduced from 16 ft x 21 ft in order to match the capacity of an aircraft cargo hold in anticipation of the piece being shipped to Osaka. See exhibition catalogue: Maurice Tuchman, *Art and Technology: A Report on the Art and Technology Program of the Los Angeles County Museum of Art 1967–71* (New York: Viking, 1971), 282.

10 Marshall McLuhan, *Understanding Media: The Extensions of Man* (Corte Madera: Gingko Press, 2003), 383 (original edition New York: McGraw-Hill, 1964).

11 Comments by Lewis Ellmore, Director of Special Programs at Teledyne, in Tuchman, *Art and Technology*, 280.

12 Letter from Lewis Ellmore, Director of Special Programs at Teledyne, to Robert Rauschenberg, dated 20 December 1968. Rauschenberg file, LACMA Archives.

13 Ellmore, letter, 1968.

14 In contrast to the more high-resolution medium of film, McLuhan says, 'The TV image is *now* a mosaic mesh of light and dark spots which a movie shot never is ...'; McLuhan, *Understanding Media*, 418.

15 From original typescript of an interview between Maurice Tuchman, Robert Rauschenberg, and Gail Scott, LACMA Archives, 2 October 1970, pp. 11–12; published in Tuchman, *Art and Technology*, 287.

16 McLuhan (2003), 468.

Eco_logics, pages 114-125

1 Manuel De Landa, 'Deleuze, Diagrams, and the Genesis of Form', in 'Diagram Work', *ANY* 23 (1998): 34.

2 Jesse Reiser, in *Crib Sheets: Notes on the Contemporary Architectural Conversation* (New York: The Monacelli Press, 2005), 18.

3 See Reyner Banham, *The Architecture of the Well-Tempered Environment* (University of Chicago Press, 1984).

4 See Furján, 'Lounge Core', Los Angeles Forum for Architecture and Urban Design, *Forum Annual*, Fall 2004: 41–6.

5 Jeffrey Kipnis, 'The Cunning of Cosmetics', *El Croquis* 84 (1997): 26.

6 Marcelyn Gow, 'Soft- and Hard-Wires: EAT's Environmental Feedback', *SITE*, 12 (2004): 10–11. The pavilion, the first to use fog technology, was in part a water vapor cloud sculpture, designed by Fujiko Nakaya, that could generate as much as a six-foot-thick cloud that responded to the existing weather conditions. Diller and Scofidio's 2002 Blur Pavilion was, of course, a direct descendant of this pavilion. The Blur dispersed the 'matter' envelope into a suspension of particulates, an ambient field in the purest sense. 'Feeling' the space (the mist hitting the surface of the skin) and 'feeling one's way' collide in a haze of atmospherics and effect, the edifice of architecture dissolving into an aerosolized matter, and in turn into the flow of media technologies to which it is wired. In the Blur's dissolution, the dominance of visuality was resisted, submerged by the ambient effects of swirling mists or pulsing colors, a blinding, disorienting immersion in which the very status of the object dissolves, dematerializing into a shifting, indeterminate 'environment'.

7 Gow (2004).

8 Constant, 'New Babylon: Outline of a Culture', exhibition catalogue (1965).

9 Ben van Berkel and Caroline Bos, 'Effects: Radiant Synthetic', *Move*, 3 (UN Studio/Goose, 1992): 27. Recent architectural experiments with affective and ambient micro-environments are linked to the projects of artists like Olafur Eliasson or the responsive simulated environments of Char Davies. Eliasson's *Weather Project*, an immersive installation for Tate Modern that utilized fog as the medium for an intensive yellow light, generates not just aerial effects but a tactile-optical space that is pure sensation – J. M. W. Turner's 'mustards' mutated through twentieth-century technology. Turner's paintings, redolent with atmosphere, were attempts to materialize sensation.

10 See translator's introduction, Gilles Deleuze, *Francis Bacon: The Logic of Sensation*, trans. Daniel Smith (Minneapolis: University of Minnesota Press, YR), p. xxvi; quotation from Henri Maldiney, *Regard Parole Espace* (1973).

11 Kevin Kelly, *Out of Control: The New Biology of Machines, Social Systems and the Economic World* (New York: Basic Books, 1994), 22.

12 Kelly (1994), 21.

13 Michael Weinstock, 'Morphogenesis and the Mathematics of Emergence', in *Emergence: Morphogenetic Design Strategies* (Architectural Design Profile 169, 2004), 11.

14 See Mark C. Taylor, *The Moment of Complexity: Emerging Network Culture* (University of Chicago Press, 2001), 146.

15 'Noise' – unexpected or unpredictable events or choices – 'simultaneously disrupts order and creates the condition of the possibility of the emergence of a new and more complex order' (Taylor (2001), 135).

16 Kelly (1994), 76–7.

17 See Félix Guattari, *The Three Ecologies* (London/New Brunswick: Athlone Press, 2000).

18 James Corner, 'Landscape Urbanism', in *Landscape Urbanism: A Manual for the Machinic Landscape* (London: AA Publications, 2003), 63.

Matter and Senses, pages 126-139

1 In a recent lecture Sanford Kwinter describes this condition in more Deleuzian terms: 'The abstract diagram has a very high degree of correspondence with its form.' Kwinter, 'Beat Science', lecture delivered at the Department of Digital Media Arts at the University of California Los Angeles, 9 May 2005.

2 Lecture delivered at the Department of Architecture and Urban Design at the University of California Los Angeles, 20 October 2003.

3 Somol contrasts these with certain 'cooler, easier' practices not involved in indexing. While these latter tendencies lie outside the scope of this essay, they are important to mention as they strengthen his argument through contrast.

4 It is unclear whether Somol himself goes this far with his argument.

Postscript: I, the Scent Cube and CSI, pages 144-147

1 Bart Lootsma, 'Auf dem Weg zu einer neuen Tektonik'[En Route to a New Tectonics], *Daidalos* 68, June 1998.

2 Lars Lerup, 'Stim and Dross: Rethinking the Metropolis', in *After the City* (Cambridge, MA, and London: MIT Press, 2000).

3 Adolf Loos, 'Das Prinzip der Bekleidung', in *Ins Leere gesprochen, 1897–1900* (Unveränderter Neudruck der Erstausgabe, 1921; Vienna: Georg Prachner Verlag, 1981).

4 Hans Hollein, 'Alles ist Architektur', *Bau*, 1968: 1–2.

5 Sean Lally, Jessica Young, 'Preface', in *Softspace*.

6 Le Corbusier, Amédée Ozenfant, 'Domaine de l'Esprit Nouveau', *Esprit Nouveau 1* (Paris, 1920).

7 Victor Basch, 'l'Esthétique nouvelle et la science de l'Art, Lettre au directeur de l'Esprit Nouveau', *Esprit Nouveau 1* (Paris, 1920).

8 Amédée Ozenfant, *Foundations of Modern Art*, (London, 1931; London, 1952).

9 Ozenfant (1931/1952).

Image and Project Credits

Photo by John Gunn, Earth & Space Research. Melting ice field in the Chukchi Sea, NW of Alaska, summer 2002. Shot with a Canon S30 digital camera during the Western Arctic Shelf-Bason Interactions Study from aboard the USCG *Healy*, funded under a National Science Foundation grant (OPP-0125252) to Earth & Space Research.

Introduction: Energies, Matter & the Gradients of Space, pages 1-7
1.1 Image courtesy of the Yves Klein Archives, Paris.
1.2 Images courtesy of Mrs. Janet Evans.
1.3 From *Architecture in the Digital Age: Design and Manufacturing*, Branko Kolarevic, © 2003, Spon Press/Taylor and Francis. Reproduced by permission of Taylor & Francis Books UK.
1.4 From Greg Lynn, *Animate Form*, Princeton Architectural Press, 1999. Reprinted by permission of Princeton Architectural Press.
1.5 From *Architecture in the Digital Age: Design and Manufacturing*, Branko Kolarevic, © 2003, Spon Press/Taylor and Francis. Reproduced by permission of Taylor & Francis Books UK.
1.6 (top left) From *Performative Architecture: Beyond Instrumentality*, Branko Kolarevic and Ali Malakawi, © 2005, Spon Press/Taylor and Francis. Reproduced by permission of Taylor & Francis Books UK.

Putting Out the Fire with Gasoline, pages 10-23
2.1 Image courtesy of Nigel Dickinson, www.nigeldickinson.com
2.2 From Reyner Banham, *The Architecture of the Well-Tempered Environment*, 2nd edn., University of Chicago Press, 1984. All rights reserved. First edition published 1969.
2.3 Image courtesy of B. & C. Alexander/Arcticphoto.

Potential Energies, pages 24-37
3.4 Image reprinted by permission, Edward R. Tufte, *Visual Explanations* (Cheshire, Connecticut, Graphics Press LLC, 1997).
3.8 Image courtesy of the National Center for Super-computing Applications and the Board of Trustees of the University of Illinois.
Project Credits
> SIM Residence, 2004 (3.2, 3.3, 3.5, 3.6, 3.7): All images, models and photography by Sean Lally.
> 'Amplification' Installation, Gen(h)ome Exhibition, 2005-06 (3.1, 3.9-3.14): Simulations, site model and prototype by Sean Lally. Assisted by Chad Loucks, Andrew Corrigan, and Maria Gabriela Flores. Photography in 3.9 and 3.12 by Chad Loucks, ©2005. Photography in 3.10, far right, by Helene Furján.

The Phenomena of the Non-Visual, pages 38-51
4.1 Image courtesy of NASA.
4.3 Image courtesy of Gary Settles, Penn State University.
4.5 Image courtesy of Ken Nakayama.
4.8B Image courtesy of Flomerics Corporation.
4.9 Image courtesy of Nasser Albuhasan and Joaquin Goicoechea.

Nested Capacities, pages 52-65
All images and photos are the property of OCEAN NORTH.
Project Credits
> Jyväskylä Music and Art Center by OCEAN NORTH
Phase 01 - 1997: Kim Bauman Larsen, Johan Bettum, Markus Holmsten and Kivi Sotamaa with Lasse Wager, Vesa Oiva and Hein van Dam.
Phase 02 - 2004: Michael Hensel, Achim Menges and Kivi Sotamaa with Hani Fallaha, Shireen Han, Andrew Kudless, Neri Oxman, Nazaneen Roxanne Shafaie, Nikolaos Stathopoulos, Mark Tynan and Muchuan Xu.
Phase 03 - 2005-06: Michael Hensel and Achim Menges with Nikolaos Stathopoulos.

Dissipative Prcedures, pages 68-85

6.1 & 6.2 Courtesy FRAC Centre Collection.

Project Credits

> Ecoscape, 2002 / Location: Sierra Nevada Mountains, California (6.1-6.7): Design concept by Open Source Architecture / Aaron Sprecher, Chandler Ahrens and Eran Neuman; Computational algorithm by Aaron Sprecher, OSA; Ecological system by Chandler Ahrens, OSA; Laser cutting and vacuum forming model by Chandler Ahrens, OSA with UCLA Model Technology Laboratory; Text by Eran Neuman and Aaron Sprecher, OSA.

> IsoMorph, 2003 / Client: Israel Gas Company / Location: Israel (6.8-6.12): Design concept by Open Source Architecture / Aaron Sprecher, Chandler Ahrens and Eran Neuman; Computational algorithm by Aaron Sprecher, OSA; Structural engineer, M. March, Tel Aviv; New material consultant, Dr. Daniel Neumann, Tel Aviv; CNC milling model by Chandler Ahrens, OSA with UCLA Model Technology Laboratory; Text by Eran Neuman and Aaron Sprecher, OSA.

> Perpetuating Particles, 2004 / Location: Maine (6.13-6.17): Design concept by Open Source Architecture; Particle system and computational scripting by Aaron Sprecher, OSA; Stereolithographic model by Chandler Ahrens, OSA with UCLA Model Technology Laboratory; Text by Eran Neuman and Aaron Sprecher, OSA.

Cybernetic Anything... pages 88-97

7.1 Courtesy Wen-Ying Tsai / Tsai Studio.

7.2 Art © Robert Rauschenberg / Licensed by VAGA, New York, NY. Image courtesy of Moderna Museet, Stockholm.

The Archoid Chimera, pages 98-111

All images and photos are the property of Tobi Schneidler / maoworks.

Project Credits

> Responsive Fields, 2004 / Client: ZKM Karlsruhe / Location: Karlsruhe, Germany / Team: Tobi Schneidler, Pablo Miranda, Loove Broms and Smart Studio.

> Remote Home, 2005 / Client: Victoria and Albert Museum / Location: London / Team: Tobi Schneidler, Loove Broms and Milo Lavén.

> Vestigii Ticker Chair, 2005 / Client: Vestigii Fashion / Location: Berlin / Team: Tobi Schneidler, Loove Broms and Milo Lavén.

Eco_logics, pages 114-125

9.1 Photograph by Helene Furján.

9.2 Art © EAT / Courtesy of: Research Library, The Getty Research Institute, Los Angeles, California. Image courtesy of Moderna Museet, Stockholm.

9.3 Images courtesy of Francois Roche / R&Sie.

9.4 Images courtesy of Winka Dubbeldam / Architectonics, New York.

9.5 Images courtesy of Future Cities Lab: Jason Johnson and Nataly Gattegno.

9.6 Photograph by Helene Furján.

Matter and Sense, pages 126-139

All images by Gnuform except as noted.

10.3 Image by Benny Chan.

10.6 Image by Deborah Bird.

10.8 Image by Deborah Bird.

10.14 Image by Deborah Bird.

Project Credits:

> Man-O-War (10.1-10.5):
Principals: Jason Payne, Heather Roberge
Assistants: Sven Neumann, Katie Fallat with UCLA students.

> NGTV (10.6-10.14)
Principals: Jason Payne, Heather Roberge
Assistants: Timothy Gorter, Adam Fure, Katie Fallat, Kelly Bair.

About the Contributors...

Michelle Addington

Michelle Addington, whose teaching and research explore the re-conceptualization of the human thermal environment, is trained both as an architect and as an engineer. Originally educated as a nuclear and mechanical engineer, she began her career with NASA, where she was a structural analyst designing components for satellites and rockets, and she later worked in the chemical industry for many years as a thermal process designer, power plant engineer, and, eventually, a manufacturing manager.

After a decade in industry she studied architecture and joined a small Philadelphia firm as an associate while simultaneously teaching design studio, building technology and building mechanical systems at Temple University. To further investigate the potential for architecture afforded by new scientific theories in heat transfer and fluid mechanics coupled with emerging technologies, she returned to Harvard to earn a doctorate.

She joined the faculty of Harvard University's Graduate School of Design in 1996, where she is an Associate Professor of Architecture teaching courses in energy, environment, advanced technologies and new materials. She recently co-authored a book titled *Smart Materials and Technologies for the Architecture and Design Professions*.

Helene Furján

Helene Furján is an Assistant Professor at the University of Pennsylvania. She held an Assistant Professorship at Rice University from 2004–2005, and has taught at UCLA, SCI-Arc (the Southern California Institute for Architecture), the Architectural Association School of Architecture in London, the Bartlett School at University College London, the Faculty of Architecture at the University of Auckland, and Princeton University. She received her Ph.D. from Princeton University in 2001, and her professional degree from Auckland University in 1990, where she graduated with Honors, *magna cum laude*.

Helene has received fellowships and grants for her scholarly work from numerous institutions, including the Paul Mellon Centre for Studies in British Art, the William Andrews Clark Memorial Library, and the Fulbright Commission. A book tracking contemporary discourse and co-edited with Sylvia Lavin – *Cribsheets: Notes on the Contemporary Architectural Conversation* – was published by Monacelli Press in 2005. Helene has had essays and reviews published in journals including *Grey Room, AAFiles, Assemblage, Casabella, Journal of Architecture, Hunch9,* and the *Los Angeles Forum for Architecture and Urban Design Annual*. She has essays forthcoming in 2006/07, including two essays on Soane to be published in *Intimate Metropolis: Constructing Public and Private in the Modern City* (Routledge) and *Interstices,* as well as essay contributions to the *Gen(H)ome* exhibition catalogue (MAK Center/Open Source Architects, 2006), and a DD monograph on servo (DD, Korea). She is currently working on a book on John Soane's house-museum, and researches the impact of atmospherics, networks, and models of complexity on contemporary architecture.

Gnuform: Jason Payne and Heather Roberge

Jason Payne and Heather Roberge established their practice in 1999 to pursue both built and speculative projects. Their work is informed by intensive research and an experimental approach primarily involving the application of material dynamics to the organization of form. They promote a new materialism – one that exploits the organizational and spatial potentials of the flows of matter and energy that constitute our environment.

Payne and Roberge consider their work part of an emerging 'vitalist-materialist' model for architectural production that privileges the role of matter in the design process. Traditionally matter in architecture has been understood as secondary to organization, its shape beholden to underlying and essential diagrams. For them there is no pre-existing diagrammatic condition. Diagrams and their progeny, organizations, are secondary and emergent, culled from the play of matter and energy in space and time. Matter first, organization second.

Ultimately this way of thinking leads to an architecture of *effective atmospheres*. We are ever more a species that thrives on immediate, sensual stimulation and material fact. It is not what it is so much as *how it feels*, and one of the things we feel most potently in buildings is their atmosphere. Therefore maintaining and extending the public role of buildings demands more than that they be merely looked at; they must produce a saturated experience so that they cling to the skin of the people moving through them.

Marcelyn Gow (servo: Los Angeles–Zurich)

Marcelyn Gow is a partner and founding member in the architecture and design collaborative servo. She received a Master of Science in Advanced Architectural Design from Columbia University and an AADipl. and RIBA II from the Architectural Association School of Architecture, and was an MFA Program Fellow at Columbia University's School of the Arts. She is currently conducting doctoral research at the ETH-Swiss Federal Institute of Technology.

Gow has taught at the Royal Institute of Technology School of Architecture in Stockholm and the ETH-Swiss Institute of Technology in Zurich, and is currently teaching design studios at the UCLA Department of Architecture and Urban Design.

Christopher Hight

Christopher Hight is an assistant professor at the Rice School of Architecture, where he is pursuing design research on emerging electronic and material urbanisms. He has been a Fulbright Scholar and obtained a masters degree in the histories and theories of architecture from the Architectural Association, and a Ph.D. from the London Consortium at the University of London. Previously he taught at the Architectural Association's Design Research Laboratory, and has worked for the Renzo Piano Building Workshop. He is currently writing a book on cybernetics, formalism and post-World War II architectural design (Routledge, 2006) and is co-editing an issue of *AD* on network design practices. He has published over thirty articles and lectured internationally. At Rice he is the editor of the Architecture at Rice book series and organized the fourth Kennon Symposium, 'Modulations'.

Sean Lally

Sean Lally founded the office Weathers (www.w-e-a-t-h-e-r-s.com) in 2004 with a focus on exploring the implications for our spatial and organizational constructs as architects continue to engage advancements in the tools and techniques available today. He received his bachelor's degree in landscape architecture from the University of Massachusetts in 1996 before practicing with Raymond Irrera + Associates. He received his Masters in architecture from the University of California in Los Angeles, was appointed the Wortham Fellow at the Rice School of Architecture in 2002, and is currently the Caudill Visiting Assistant Professor at Rice. Sean Lally / Weathers' recent projects include an installation at the upcoming Gen(H)ome project at the Schindler house (Fall 2006), the SIV House (2004), the SIM Residence (2004), and the Cushioning of Space (2003). Sean's work has been featured in exhibitions at Rice University and the University of Minnesota, The Past/Present/Future Exhibition in Los Angeles, and the 2003 Possible Futures Exhibition for the Bienal Miami. Recent lectures and conferences include the Kennon Symposium and the Form D conference at the Technion in Israel.

OCEAN NORTH

OCEAN NORTH is an experimental and multidisci-
plinary design collective, which undertakes design
research, projects, and consultancy in the intersection
between urban design, architecture, industrial design, and cultural production. Michael Hensel, Achim
Menges and Birger Sevaldson organize the think tank.
OCEAN NORTH's work has been widely published and
exhibited in Europe, Asia and the Americas. Recent
projects include the *World Center for Human Affairs*,
exhibited in the A New World Trade Center exhibition
at the Max Protetch Gallery in New York, the Venice
Architecture Biennale in 2002 and the Blobjects exhibition at San Jose Museum of Art in 2005, as well
as the *Jyväskylä Music and Art Center*, exhibited at
the Venice Architecture Biennale in 2004. For further
information see: www.ocean-north.net

Open Source Architecture (OSA)

OSA is an international research practice dedicated
to the production of dynamic and fluid architectural
systems based on inclusive processes of data treatment and technological operators. Its explorative team
– founded by Aaron Sprecher, Chandler Ahrens and
Eran Neuman – undertakes experimental design with
the aim of establishing synergetic relations between
architectural theory and history, design methods, and
technological research and design (R&D). Since OSA
was established in 2003, founders have taught and
lectured throughout the world in leading schools and
conferences such as at Princeton University, Rice University, Syracuse University, Ohio State University, and
the Technion – Israel Institute of Technology. OSA's
work has already been presented in many exhibitions,
including AIA ACADIA's Fabrication (2004), Softspace
at Rice University (2004) and Past, Present, Future at
UCLA (2003). Currently, OSA is curating an exhibition
at the MAK Center for Art and Architecture, in Los
Angeles, titled The Gen[H]ome Project: Genetic and
Domesticity, to be opened in Fall 2006.

Tobi Schneidler / maoworks

maoworks is a design strategy company, inventing intriguing new types of environments that combine service, interactivity and emotional qualities to encourage communication and play. maoworks collaborates with commercial, research, and cultural clients to connect people, places, and information through situated interactive experiences. maoworks stands for the Office for Mediating Architecture and Objects. It was founded in London in 2004.

maoworks is currently involved in a British government-funded innovation project on the use of Smart Dust in Knowledge Workplaces and the design of a creative meeting place for the Swedish Design Council, as well as the in-house development of interactive interior design products. maoworks also facilitates innovation workshops with companies and public organizations.

maoworks founder Tobi Schneidler graduated as an architect from the Architectural Association in London. He then initiated various applied research projects within tangible media and interactive architecture as well as pursuing independent design consultancy work on an international level. Tobi has also been teaching and lecturing at various design and architecture universities in Europe, the US and Asia, such as the Royal College of Art in London and the Royal institute of Technology (KTH) in Stockholm. His installation work has been shown al venues such as the Institute of Contemporary Art (ICA) and the Victoria and Albert Museum (V&A) in London.

Jessica Young

Jessica Young is a designer living in Houston, Texas. She is the Director of Publications at Rice School of Architecture, where she is also the managing editor for the Architecture at Rice book series, and has taught with Mark Wamble. She received her Master's in architecture from Rice, and her Bachelor of Arts from Lehigh University in Pennsylvania. She has collaborated on various types of projects with Lars Lerup, Interloop Architecture and Design, David Guthrie Studio and Workshop, Thumb Projects and Philip Lee, among others. At present, she is working with Lars Lerup on his current book, *Stim and Dross*, and on an ongoing urban landscape project.

Preceding pages: Melting ice
field in the Chukchi Sea, northwest of Alaska, 2002.